To Elwyn
With all good wishes
from
Norman
NRCDockeray
15th November 1994

THE POWER OF MIRACLE

Also by Norman Dockeray:

An Elementary Treatise on Pure Mathematics,
G. Bell & Sons 1934
Elementary Mechanics, Edward Arnold & Co.
1936 (Co-author)
Further Mechanics and Hydrostatics,
Edward Arnold & Co. 1937 (Co-author)
Various articles in the *Mathematical Gazette*
An Anglican's Reflections on Humanae Vitae,
Downside Review, July 1970
An article on *The Fatherhood of God*, published in
local Parish Magazine, June 1971
Tentative Answers to Ten Questions,
The Book Guild Ltd. 1988
Thy Kingdom Come, on Earth, Fairacres
Chronicle, Spring 1989

THE POWER OF MIRACLE

Norman R.C. Dockeray, C.B.E.

The Book Guild Ltd.
Sussex, England

Dedicated to the Lord Archbishop of Canterbury, the Most Reverend and Right Honourable Robert Runcie

This book is sold subject to the condition that it shall not, by way of trade or otherwise, be lent, re-sold, hired out, photocopied or held in any retrieval system, or otherwise circulated without the publisher's prior consent or otherwise circulated in any form of binding or cover other than that in which this is published and without a similar condition including this condition being imposed on the subsequent purchaser.

The Book Guild Ltd.
25 High Street,
Lewes, Sussex.

First published 1991
© Norman R.C. Dockeray, C.B.E. 1991
Set in Baskerville
Typesetting by APS,
Salisbury, Wiltshire,
Printed in Great Britain by
Antony Rowe Ltd.,
Chippenham, Wiltshire.

British Library Cataloguing in Publication Data
Dockeray, Norman R.C.
  The power of miracle
  1. Christian theology
  I. Title
  230

ISBN 0 86332 521 1

CONTENTS

		Page	Paragraph
PREFACE		7	
CHAPTER ONE	**THE THREE TRINITIES**		
I	The Trinity of Being	11	1
II	The Trinity of Man	26	24
III	The Trinity	31	35
	Notes and References	38	
CHAPTER TWO	**MIRACLES AND FREEDOM**		
I	The Meaning of Miracle	43	42
II	Divine Miracles	49	52
III	Miracles and Man	53	56
IV	The Meaning of Freedom	54	57
V	The Two Classes of Miracle	65	75
	Notes and References	67	
CHAPTER THREE	**THE CREATION OF CHARACTER**	77	77
	Notes and References	89	
CHAPTER FOUR	**THE MASTERY OF EVOLUTION**	93	96
	Notes and References	120	
CHAPTER FIVE	**THE TRANSFORMATION OF BEING**		
I	The Meaning of Resurrection	130	134
II	Recognition and Communication	140	149
III	The Metaphysics of Consciousness	156	175
	Notes and References	160	
CHAPTER SIX	**APOTHAUMATA**		
I	Definition	173	180

II	The Range of Apothaumatic Power	175	185
III	The Miracles of Jesus	182	199
IV	Healing Miracles	186	209
V	Human Apothaumatic Power – the Need for Recovery	189	215
	Notes and References	197	
CHAPTER SEVEN	**THE TWO GREAT MIRACLES**		
I	The Virgin Birth	206	230
II	The Resurrection	213	243
	Notes and References	227	
SUBJECT INDEX		232	
INDEX OF BIBLICAL REFERENCES		241	

PREFACE

C.S. Lewis, in his book *Miracle, a Preliminary Study* (Geoffrey Bles, 1947), defines miracle as 'an interference with Nature by a supernatural power', and this is substantially the definition I have adopted, though I have found it necessary to express it in more formal terms (paragraph 48). It is probably what most people understand when they use the word, and those who deny that miracles occur usually do so either on the ground that belief in the existence of a supernatural power (either as an existent being or as an attribute inherent in or conferred on an existent being or beings) is a false belief, or on the ground that if such a power does exist, he or it does not interfere with natural law. Obviously, since in this book I have set myself the task of investigating the power of miracle, I reject the hypothesis that miracles do not occur, and the questions to which I have tried to provide answers are: who has the power to perform miracles, how is this power exercised, and in what manner does it display itself? To the first question I think that among those people who accept the possibility of miracle most would answer that the power resides in God alone; and this limitation is reflected in the popular use of the word in such expressions as 'his recovery from such a serious operation was miraculous' or, on reading of a railway accident, 'it was only by a miracle that I decided to travel by a later train'. Underlying these remarks is the idea of God as Providence – it is supposed that God, for reasons known only to himself, has decided that a particular human life must be preserved on earth a little longer, and that this requires his intervention. C.S. Lewis also assumes that God is the only being endowed with supernatural power to interfere with Nature, although he allows (p. 162) that 'whatever may have been the powers of unfallen man, it appears that those of redeemed Man will be almost unlimited', and he cites Matthew xvii, 20 and a number of other scriptural references in support of this thesis. But he does not appear to consider the possibility that miracles can be performed by man in his present fallen condition.

I do not think that this limitation of the incidence of thaumaturgic power can be sustained. If we try to analyse the principles by which the sequence of events in the universe is governed, we are forced to the conclusion that the relation between the total state of the universe (including its mental as well as its physical constituents) at any given moment and its state at the next succeeding moment is either random, or is governed by inviolable law, or is the result of miracle, or is one in which two or more of these possibilities have played some part. Unless therefore we are willing to admit that human beings have no more control over the march of events than any other animal, we must believe that they have the power to perform miracles. This is the premise on which the argument of the present book is based, and it is hoped that the argument will justify both the premise itself and the conclusions drawn from it, in particular the fact that it is man's ability to control his own development by using his miraculous powers that has been the most potent factor in bringing about his present condition. From this fact it follows that the study of miracle ranks among the most important tasks to which it is possible to apply one's mind. For it is nothing less than to provide a very significant part of the answer to the question 'What is man?'

It would obviously be useless to tackle the issues involved in a study of miracle by observation or experiment, for observation could only show that an event is mysterious or inexplicable on the basis of what is known, and not that it is miraculous, and if experiment could produce foreseeable results these would clearly not be miraculous. The method I have adopted has therefore been that of reasoning from first principles. For this purpose some basic assumptions must be made, but these should be as few as possible. Nevertheless, one must start from some hypotheses, and the hypotheses on which my argument is based may be summed up in the statements that (i) God exists and is not a mere demiurge; (ii) God is rational and therefore what takes place in the universe and in heaven is not random;

and (iii) when Jesus instructed his disciples to address God as 'Father', he meant precisely what he said and he meant his words to apply to all mankind. Thus I have to this extent assumed a Christian standpoint, and I have analysed (and supported) the miraculous claims made in the New Testament, but I have not otherwise based the argument of the book on the truth of Christianity, and I hope that this fact will induce others besides Christians to read the book and to consider whether it may not persuade them that the humanist point of view is inadequate and, in particular, that belief in the occurrence of miracles is neither irrational nor evidence of gullibility.

From the assumptions made the conclusions reached follow by straightforward reasoning, but as the issues are those of eternity rather than of time so also the logic employed must be the logic of eternity and not the logic of time. The logic of eternity is more flexible than the logic of time as it is free from the limitations which attach to the latter by reason of the fact that time is linear. Thus instead of proceeding from simple assumptions by linear progression to complex conclusions, which is the typical method of temporal logic, the logic of eternity is concerned rather with the relations between different truths, all of which lie at substantially the same level of complexity and profundity, and are both the focal points of this logic and the inescapable consequences of its application.

We may expect to find, therefore, that these truths will be readily accepted, even as being almost axiomatic, by those who are familiar with or whose minds are attuned to this eternal logic, but it must be admitted, regrettably, that both they and their logical interrelations arouse less interest and are consequently less familiar today, even among those who profess a religious belief, than at some earlier periods in man's history. It is easy to account for this decline in interest, but explanation of its causes does not render it less potentially harmful.

The secular priorities that characterise so much of modern thought have led those whose duty it is to interpret the gospel to lay great emphasis on the parable of the sheep and the goats (Matthew xxv, 31-46), and in the tragic circumstances that prevail over a large part of the world it is right that this should be done; but we ought not to lose sight of the fact that this parable has an eternal as well as a temporal message and that it is the former that is fundamental. Nor is this order of priority peculiar to Christianity, for while most, if not all, religions rightly lay stress on the moral virtues of self-sacrifice and altruism, in fact of loving one's neighbour, they set these virtues in an eternal context which, being unbounded, transcends the values of our earthly life. It is with the hope of making a small contribution towards restoring belief in the primacy of the eternal realm, both as an intrinsic fact of reality and because it is the source of our earthly values, that this book has been written.

January 1990

1

THE THREE TRINITIES

I. The Trinity of Being

1. God can, of course, perform miracles, but the only creature known to us who is endowed with a similar power is man. If, therefore, we set ourselves the task of studying and explaining in rational terms the phenomenon of miracles we cannot avoid including in our study an examination of the nature of man. And conversely, if we seek to discover what man is, we shall be led to consider the powers which, among all creatures known to us[1], he alone possesses, the powers which serve to distinguish him from all other creatures, and in particular from all other animals, and among those powers we must include the power of performing miracles. Since it will hardly be denied that the nature of man is a proper and very important field of study (indeed Alexander Pope asserted that it was the *only* proper field[2]), it follows that the nature and meaning of miracles must also engage our attention.

2. There are, of course, those who deny that man possesses any special features, that is to say, any features which distinguish him *in kind* from other species of living beings. There are even those who deny that there is any difference in kind between living and non-living matter, holding that the only distinction is that in the former the peculiar properties of carbon, including in particular its power to combine in an enormous number and variety of ways with hydrogen, oxygen, nitrogen and other elements to form immensely complex molecules, have been utilized by the forces of evolution to develop the powers of

reproduction, locomotion, awareness of the outside world, and all the other properties which seem to demarcate living organisms as being distinct from all other material structures. Those who hold this view would maintain that in passing from the simplest chemical compounds, such as water or carbon monoxide, to the most complex proteins, and beyond the proteins to the assemblages of proteins which we describe as living beings, there is no Rubicon to be crossed, that the whole process is continuous, and that at no point do we have to postulate any new force or entity, or even any new principle; and they would point to the viruses as partial evidence of the truth of their opinion. They might also defend their argument by appealing to the principle enunciated by William of Occam[3], namely, that it is improper, in philosophical reasoning, to postulate the existence of any unnecessary entities, a principle to which all scientists would give at least qualified approval[4].

3. Those who hold the view that all material structures, whether living or non-living, whether able to move independently or only in response to external forces, whether endowed with senses or not, and whether they are intelligent, able to reason and to plan the future, or merely react to the circumstances in which they happen to find themselves, are all essentially the same, differing only in the degree of complexity of their structure, will find no use, and therefore no place, for any supernatural agency, and will almost certainly deny the possibility of miracles; and the same is true of those who, while admitting that living matter differs from non-living matter in some real but undefined (and perhaps indefinable) way, nevertheless regard man as in no way distinct, other than in degree, from other animals. These latter would of course admit that man differs from the lower animals in that he possesses an immensely larger and more complex brain, but difference in size, they would maintain, does not necessarily or even generally spring from, and certainly does not prove the existence of, any essential difference.

4. It is necessary to mention such views as these, because they are very widely held, often by people who are quite unaware that they are thereby committing themselves to a deterministic interpretation not only of nature in general but also of man.

But this is in fact the case, for it is very difficult, if not absolutely impossible, to reconcile the view that man is no more than an animal, differing from other animals only in the degree to which, under the influence of evolutionary forces, certain organs and faculties have developed, with the view that he possesses free will.

5. Now, as we shall see in the following chapter, a belief in the occurrence of miracles is not inconsistent with holding that the universe as revealed to our senses is subject to a system of law, provided that we are prepared to admit the existence of a level (or levels) of reality to which our senses do not directly respond. But if we wish to claim, not merely that miracles can occur, but that men and women, alone among created (earthly) beings, can and sometimes do perform them, we must also admit that human beings have access to this second level of reality. Or, to put the matter conversely, if we rule out *a priori* the possibility that man is in some way, yet to be defined, essentially different from other animals, that is to say, if we deny that there was an event in the process of evolution whereby man was *created* by the implantation into the evolving species of some additional feature or faculty, then we must also exclude the possibility that he can perform miracles. And since it is my purpose to expound the Christian and not merely a theistic account of miracles, and since the Christian tradition holds that men and women have frequently performed overt miracles, miracles which were apparent to any onlooker, and are also constantly performing miracles which take place within their own personalities and are not plainly visible to the onlooker, we must reject at the outset the notion that the evolution of man from his animal ancestors has been entirely a continuous process, in favour of the view that at some point of time a discontinuity took place whereby he became, from that moment, a unique creature, not merely a new and distinct species, but a creature essentially different from the rest of the terrestrial creation, because he has had added to him a faculty enabling him to exercise powers which, though undoubtedly limited and exercisable only in a narrow field, are similar to a power, unlimited in range and magnitude, inhering in his Creator.

6. We must therefore seek to discover and describe the nature of this unique feature in the composition of man, and it need occasion no surprise to find that the most fruitful starting point for the analysis is the opening phrase of the Lord's Prayer – 'Our Father, which art in heaven'. For no other creature is instructed to address God as 'Father'[5], and to no other creature is it revealed that God is 'in heaven'. However, both these points need to be interpreted, and when we come to study them we find that these six words contain almost all the information needed for the understanding of God and man and of their mutual relationship. They are, in fact, probably the most comprehensive, profound and fruitful words ever uttered.

7. We take first the second part of the phrase, the words 'which art in heaven' which are used to describe God. Clearly these words are not to be read as meaning that God is in some place, a place, for example, 'above the sky', somewhere in outer space. Whatever pictorial language may have been used to try to portray God to a largely illiterate (but not, because of illiteracy, necessarily unintelligent) peasantry, no one with any pretension to learning has at any time supposed that heaven is a place. In fact the widespread belief among those whose knowledge of Christianity is almost non-existent (and this includes a large proportion of our so-called intelligentsia), the belief that Christians are *required* to think of heaven as a place, coupled with the belief that it is this, together with other equally absurd doctrinal requirements, that has alienated so many people from the Christian faith, is indicative of the extreme gullibility that is so characteristic of the twentieth century[6]. On the other hand, the fact that heaven is not, and never has been supposed to be, an actual location, somewhere in, or even outside, the physical universe, is not to be interpreted as implying that God is a purely subjective phenomenon, a condition of the minds of men. The efforts of some modern theological writers to persuade their readers that this is the case, that God is not transcendent but merely immanent, and not even, strictly speaking, an immanent being but only a postulate to be made because man is 'a religious animal', have done as much damage to Christianity as the erroneous beliefs (admittedly springing largely from the unscientific, or rather

anti-scientific, attitude of some nineteenth-century ecclesiastics) now held about the amount of irrational nonsense Christians are required by their faith to accept as true.

8. If then heaven is not a place in which God is to be found, how are we to interpret the phrase 'which art in heaven'? Does 'in heaven' denote a state of mind, as when we say 'I was in heaven when I learned that I had got the job', or 'when I realized that I was going to have a baby'? Clearly this is also impossible. For states of mind are ephemeral and are continually changing, whereas God is unchangeable[7]. Moreover, although God may comprehend all mind, he is not a psychical entity, any more than, although he may comprehend all matter, he is a physical entity. For we are told that God is a spirit[8], and spirit must be clearly distinguished from mind[9]. Even more positively we must distinguish spirit from a *state* of mind. Indeed the whole concept of a state is inapplicable to God, for if we have to mention a particular state we imply that there are other possible states, and the idea that there are, at the level of God, a number of different states which he might adopt cannot be reconciled with the fact that he is unchangeable; it is manifestly absurd. God is as he is, and cannot be other than he is, because at his level there is only God; there are no other beings with which he might be compared, and there are no characteristics[10] other than those inhering in him to allow the possibility of any variation. When, therefore, we say that God, who is our Father, is 'in heaven', there can be only one possible interpretation, and that is that we are speaking of the nature of the *being* of God. We are saying that the being of God is unique, that it is a type of being which other beings do not share, although since God is our Father our being must be in some way related to the being of God[11]. We may anticipate the conclusion we shall later reach by saying that God has *supra-eternal* being whereas his creatures have only eternal or temporal being or, in the case of man, a measure of both temporal and eternal being.

9. It is an essential article of Christian belief that God is active. The most obvious example of his activity is creation; in fact all theists, including those who are not Christians, agree that the universe owes its origin to the creative activity of God. When

we speak of 'the Creation' it is this we have in mind, but God's creative activity did not cease when the task of constructing the universe, together with space and time, had been completed[12]. God may have 'rested on the seventh day'[13], that is to say, he may have allowed the universe to unfold itself for some time in accordance with the divine laws implanted in it, but he was not inactive, for what he had created had to be maintained in being; moreover when the time was ripe the active work of creation was resumed. The creation of mind and its association with matter probably constituted such a separate act, and it is held as an undeniable truth by all Christians, and by many who are not Christians, that every human soul is the product of an individual act of creation by God[14].

10. Creation, however, (as we shall see later[15]) is not the only manifestation of God's activity. The Christian God is continuously active, and although the activity of creation is exercised *ex nihilo*, all other activity requires not only a subject by whom it is performed, but also an object who (or which) is affected by it. In the world as we know it there is no difficulty about supplying the object; it is the whole created universe, and more particularly that part of it which appears to possess a certain degree of autonomy, and which we distinguish from the rest of the universe by applying to it the term 'living'. Most particularly of all, the object of God's activity is, according to Christian teaching, the human race, which has been singled out for special recognition by the fact of the Incarnation. So long therefore as the universe has existed there is no difficulty about supplying the object of God's activity. But unless we regard time as stretching infinitely back into the past, a supposition which involves great philosophical and scientific difficulties, there must have been, outside time, circumstances in which time and space and, *a fortiori*, the universe did not exist. And from this it follows that there must be, in the absence of the universe, beings on whom God's activity is directed and who are affected by that activity. The kind of existence which these beings (we may assume that there are more than one) enjoy must be inferior to that of God, since God is unique, but must be superior to that of the physical universe known to us, because it is independent of, and therefore unconditioned by,

time and space. They must be able to receive, absorb and respond to the outpouring of God's activity, and must therefore at least be persons, for the capacity to respond to God's activity is one of the major characteristics of personality. For although everything in the created universe receives and absorbs the activity of God, indeed necessarily does so as a condition of its continued existence, only human beings can respond to it, only human beings can receive it other than passively. The inanimate world receives it and by receiving it is maintained in existence; the living world receives it and, in greater or lesser degree, *enjoys* it[16]; but men and women seek to understand it, and in so doing analyse it into component parts falling within their powers of comprehension, and having understood it, however imperfectly, make some response, even if in some cases it is the response of rejection. Likewise those beings who, outside the confines of the universe, outside the realm of space and time, receive the outpouring of God's activity, must have the power of responding to it. For a Supreme Being who radiates to beings created by him activity which they absorb but to which they do not respond, is a mere demiurge, and is infinitely less than the Christian God. These responsive beings are the angels, and we thus see that the existence of angels is a direct and logical consequence of the uniqueness of the being of God. The mode or level of being (or existence) enjoyed by the angels is clearly at least equal to that of human beings; it must in fact be superior, since it is not conditioned by the laws of time, space and energy which govern the universe. The conclusion we reach, therefore, is that there must be three levels of being, namely that of God, that of the angels and that of the physical universe. To these three levels we give the names supra-eternal, eternal and temporal. This is the first trinity, the trinity of being, and a recognition and understanding of the existence of these three levels of being is essential to an understanding of the nature and significance of man, and therefore also of miracles.

11. The abstract concept of 'being' which is here referred to must of course be distinguished from the concrete manifestations of being in existing things for which, unfortunately, we often use the same word, as when we speak of a human being or

an inanimate being. In order to distinguish between the two meanings of 'being' I have used the expression 'mode of being' or 'level of being' to denote the abstract concept, but if this designation is used we must be careful to avoid falling into the error of supposing that the mode of being of a thing can change (as the word 'mode' might seem to imply), whether by a change in the outside circumstances or at the volition of the thing itself. This is not the case. The mode of being (or simply 'the being') of anything is simply that by virtue of which it exists[17]; it is conferred by God and, except in the case of one very important class of entities, as will be explained later[18], can only be changed by God. Thus the mode of being of a stone is temporal being, and this cannot be changed by itself or by any other creature into another mode of being; this is also the mode of being, and the statement is also true, of a tree or a dog, and in fact of all living beings, including those having minds, other than man.

12. Abstract concepts are notoriously elusive, and although they may be clearly grasped when one's concentration is focused on them they easily escape as soon as the attention is directed elsewhere. The difficulty of holding in the mind the abstract concept of being and in particular the idea of different modes or levels of being may, however, be partially lifted by drawing an analogy with the concept of life. It can be argued that, although there are some beings which are clearly living beings and others which are clearly inanimate, life itself is not a substantive thing but only a word used to distinguish between the two classes[19]. But although this may be argued it cannot be proved, and as the mind finds it easier to grasp abstract concepts if they are regarded as having substantive reality and not merely as mental figments it is certainly permissible, as an aid to thinking if for no other purpose, to speak of life as something which living beings 'possess' but non-living beings do not possess. And we can go on from this to speak or at least think of the 'mode of life' possessed by a horse or a dog, or any of the so-called higher animal species, as being in some essential way different from the mode of life possessed by a plant, and as being even more different from the mode of life possessed by a bacillus or a bacterium. In the same way we can aid our grasp

of the concept of being if we regard it as something 'possessed' by all existing things, and this hypostatization of the being (or mode of being) of existing things may be extended to include the idea of different modes of being possessed by different existing things. It is, however, important to bear in mind that although the concept of different modes of life attaching to different living beings may be no more than an aid to thought, the distinction between the three modes of being is a real distinction, each mode having its own distinctive properties.

13. Corresponding to the three different modes of being we recognize the existence of three different 'media' or 'orders of reality' in which the things which manifest these different modes of being exist or 'have their being'[20]. We may speak of these as the supra-eternal order, the eternal order (or eternity) and the temporal (or spatio-temporal) order. But it is obviously not enough to state that there are three different orders of reality, in which the beings possessing the different modes of being exist, we must also indicate in what way these three orders and the beings inhabiting them differ from one another, that is to say, differ *essentially*, so that there can be no transition from one mode (or order) to another[21]. This is easy in the case of the two extreme orders; consideration of the intermediate order, the eternal order, presents greater difficulties and the specification is both less precise and less cogent.

14. The essential feature of the supra-eternal order is utter and complete changelessness, and the only being satisfying such a criterion of changelessness is God. God is the only supra-eternal being, and is thus the only inhabitant of the supra-eternal order[22]. But God exhibits also the characteristic of activity (although this is not peculiar to him but is exhibited also by the inhabitants of the other two orders), and by combining the fact of activity with the fact of changelessness we see also that God is infinite. For by virtue of his activity God is continually radiating spiritual energy, but is in no way lessened thereby, and the only concept that remains unaltered when part of its essence is subtracted from it is infinity.

15. By contrast with the changelessness of God, the essential characteristic of the spatio-temporal order, the order which 'houses' those things whose mode of being is temporal being, is

change, continuous and unceasing change. For temporal being (or, if we prefer, everything whose being is temporal being) is lodged in and conditioned by time, and time has no meaning apart from change. In fact, time and change are interdependent; conceptually each implies the other, and ontologically neither can exist without the other. Moreover, since change cannot be random, otherwise the whole universe would be chaotic, which it manifestly is not, it follows that change is governed by law. Thus the observable characteristic of temporal being is that it is subject to law, and a great part of the activity of human beings has been, and must always be, devoted to the attempt to discover the laws by which the universe, which is the visible manifestation of temporal being, is governed, and to using the laws thus discovered to adapt the universe towards the achievement of those ends which men and women have selected as being desirable.

16. We are, of course, familiar with the temporal order, and while many of its laws are elusive we feel that they lie within the bounds of our powers of understanding. It is possible – indeed it is probable – that we shall never be able to say, with truth, that there is nothing in nature remaining to be discovered, particularly if we bear in mind that, as we shall see[23], we must include under the heading 'nature' the psychical world, or a large part of that world. Nevertheless, there is no reason, in principle, to assign any limit to the advance of our knowledge of the laws of the temporal order, that is to say, of science. Whatever may be the truth of this matter, however, we are well able to grasp the basic truth that the essential characteristic of the temporal order (and of temporal being) is incessant change in accordance with law.

17. Likewise, although the totality of the nature of the supra-eternal order must for ever remain a mystery, we can readily grasp the meaning of the statement that the essential characteristics of God are changelessness and activity. Moreover we can experience and partially understand the nature of these characteristics in so far as God considers it good to reveal himself to us. To aid in this understanding we analyse his activity into categories suited to the powers of our finite minds, naming them as Truth[24], Beauty, Goodness, Love, Wisdom,

Power, Authority, and so on; and in our most penetrating moments we recognize these manifestations of his activity as universal and changeless. Moreover, we can respond to this activity to the extent that and in such manner as we ourselves decide.

18. Thus the meaning of the essential characteristics of the two outer orders of reality, the supra-eternal and the temporal orders, lies within our grasp. It is the intermediate order, the eternal order (and with it the nature of eternal being), that is most difficult to understand. For the eternal order is certainly not changeless, as God is changeless, nor is it subject to change, as is the temporal order, since eternity is not time – not even endless time – nor is it comprehended in or conditioned by time. Obviously the problem thus posed must have a solution, but the solution is not easy to express in words, because our language has developed out of our experience, which is temporal experience. We can, however, indicate by analogy the lines along which the solution may be partially grasped. We start by noting that our experience of time is one-dimensional – it proceeds continuously from past to future and does not branch off or return on itself. This characteristic of time is summed up in the fact that, once a reference moment has been decided on (e.g., the moment when the year 1 BC ended and the year AD 1 commenced) only *one* measurement is needed to specify any other moment of time. In space the one-dimensional element is the line, and we may therefore picture time as the tracing out of a line by a moving point in space. The part of the line already traced out represents the past, the position of the moving point represents the present and the part yet to be traced represents the future. (It is not necessary to think of the line being traced out as a straight line; in fact it is best to think of the point as following any kind of path in space, as this emphasizes the fact that the future is undetermined.) Having fixed in our minds this picture of time, we may think of eternity (or the eternal order) as the space in which this unfolding of time takes place. It must be understood that this representation is advanced only as a pictorial aid to thought; it is not suggested that it is a true description of the relation between eternity and time, for in fact the distinction between these two

media is not geometrical or structural, but ontological. It would certainly be wrong to say that eternity is three-dimensional time, but it is as legitimate to use this graphical illustration of a three-dimensional (or multi-dimensional) space to represent eternity and a moving point in that space to represent time as it is in everyday life to draw a graph to show the manner in which two changing quantities are related. Furthermore, the picture, though admittedly inadequate, enables us to reach certain conclusions about the nature of eternity and its properties. First, although the beings whose mode of being is eternal being, whom we may call the inhabitants of the eternal order, cannot be subject to change, in the ordinary sense of that word, because change is indissolubly linked with time, their existence is certainly not static. We can say this with absolute confidence, not only because it is a deduction from the graphical representation of the relation between eternity and time, but also because it would be absurd, it would in fact be unthinkable, to suppose that the angels are inactive. This flows from the fact that their existence has been established by the need to postulate beings completely independent of the created universe of time, space, matter and mind, who are capable of responding to the outpoured activity of God, and the notion of response involves that of activity of some kind which is incompatible with a static existence. Secondly, the idea of time as being comprehended in eternity and as being unfolded in eternity as a moving point might trace out a line in space leads to the further conclusion that the eternal order itself, and not only the inhabitants of that order, is in a state of development, since the creation of the line as the point moves involves a modification of the condition of the order that contains it. Thus there is not only development *in* eternity, there is also development *of* eternity.

19. This argument would seem to show that, contrary to what has been said, eternity is subject to change and is therefore of the same nature as space-time, both being realms in which change takes place. But if we use the word 'change' to describe the kind of development that takes place in the eternal order we run into difficulties, because change in time is linear whereas what takes place in the eternal order is not linear. We

might distinguish between change in time and development in eternity by referring to the former as temporal change and to the latter as eternal change, but this would not only tend to mask the distinction but might also give rise to misunderstanding, as the expression 'eternal change' might be understood to mean change that goes on for ever, which would involve a misunderstanding of eternity. Or it might be held to mean irreversible change in the structure of eternity or in the condition of its inhabitants, an interpretation that is precisely the reverse of the truth. It is change in time that is irreversible[25], whereas development in eternity can turn back on itself so that modifications, whether of the eternal order or of eternal being can be wiped out. Thus the temporal consequences of sin must be suffered, but its eternal consequences can be avoided by repentance and divine forgiveness. It is therefore necessary to coin an entirely new word to denote the fact that neither the eternal order nor its inhabitants is subject to change, and yet neither is static. For this property of eternity I shall use the word *metallassis* (from the Greek *allassein*, to change), which we may define as the mode of development in eternity which corresponds to change in time.

20. The apparent anomaly in the statement that the beings which inhabit the eternal order, and the eternal order itself, are neither changeless nor subject to change is thus resolved. There are in fact three states of activity, namely activity involving change, which is the condition in the temporal order, activity involving metallassis, which is the condition in the eternal order, and activity involving neither change nor metallassis, which is the condition of God.

21. Another equally important characteristic of the eternal order can be deduced from the picture of that order as a multidimensional manifold embracing time, and time as the path traced out by a moving point in that manifold. This is that, whereas change in time must be ordered and therefore subject to pre-ordained law (else it would be chaotic), this requirement does not obtain in the eternal order. It is indeed certain that, since development cannot be random[26], there is in eternity a principle governing metallassis, that is, a principle of development corresponding to natural law in the temporal order, but

whatever that principle may be, it is certain that it differs fundamentally from the law of cause and effect which prevails in the temporal order, for this law is unbreakably linked with time, in fact the notion of natural law cannot be defined otherwise than by reference to time. Thus the concept of an inevitable effect following on a given cause has no meaning in eternity, and we deduce from this that the principle by which development takes place in the eternal order must be such as to allow a very wide measure of freedom to its inhabitants. This is a fundamental property of eternity and it follows that, as the being of man is in part eternal being (a fact that will be established in section II of this chapter), a clear understanding of the link between eternal being and freedom is essential to our understanding of man. Freedom cannot, however, be absolute, otherwise the beings possessing it would be equal to God. It is a privilege conferred by God and is limited by the power of God to withdraw it or to override its effects. Thus, whereas in the temporal order the past cannot be undone, development in the eternal order which is consequent on the exercise by the possessors of eternal being of their freedom may, if God so decides, be reversed and even entirely expunged. This has an important bearing on the meaning of divine forgiveness, for it shows that although the temporal consequences of sin or error cannot be undone its consequences in eternity can be prevented or obliterated.

22. The distinctive properties of the three orders are parallelled and complemented by important ontological differences. Obviously, the supra-eternal order, which coincides with God, the only supra-eternal being, stands alone. God is not only the Supreme Being, he is also the source of all being; consequently the eternal and temporal orders both derive from him. We can, however, see, from the argument of paragraph 10, that the mode of derivation of the eternal order is more direct than that of the temporal order. For the existence of the temporal order is *contingent*; God is entirely independent of time and space and the whole physical universe, and would be in no way diminished (or increased) if these entities did not exist. They owe their being to a positive act on the part of God; in other words, they are *created*. The eternal order, on the other hand, has

necessary existence. For the angels, whose being is eternal being, are required, independently of the existence of the temporal order, to be the recipients of and respondents to the activity of God, and the medium of their existence, which is the eternal order, is therefore a necessary concomitant of the existence of God. If this were not so, we would be forced to postulate the existence of another order and other beings, to act as the recipients of God's activity in the absence of the angels. We can best express the special derivation of the eternal order by saying that it *proceeds* from God[27]. It should be noted, however, that although the eternal order is not created, its inhabitants, the angels, must be created, for otherwise they would be in some sense emanations from God and would not have independent wills, whereas we know from the fact that Satan exists that their wills are entirely free, even to the extent of enabling them to reject God. Indeed we shall see in the following chapter that free will is an inescapable characteristic of eternal being. The fact that the angels are created does not give rise to any question as to how God's activity was absorbed before their creation, for this act of God is an occasion in eternity and not an event in time, and therefore the concepts of 'before' and 'after' cannot be applied to it.

23. The conclusions of the preceding paragraphs, in so far as they relate to the eternal order, can be summarized by defining the principle governing development in that order as freedom subject to the overriding power of God. This however is not all. Freedom from causal law is not the only, nor is it the most fundamental, freedom enjoyed by the possessors of eternal being; there is also freedom of being itself. By this I mean that whereas temporal being is maintained only by the continuous activity of God, so that if God withheld his activity from any existing temporal thing, that thing would instantly cease to exist, eternal being is a gift which can only be withdrawn by a positive act on the part of God. We have seen that the possessors of eternal being are free to reject God, and we now see also that they can do so without thereby ceasing to exist, unless God, in consequence of that rejection of him, positively withdraws the gift of being. It is possible that this statement cannot be rigorously proved, but its justification lies in the fact

that if its truth is taken as a hypothesis the consequences that flow from it enable us to understand much that would otherwise be puzzling. In particular it accounts for the continued existence of Satan and should therefore be accepted by all Christians; moreover, as God has not annihilated Satan, as he obviously could, we draw the vitally important conclusion that he does not necessarily withdraw the gift of eternal being solely on the ground that the possessor of that mode of being has rejected him. In other words, no-one, however evil, is irredeemable. Even rejection of God does not lead to final condemnation. And with this important and reassuring conclusion we may leave our analysis of the three orders of being which comprise the 'trinity of being', and may proceed to consider the nature of man.

II. The Trinity of Man

24. It is generally (though perhaps not universally) acknowledged that man is a trinity, consisting of body, mind and soul (or spirit), but the words 'mind', 'soul' and 'spirit' are not used with any precision, 'mind' and 'soul' being sometimes used as though they were interchangeable terms for the same thing, and similarly with 'soul' and 'spirit'. It is much less usual to speak of 'spirit' where 'mind' is clearly intended, or *vice versa*, and it might be thought therefore that the best way to avoid confusion would be to use the words 'body', 'mind' and 'spirit' only, leaving the word 'soul' to discharge the functions of 'mind' or 'spirit' as the occasion or the context might require. I shall not, however, do this, partly because, as I have already pointed out[28], the Greek text of the New Testament distinguishes between 'soul' (*psuche*) and 'spirit' (*pneuma*), partly because, following on this distinction, it seems best to reserve the word 'spirit' for the outpouring activity of the soul, and partly because of the need to avoid confusion between the Holy Spirit (or the Holy Ghost) and the soul of man, which might arise if the word 'spirit' were used for the latter.
25. Thus we shall speak of the trinity of man as being his resolution into body, mind and soul, and the task to which we

have to address ourselves is to specify the particulars in which these are essentially distinct. In fact this task cannot be completely accomplished, but we are concerned with the ability of man to perform miracles, and the essential differences can be sufficiently defined for this purpose. We do this by considering the modes of being possessed by these three elements.

26. Starting with the body, it is clear that, as the bodies of all living creatures (on this earth) die and, even while living, are governed by the laws of physics and chemistry, their mode of being is the temporal mode. On the other hand, since we know that man has some sort of relationship with God, and since this relationship cannot be merely temporal, at least one element in the trinity of which man is composed must be entirely free from the restrictions imposed by the temporal order. As we shall see, this is not true of the mind; it follows therefore that the element that enters into relationship with God and responds to his activity is the soul. Thus the mode of being of the soul is not temporal, but clearly also it cannot be supra-eternal, else man would be on a level with God; it follows that the mode of being of the soul is eternal being. And from this the vital conclusion is drawn that the soul of man is free[29].

27. The nature of the being of mind is less easy to determine. It might be thought that mind and body are so clearly distinct that their modes of being must be different and that the being of mind must accordingly be eternal being. But a little reflection will show that the matter is not so simple. For it is easy to see that over a large field the mental responses to physical stimuli are governed by causal law. This causal interaction between mind and matter displays itself in a number of ways. It displays itself particularly in sensory experience, for sight, hearing, the senses of smell, taste and touch, also pain, hunger, thirst and sexual desire are all mental experiences, and all are deterministically caused by the physical condition, or changes in the physical condition, of the body (particularly of the brain), and these conditions or changes of condition are themselves the consequences of activity taking place either in the body itself or in the outside world. The relationship between body and mind disclosed in sensory experience must

be causal, otherwise the world as revealed to us by our senses would not be rational.

28. The causal relation between matter and mind is also illustrated by the facts that our emotional states are largely governed by the state of our bodies – as is recognized by the use of such words as 'sanguine' or 'melancholic' – and that certain mental disorders can be cured by the use of drugs. As examples of causal action in the reverse direction we may point to the facts that some illnesses are classified as 'psychosomatic', implying that the physical illness is the consequence of the mental condition (e.g., severe depression) of the patient, and that recovery from illness is often aided or hampered by the desire, or the lack of desire, for health, or by what is sometimes referred to as the 'will to live'.

29. These considerations lead to the conclusion that matter and mind interact in accordance with a system of law, and that accordingly the being of mind is temporal being, so that matter and mind are ontologically on the same level. This, of course, must not be taken as implying that they are identical or that one is merely a particular instance of the other. It would, for example, be both wrong and incompatible with Christian theory to suppose that mind is a specially rarefied form of matter, or that matter is a mere figment of the imagination. It is true that philosophical systems may be constructed on the basis that one or other of these suppositions is valid, but from the point of view of common sense, and still more from the point of view of anyone desiring to make deductions of practical value in understanding the nature of God, man and the world and their mutual relationships, the construction of such systems is best held to be no more than an interesting logical exercise. We must therefore hold that matter and mind both exist and are distinct entities, not convertible one into the other, but also that as their interactions are governed by causal law they must belong to the same ontological order. And this conclusion is reinforced by the fact that all the higher animals, down to a level which we cannot and need not attempt to determine, have mental experiences and are therefore endowed with minds, yet no animal other than man has any part in the eternal order.

30. Nevertheless this is obviously not the whole picture. For there are other faculties associated with the human mind (but not with the minds of animals) whose activity is not merely a direct reaction to external stimuli, although it is often triggered by such stimuli and is usually associated with conditions in the external world, and in particular cases with the behaviour of living beings in that world. Such faculties include the faculty or sense by which we recognize the validity of analytic and logical thought, the aesthetic sense (in all its manifestations), the moral sense, and the abstract counterparts of these, namely the recognition of the existence, in some form that is not merely subjective, of the concepts of truth, beauty and goodness; and, flowing from this last, conscience and the sense of obligation.
31. These reactions and activities have two important characteristics. The first is that as they are peculiar to the human race we regard them as being of a higher order than the experiences we obtain through our physical senses, which we share with the animal creation. This is reflected in everyday speech, as when we refer, pejoratively, to someone as being sensual or materialistic. And the second characteristic is that we feel, so strongly that we may say we *know*, that the manner in which these faculties are exercised is, at any rate to some extent, under our control, and is therefore not the same for all individuals. This characteristic distinguishes these 'higher' faculties markedly from sensory experiences. Thus a person who is not blind and who, with his eyes open, looks at something, cannot avoid seeing it (though he may of course not *attend to* what he sees), and the same is true for the other senses by which we are aware of the external world[30]. But the response of different people to a poem, a picture or a piece of music may range from rapturous enjoyment to active dislike, and an equal range may divide one man's moral sense from that of another.
32. There is a real ontological distinction here, a distinction in kind, not merely in degree. But this is often obscured in ordinary speech. We tend to regard our appreciation of a beautiful landscape or of a symphony as a mental experience, and as nothing more than that. In this assessment we are certainly in error, for when we speak of truth, beauty or goodness we are dealing with the realm where the soul and the

mind are, as it were, in contact, and with a process whereby the former exerts an influence on the latter. But our obsession with the material world has led us to develop the sensory faculties of the mind to such an extent that we have almost lost sight of the existence of the soul as a distinct part of our being, and as a result are prone to describe as mental activities, or to attribute to the operation of the mind, various activities which are in reality spiritual, and which spring from the activity of the soul. If we restore the distinction between these two essential parts of our being, recognizing that they not only differ in the faculties they embody, the manner in which they exercise those faculties and the purposes they serve, but also differ *ontologically*, we shall have a very much clearer picture of the nature of that remarkable being 'man' and, as we shall see later, we shall also have gone a long way towards unravelling the mystery of miracles.

33. With these considerations in mind we may *define* mind as that part of the make-up of human beings which has temporal being, but is not material and is therefore not comprised in the body. All activities, which in colloquial speech we may unthinkingly refer to as mental activities but which are exercisable in a manner that is unconditioned by the temporal order, must be ascribed to the soul, which has eternal being. Since then the being of the mind is temporal being it follows that the body and the mind, and in fact the whole physical and psychical world, are subject to a system of law[31]. We may, for convenience, regard this system as consisting of three categories – (a) physical law, i.e., the laws governing the interactions of matter and radiation with each other and with space and time, in the absence of interference from the psychical world; (b) psychical law, i.e., the laws governing the interactions of the various elements of which mind and mental activity are composed, and which manifest themselves as thought, emotion, desire, and so on, with each other and with space and time, in the absence of interference from the physical world (if such be possible) *and also from the eternal order*; and (c) interactive law, i.e., the laws governing the interactions of the physical and psychical worlds[32]. Of these three categories our knowledge of the first is both extensive and systematized, of the

second almost non-existent and of the third very sketchy, almost entirely empirical and not in any way systematized. It is clear therefore that an enormous field yet remains for scientific investigation, but in pursuing such investigation it must be borne in mind that the boundaries of the categories may not be very precise.

34. The definition of mind given in the preceding paragraph might be thought to be too restrictive, in that it would seem to imply that, as mental activity is part of the activity of the temporal order, its products must also be linked to that order and must therefore cease when the body (and the mind) dies. This, however, is not a necessary inference. For the products of mental activity may, at the discretion of the soul, be taken over by the soul into the eternal order, and may thereby be made the possessors of eternal being[33]; and on any reasonable interpretation of man's association with the eternal order and his power, by virtue of his possession of eternal being, to transcend the limitations of time and space, we must hold that this transference does in fact take place. The true inference to be drawn from the definition of mind is that the statement made earlier[34] that the soul of man is free may be supplemented by the inverse statement that it is in his soul, and only there, that man's true freedom is to be found.

III. The Trinity

35. It is a fundamental and vital doctrine of Christianity that God is triune – three in one and one in three. We know this by revelation, not by reasoning from first principles, but it is both interesting and instructive to note that at least some part of the doctrine of the Trinity is deducible from the opening words of the Lord's Prayer, which we invoked earlier to establish the truth that God is supra-eternal. For our former purpose we analysed the phrase 'which art in heaven'; for our present purpose we examine the content and meaning of the words 'Our Father'.

36. Now it is obvious that when we say 'Our Father' we are not using the word 'father' in its ordinary sense. The explanation

usually given is that when we address God in this way we are speaking metaphorically, and we interpret the metaphor by ascribing to the phrase two meanings – first, that we should look to God as a source of love, authority and power, as a child ought to look on his parents both as loving him and as directing and controlling his development; and secondly, that God provides the model for earthly parents, the ideal towards which they should strive in their relation to their children. No doubt these are justifiable interpretations, but they certainly do not exhaust the meaning of the invocation with which the Lord's Prayer opens, nor do they express the most important truth contained in it. In fact they invert reality by explaining the supra-eternal in terms of the temporal and the eternal, and they do less than justice to him who taught his disciples how to pray. For Jesus did not say, 'Your relation to God should be similar to that which, when you were children, you bore towards your parents, and if you yourselves are parents you should model your treatment of your children on God's treatment of you'. He said, quite simply, 'God is your Father'. We can only interpret this uncompromising statement correctly by recognizing two things: first, that (as is obvious enough) 'fatherhood' is a relation between two beings, and secondly, that its essence is not fully contained or expressed in the relation between an earthly parent and his (or her) child, which is only the manifestation in the temporal order of a much more fundamental relationship having its being in the supra-eternal order. This relationship is a principle inhering in God himself, a principle which, when he created the natural world, he decided to incorporate, in an appropriate form, in living creatures.

37. At the earthly level, that is, the temporal level of matter and mind, fatherhood is associated with the process of begetting. We know a great deal about the physical reactions which take place when this process is set in motion, and we know by experience the desires, that is, the mental conditions, by which we are impelled to initiate the process. We can reasonably suppose that the higher animals are impelled by similar desires (although in their case the desires are probably wholly epiphenomenal). We also know a great deal about the physical

means by which characteristics are transmitted from father and mother to son or daughter, but we know, as yet, virtually nothing of the laws of psychical heredity, in so far as these are not entirely linked with physical heredity. We are, of course, under a duty to extend the bounds of our knowledge as far as possible, but the fact that our understanding of the physical and psychical laws whereby life, and the characteristics of living beings, are carried on from generation to generation is limited in no way hampers our present inquiry. For this rests, not on a full knowledge of the laws implanted by God into the temporal world to enable his plan of evolutionary development to be carried forward, but on the existence of one feature of the concept of begetting about which there can be no doubt, a feature which lies at the root of and informs all the processes, both experienced and not experienced, both physical and psychical, involved in its temporal manifestation, whether in human beings or in other animals or in the plant world. This is that begetting is a means of self-expression. It displays this feature at three levels: first, it is the means whereby self-expression is given to the principle of life itself, the principle which imbues all living matter and distinguishes it from non-living matter; secondly, it is the vehicle for the self-expression of the individuality by which the various species of the vegetable and animal worlds are differentiated and by which the essential feature of variety is maintained within the unity of the ecological system; and thirdly, in human beings, it is also the process whereby personality, which is the possession of eternal being, is enabled to express itself (or to be transmitted) from generation to generation.

38. In our experience of living creatures begetting is a process, but the word 'process' is linked with space and time and cannot be applied outside the temporal order. Since, however, God is our Father, we must, in some measure, be begotten by him, thus the processes of reproduction with which we are familiar do not comprise the essence of begetting, they are in fact no more than the manifestation in the temporal order of a principle of self-expression which is independent of the existence of that order, a principle whose essence is supra-eternal. From this fact the very important deduction can be made that

although, in common with the whole of the temporal world and the beings who inhabit the eternal order, we are created beings[35], we are also beings in whom God has, to some extent and in some manner which we need not here attempt to define, expressed himself. It is in this fact, combined with the fact that we are, in part, possessed of eternal being and therefore of the power of response, that we find the source of our duty to God and of our sense of obligation; it is therefore the foundation on which the whole moral law rests. It is in this fact also that, as eternal being confers on those possessing it the gift of freedom, we find the source of the tension between duty and desire, the tension, subsisting in the will itself, between submission to the will of God and the lure of self-aggrandizement, from which we can never escape. But these deductions, important though they are, are not the only or even the most basic conclusions to be drawn from the fact that the principle of self-expression to which the name 'begetting' is applied inheres in God himself. For we learn from it that the activity of God finds expression, not only in creation, in maintaining the created world in being and in pouring out the essence of his Being, the Holy Spirit, on those who can receive and respond to it, it expresses itself also in the principle of begetting; and since God exists independently of the created world, this principle must also reveal itself without reference to the created world. In other words, God is Father, not only to human beings, but also before there were any human beings; he is Father in himself, in the absence of any created beings, whether living or not living, whether material or immaterial, he is Father 'before all worlds'. And since fatherhood is a relationship, God is also Son, thus the existence of at least two Persons in the Godhead is established.

39. The begetting of the Son by the Father is therefore a characteristic inhering in God. It is an event in supra-eternity and is therefore not translatable into the language of space and time. Nevertheless it is our duty to try to understand God to the best of our ability, and accordingly we are not entitled simply to assert that the Son is begotten by the Father and to regard this as a statement to which no meaning can be attached. On the other hand, as our intellectual powers are limited by the facts that our minds have temporal being and that, conse-

quently, in our efforts to grasp the reality and meaning of the supra-eternal and eternal orders, we find it impossible to eliminate completely the concept of time, we may legitimately think of the begetting of the Son by the Father as being not only an event which took place before all worlds, but also as a process taking place continuously, now and throughout all time, provided that we bear in mind that this is no more than a way of bringing an incomprehensible truth within the scope of our comprehension.

40. The existence of the third Person of the Trinity may be inferred from the facts that God is active and that his activity is, in part, directed to making himself known to man. To see this we consider the two manifestations of his activity already mentioned, namely creation and begetting. Neither of these is easily intelligible to the human mind, and indeed any definition that may be attempted must be incomplete, for although men and women can and do exercise activities akin to creation (as, for example, when they produce true works of art) and begetting, these are in reality the expression, within the limits of the eternal and temporal orders, of activities in the supra-eternal order which our minds cannot fully grasp. Creation and begetting are, however, not the only manifestations of God's activity; if they were, our knowledge of him would only extend to the fact that it is his will that the human species should exist and should be maintained in being, and this is by no means the case. We rightly claim to have some further understanding of God's nature, as, for instance, in our ability to discern some purpose underlying the development of the human race, in our conviction that this development is in some sense *willed*[36], and in our recognition of the existence of a moral law. These and, so far as God deems it right to reveal himself to us, other insights come to us by virtue of the Holy Spirit, which is the third Person of the Trinity. The Holy Spirit is clearly not created, since it is supra-eternal and embodies the essence of God himself, nor is it begotten, because it is not identical with the Son; its relation to the other two Persons of the Trinity is described as *proceeding*, by which is meant that it is continually poured out from both the Father and the Son[37]. The Holy Spirit is thus the form in which the activity of the triune God

manifests itself; it is this Spirit which is projected into the angels and into the souls of men and women and enables them to grasp, however dimly, the nature of the divine Being from whom it proceeds. The revelation of the nature of God to the souls and minds of men is not, however, the only function of the Holy Spirit, for it is also the Paraclete, the Advocate, the Intercessor, by means of which the response of human beings to God's activity is conveyed back to him. It is thus the medium of communication between God and man, maintaining them in contact and carrying messages in both directions, thereby ensuring that, while God will certainly never forget man, neither can man ever forget God.

41. It is customary to speak of the three elements of which the Godhead is composed as Persons, and this usage has become enshrined in statements of orthodox belief, but it must be understood that the word 'person' as ordinarily used by human beings is as inadequate to describe the mystery of the divine Being as is the word 'begetting', in its human connotation, to describe the relation of the Father to the Son. For 'person' to us means a human being, and the essence of personality, the characteristic which distinguishes those beings who are persons from those who, though individuals, are not persons, is the possession of eternal being. Human beings possess this mode of being in part, but the angels possess it wholly, having no part in the temporal order. Thus we must admit angels also into the category of persons. But the being of God is supra-eternal, and it is therefore supra-personality, a form of personality unimaginable by us, that is shared by the members of the Trinity. These three Persons (or supra-persons) share the same 'substance' – in the medieval sense of that word; but although this fact is proclaimed in the Nicene Creed[38] it is a statement that can give rise to misunderstanding, because the substance of anything is defined as the unchanging and wholly immaterial substratum on which the accidents, i.e., the properties of that thing as revealed to our senses and to scientific investigation, are based, or in which they inhere; but in God there are no accidents; he is in fact pure Substance, the source of all substance, and pure Being, the source of all being. It has been said that in him substance and accident, subject and object,

being and becoming, all coincide. These are mysteries which can be stated in words, but the verbal expression does not convey their full meaning, serving only to perform the negative (though important) function of reminding us that the philosophic concepts which the words are designed to embody do not originate with us, but are the incomplete, fragmented and distorted image constructed by our finite mental powers of the transcendent and unified reality of God conveyed to us by the Holy Spirit.

CHAPTER ONE

NOTES AND REFERENCES

(The numbers in brackets indicate the paragraphs in which the references occur)

1. (1) Whenever the word 'creature' is used in this book, it should be read as being qualified by the words 'known to us'. For we shall be considering the powers available to human beings, and we do not know whether created beings having similar powers exist now, or have existed in the past, or will exist in the future, in other parts of the universe. We cannot rule out the possible existence of beings possessing the power to work miracles, but we can speak only of beings known to us, that is, of beings living on the earth. See also Note 35 below.
2. (1) *Essay on Man*, Epistle ii, lines 1, 2.
3. (2) William of Occam (or Ockham), born c. 1290 at Ockham, Surrey, died 1349 at Munich. The words in which he expressed his principle, often known as Occam's Razor, are 'Entia non multiplicanda sunt praeter necessitatem'.
4. (2) It is a major object of scientists, when formulating new theories, to include the greatest number and variety of phenomena under the smallest number of principles. It is a great triumph when two sets of apparently unrelated phenomena are shown to be different instances of the operation of some wider law. Thus Occam's Razor is a basic feature of scientific investigation; but its application is nevertheless qualified, because a hypothesis will sometimes be held to be true even though its adoption is not strictly necessary for the explanation of phenomena, if explanation is thereby greatly simplified.
5. (6) Thus when Jesus told his disciples that God takes note of the fall of a sparrow (Matthew x, 29), he referred to God as 'your Father', not as 'its Father'.

6. (7) This is evidenced by the widespread belief in astrology and other irrational occult creeds. Such beliefs, though firmly held, are often admitted only with reluctance or with some degree of shame.
7. (8) Malachi iii, 6.
8. (8) John iv, 24.
9. (8) The Greek word which in the New Testament is translated 'spirit' is *pneuma*, a word which also means 'breath' and carries with it the notion of something emanating or outpoured. A number of different Greek words are translated 'mind'; these include *noos* (whence the English word 'nous'), *gnome, dianoia* and *psuche*, but this last is usually translated 'soul'. In Mark xii, 30 – 'Thou shalt love the Lord thy God with all thy heart, and with all thy soul, and with all thy mind, and with all thy strength' – the words translated as 'soul' and 'mind' are, respectively, *psuche* and *dianoia*.
10. (8) In fact God does not have a variety of characteristics; we are told that he is love (*agape*) (1 John iv, 8), and it is our finite minds that analyse this agapeic activity into the various attributes that we associate with God. See paragraph 17.
11. (8) See paragraphs 26 and 36-38.
12. (9) The deistic notion, which found favour among some eighteenth-century writers, that God was once active but that his activity ceased when he had created the universe and imposed on it the laws by which it is governed, has always been regarded as being closely akin to heresy, and certainly has no place in orthodox Christian belief.
13. (9) Genesis ii, 2.
14. (9) The same may be true of beings in other parts of the universe who, like human beings, are endowed with souls or with some similar manifestation of God's creative activity. See paragraph 26 and Note 35 below.
15. (10) See paragraphs 38 and 40.
16. (10) The Psalms constantly repeat this theme: see, for example, Psalm lxv, 12, 13; Psalm xcvi, 11, 12; Psalm cxiv, 4,6; Psalm cl, 6.
17. (11) The *being* of a thing is that by virtue of which that thing *is*, its *essence* is that by virtue of which it is *what it is*.
18. (11) In Chapter V; see also paragraph 34.

19. (12) Obviously those people who regard the whole creation as the product of a continuous process of evolution must deny the reality of 'life' as anything other than a descriptive term; there can in fact be no doubt that such people are in error, even though they might be able to cite evidence in support of their point of view, e.g., that plants transform inorganic matter into organic matter and that in this process nothing more than chemical change under the action of light is involved.
20. (13) cf. Acts xvii, 28. This text provides scriptural evidence for the statements in paragraphs 8 and 38 that there is a positive relation between the being of man and that of God. Note also that in this same text St Paul points out that the Athenian poets have recognized this fundamental truth.
21. (13) This negative statement must be qualified by the exception already referred to in paragraph 11, which is developed in Chapter V. It should also be noted that in spite of the essential differences between the modes of being, each of the two higher modes can affect beings of lower order.
22. (14) Although we may, for convenience, speak of God as inhabiting the supra-eternal order, he is of course not contained in or conditioned by it; in fact God and the supra-eternal order coincide.
23. (16) See paragraph 33.
24. (17) It should not be forgotten that part of the revelation of God falling under the heading 'Truth' is knowledge of the laws of the created (temporal) universe, which we discover by scientific investigation. It is therefore quite wrong to suppose (as some people do even today) that science and Christianity can ever be opposed.
25. (19) We can, of course, try to remedy mistakes, but this is not the same as reversing time; we can never restore the *status quo ante*, for whatever we may do with this object in view we, and the objects on which we are working, are older when the operation is completed than before it began.
26. (21) See Chapter II, Note 3.
27. (22) See paragraph 40 and Note 37 below.
28. (24) In Note 9 above.
29. (26) It is evident (the point has already been partially made in paragraph 23) that freedom is not a simple concept.

The nature of the freedom enjoyed by the human soul is explained in Chapter II, paragraphs 60-67. It should also be noted that, as the soul has eternal being, the birth of every human baby is, in the strict sense of the word as defined in the following chapter, a miracle, since it involves the implantation by God of an eternal element into what is otherwise a process in temporal reality.

30. (31) It is reasonable to suppose that when two people see the same colour, or hear the same sound, each has a sensory experience which is in some sense identical with, or at least similar or akin to, that of the other, although their emotional or aesthetic experiences may be very different. I think that most people feel instinctively that this is the case, and that if it were otherwise the world would not make sense, although it is obviously impossible to prove the statement, since the experiences of the two people cannot be placed side by side for comparison by a third person or for assessment and measurement by an instrument; and indeed it is difficult (though not, I think, impossible) to define with precision what, in the statement, is meant by the words 'identical', 'similar', and 'akin'. Nevertheless there can be no doubt that our ethical, aesthetic and intellectual activities are free in a way that does not apply to our sensory responses to stimuli.

31. (33) See paragraph 15.

32. (33) In this formulation it is assumed that the eternal order does not act directly on the physical world, but only through the intermediacy of the psychical world. It seems to me that this assumption is probably valid, although it may be unprovable.

33. (34) See paragraph 136.

34. (34) In paragraph 26.

35. (38) We have already seen (in paragraph 22) that, although the inhabitants of the eternal order, i.e., the angels and the souls of human beings (and of any other beings in the universe on whom eternal being and the gifts associated with it have been conferred) are created, the eternal order itself *proceeds* from God (John xv, 26). The reference to beings other than angels and human beings leads to the observation that, when the possible existence of beings outside the Solar System

with whom we might learn to communicate is discussed, the question posed is usually whether such beings, if they exist, are *intelligent*, and although this is very relevant in relation to establishing a means of communication, it is not the most important, or even the most interesting, question. The really fundamental issue is whether they share with human beings the gift of *personality*, that is, whether they are, in whole or in part, possessed of eternal being, and are therefore able to respond to the activity of God.

36. (40) This is not to say that the development of the human race has taken place in accordance with the absolute will of God. In fact, as we shall see in Chapters III and IV, it is *human* wills that have exerted the paramount influence, although in the ultimate God cannot allow his will to be frustrated.

37. (40) From this it appears that eternity is part of, or results from, the activity of the Holy Spirit. It is not, however, to be identified with the Holy Spirit; the two are distinct and eternity does not share the essence of the Holy Spirit. For if, as suggested in paragraph 18, there is development *of* eternity as well as *in* eternity, any blurring of the distinction would involve ascribing development to God, and this is a logical impossibility, as God is all-embracing at his own level of being.

38. (41) In the Christian creeds it is only the Father and the Son who are declared to be 'consubstantial', but I cannot myself see how the Holy Spirit can be excluded from this statement.

2

MIRACLES AND FREEDOM

I. The Meaning of Miracle

42. The word 'miracle' is defined in *The Shorter Oxford English Dictionary* as 'a marvellous event exceeding the known powers of nature, and therefore supposed to be due to the special intervention of the Deity or of some supernatural agency'. Two points arising from this definition are worthy of mention. The first is that in order to understand it fully we must first know precisely what is meant by 'supernatural', but when we again seek enlightenment from the dictionary we are given the apparently tautological definition 'that is above nature; transcending the powers of the ordinary course of nature'. I call this definition '*apparently* tautological' because although it is tautological in form it does bring out the important point that the existence of an ordinary course of nature is assumed. In other words it contains the implicit assumption that events in the natural world are subject to laws and that, from time to time, incidents are or may be observed which appear to conflict with those laws.

43. The second point of interest is that the definition contains, implicitly, a relativistic element. It presupposes the existence of an observer. An event is miraculous if it exceeds the *known* powers of nature, and is therefore *supposed* to be due to an external agency. The italicized words require that there shall be persons who know and suppose, and not all persons may know or suppose the same things. Thus what is a miracle to one man may be a natural event to another, and what is held to be

miraculous at one time may lose that status at a later time. There is no suggestion in the definition that the word 'miracle' may have an absolute meaning – that an event may be miraculous, quite independently of the existence, whether at the time of its occurrence or at any other time, of beings capable of knowing or supposing that it does or does not 'exceed the powers of nature'.

44. It may be said that we have no right to quarrel with the compilers of the dictionary for defining the word in this way. They have quite properly defined it as it is used, and it is not their business to discuss whether people ought to assign to it an absolute meaning, or whether there is a Platonic Idea of miracle existing independently of the existence of beings who may describe any particular event as miraculous[1].

45. There are indeed many people who would not only deny that absolute miracles can occur, but would also assert that the definition is already too wide, on the ground that miracles (so-called) are simply events that are for the time being inexplicable, and that accordingly the word cannot be given an absolute meaning. These are they who, having regard to the rapid expansion of scientific knowledge, and holding that many phenomena, at present appearing to be mysterious (e.g., telepathic communication, psychokinesis, and other similar unexplained phenomena[2]), will in due course be brought within the range of scientific explanation, would wish to add to the definition, after the word 'known', the words 'or knowable, whether in theory or in practice', so that the definition might be revised to read 'an event exceeding the powers of nature, whether those powers are now known or will become known or will be in theory knowable in the future, which is consequently supposed to be due to the action of an agency external to nature.' Moreover, most of those who adopt this position would almost certainly go on to say that the effect of this alteration would be to eliminate miracle entirely (other than as a false concept), since they would argue that all phenomena, however inexplicable they may at present appear to be, are instances of the operation of the laws of nature, and that these laws are all, in theory at least, within the grasp of the human intellect.

46. On the other hand, those who have thought more deeply about the matter would regard the exclusion of a possible absolute meaning of 'miracle' from the dictionary definition as a defect. They would claim that some phenomena cannot be explained by appeal to natural law and that this impossibility is inherent in the phenomena themselves and in the nature of reality. It is not relative to the state of our knowledge, nor does it arise because our minds are finite and therefore unable to grasp the whole of natural law, which may be infinite. Rather it is a consequence of the fact that, although the phenomena may involve natural law, they are not wholly manifestations of that law but are, in part at least, the result of the operation of forces to which natural law is not applicable. It may be contended that those who take this view can do so only as an article of faith, but it must be recognized that the same is true of those who deny that 'miracle' can have an absolute meaning, or assert that such a meaning can be no more than conceptual and can never be realized. What is claimed by these latter people is no more capable of being proved than is the contrary assertion that the range of truth over which the methods of scientific inquiry are effective is not co-extensive with the whole of reality. Such people often adopt an attitude of intellectual superiority towards their opponents, regarding those who believe in the possible or actual occurrence of miracles as unscientific and credulous. But in fact they themselves are on very weak ground and can properly be charged with illogicality. For their argument is based on extrapolation from what they would claim to be known facts, and extrapolation, being a form of induction, is notoriously an unreliable method of argument. Essentially their contention is that because more and more phenomena are being shown to fall within the scope of natural law, this must be true of all phenomena, and the fallacy in this argument is obvious. On the other hand, those who believe that miracles can and do occur are on firmer ground, for their argument, though more subtle, is immune from the charge of illogicality. This argument is that, in the sequence of events (in the physical and psychical worlds and their interactions) the relation between the situation at one moment and that at the immediately

preceding moment must be characterized by one or more of the following three principles: (a) deterministic law, (b) some principle of random behaviour, or (c) some other principle whose operation, though rational (i.e., not random), is external to natural law, a principle to which, anticipating the definition given below, we may give the name 'miracle'. If the range over which deterministic law prevails is all-embracing no room is left for the operation of free will (however that difficult concept is defined); this hypothesis is therefore quite rightly discarded. Likewise the principle of randomness is rejected, except possibly in the interior of enclosed packages of physical or psychical reality, from which there is no means of escape whereby the operation of the principle might be observed, for otherwise those parts of the world in which the principle is the ruling factor would be seen to be chaotic, which is not the case[3]. It follows that to some extent at least the sequence of events is controlled by a principle which is neither random nor the expression of natural law, a principle to which, in fact, natural law must itself be in part subject. It may be added that, as we shall see later[4], denial of the assertion that events are not wholly governed by natural law is incompatible with belief in any God who is more than a mere demiurge.

47. It will be my object in this book to develop the idea of miracle as an active force, having at least as much influence in determining the course of events as the laws of nature, the function of which is indeed, in the most important matters, only the subordinate one of providing the framework in which miracle may act and the 'mechanism' whereby the objectives sought by the miracle-working faculties may be achieved. It will be clear from what has been said above that we are justified in rejecting the argument that the word 'miracle' can only be given a meaning which is relative to the state of human knowledge at a particular time, and that with the advance of science such meaning as it now has will, like the state in Marxist theory, wither away. When the methods of scientific inquiry, and the explanation of events as a linear sequence of cause and effect, have been extended to their utmost limits, we shall find that we are left with a residuum which is truly miraculous; that there are some events, or aspects of the

sequence of events, which cannot, either now or at any future time, be brought within the scope of natural law, and for which, therefore, if an explanation is sought, we must, quite literally, assume the intervention of a supernatural agency. Three outstanding events in the history of the world (apart from its actual creation) may in fact be cited as falling in this category; they are (i) the implantation of life into appropriately complex chemical organisms; (ii) the association of mind with matter in appropriately complex living organisms; and (iii) the association of eternal being with temporal being in appropriately complex higher animals, in other words, the creation of man. As will appear, however, these divine miracles do not exhaust the category, for miracles can be, and in fact frequently are, performed by human beings themselves.

48. It is clear from these preliminary considerations that we need a definition of miracle which is free from the defect of relativity to human knowledge; also, to avoid the accusation of provincialism we should seek to achieve the widest possible generality. Both these conditions are satisfied by the following definition: suppose there is a system A, existing in space and time, or in an order structurally similar to space and time[5], and suppose that the motions, actions and reactions of the elements of which this system is composed are governed by laws which, in the absence of interference from outside the system, completely determine those motions, actions and reactions. Suppose further that there is another system B, external to A, the elements of which can act on those of A, *without reaction in B* (or if there is such a reaction it is independent of the laws of A[6]). Then any such action of B on A is a miracle in A[7].

49. This symbolical definition can be illustrated by an analogy in which, by the introduction of an observer (which in no way limits its generality), its meaning can be clarified. Let us imagine a complex mechanical system consisting of wheels, levers, cylinders in which pistons are oscillating, and so on. This machine is to be taken as representing the system A of the definition, and so long as it is not subjected to any interference the motions of its various parts are subject to the laws of mechanics and are therefore determined, so that if their configuration at any time is known the configuration at any

future time can be calculated. But alongside this machine there is a large chamber containing gas under pressure, and this chamber is connected with several of the cylinders of the machine by pipes, through which the gas in the chamber can be admitted to any one or more of the cylinders by means of valves. We have to imagine that the existence of the chamber and of the pipes and valves is unknown to an observer of the machine, as there is a 'barrier of knowledge' imposed between them and the machine, which his intellect cannot penetrate. The valves can, however, be opened and closed by a man on the other side of the barrier (whose existence is therefore also unknown to the observer), and his control of them is entirely unconstrained. Every time he opens or closes a valve the motions of the various parts of the machine are modified, and the modification will appear to the observer to fall outside the laws by which the machine is governed. It will in fact be a miracle in the system of the machine taken by itself, and will be accounted by the observer as such.

50. It follows that for miracles to occur there must be two systems, one of which is, normally, a determinate system, while the other may or may not be deterministic; if it is, then the laws by which it is governed must be independent of and entirely distinct from those governing the first system. It must also be possible for the second system to act on the first, causing a suspension or modification of its laws, while action by the first system on the second can only take place (if at all) in accordance with the laws of, or as may be freely determined by, the second system. But, as I have shown in Chapter I[8], the first of these requirements is precisely satisfied in the totality of reality as disclosed to our senses and as further revealed by analysis of the words 'Our Father'. The system A is the temporal created order and the temporal beings which inhabit it[9]; that is, the natural order of space and time, energy and mind, plants and animals, which is governed by law; and the system B consists of the supra-eternal and eternal orders and the Being and beings who inhabit them.

51. Moreover if we assume that in the case of systems A and B thus identified the second requirement is also satisfied, i.e., that B can act (conditionally) on A, we can apply the general

definition to the particular case of the universe as known to us; this leads to our defining a miracle as an event in the temporal order involving interference by the supra-eternal order or by beings in the eternal order on the elements of the temporal order, whereby the laws governing the actions, reactions and motions of those elements are (possibly only momentarily, and possibly only at sub-atomic level) suspended or modified. In the case of interference by the supra-eternal order there can be no reaction in that order, since God is not subject to change or metallassis; in the case of interference emanating from the eternal order either there is no reaction or, if there is a reaction, it is because an inhabitant of that order has so determined, moreover, it must be in accordance with the laws of that order and not of the temporal order. The question whether we are justified in making the assumption as to the relation between the systems A and B is thus seen to be the same as the question whether God and the inhabitants of the eternal order can perform miracles. It is to this question that we now turn and, although such proofs as can be given must necessarily rest on the metaphysical 'logic of eternity' rather than on observation, the reasonableness of an affirmative answer in both cases, and its agreement with observation, will, I hope, be sufficiently established.

II. Divine Miracles

52. God is the only supra-eternal Being; he contains, is contained in, and coincides with, the supra-eternal order. Hence a divine miracle is an event in which the supra-eternal order acts, without reaction, on the temporal order[10]. Since God is the Creator of the temporal order and of everything whose being is temporal being, and as it is by his activity that the being of all temporal beings is maintained and by his ordinance that the laws governing the motions of those beings were laid down and maintain their status and power, the fact that he can perform miracles should occasion no surprise. Rather it is the denial of that fact that should cause us to express astonishment. For if God cannot perform miracles then

either his connection with his creation has been severed or else he himself is subject to natural law. In the latter case not only the concept of law but also the actual form and content of natural law must be greater than or at least ontologically prior to God, and in order to provide for its existence we would have to posit a super-God. This super-God must be independent of natural law, otherwise the hypothesis leads to an infinite regress; he therefore becomes the true God, and this conclusion contradicts the assumption that divine miracles are impossible. If, on the other hand, God is not subject to natural law but has severed the connection with his temporal created universe (we can, for the reason just given, rule out the possibility that the severance was effected by a super-God), then we have to face the problem of explaining how and why the universe is maintained in being. To the first question the only possible answer is that, when God had completed the task of creation, he retired from the scene, having implanted in his creation sufficient ontological energy to enable it to continue its being, unaided by him, for a limited time, at the end of which the whole temporal structure, consisting of the physical and psychical worlds, together with space and time, would cease to be. And to the second question no very intelligible answer can be given. We would have to suppose that God created the temporal universe for some inscrutable reason of his own, a reason from which all reference to the elements and organized structures making up that universe, whether living or nonliving, is entirely excluded. His position would be similar to that of a man who spent his life constructing artifacts, not for the purpose of contemplating and enjoying them, or of enabling them to be enjoyed by others, but nevertheless ensuring that they are preserved, unseen, for a limited time and then destroyed. The departure from rationality and intelligibility is in fact even greater than is indicated by this illustration, for a human artifact is inanimate, whereas God's creation contains living beings: in particular it contains ourselves, who are not only living but are capable of entertaining purposes and interests, which we would have to suppose are entirely irrelevant to God's inscrutable purpose. Our status would therefore be that of creatures endowed with faculties which, though rational and purposive, are destined to frustration, since they can play no part in any rational or purposive scheme, either temporal or eternal. God himself is reduced, in his relation to the earth, and possibly also to the whole temporal universe known to us, to a demiurge, and mankind to a purposeless and pointless folly[11].

53. There is, however, an even more fundamental objection to the supposition that God has severed the connection with his temporal creation. This is that the severance would have to be irrevocable, for otherwise God could, at will, restore the connection, and this is equivalent to saying that his power to override the laws of nature is merely in suspense, that he can perform miracles but does not choose to do so. Thus the severance hypothesis involves the implication that God has voluntarily and irrevocably divested himself of certain powers in relation to his creation, and as God is free from both change and metallassis this is a contradiction in terms[12].

54. The fact that God can perform miracles does not, of course, *logically* prove that he actually does so. But the arguments of the preceding paragraphs show that to deny that he intervenes from time to time in the ordering of events is open to the same objection as the claim that he cannot do so. It is indeed difficult if not impossible to imagine a Supreme Being as possessing a power which is never exercised, and we may therefore assume, without fear of contradiction on any rational ground, that divine miracles do occur. In fact three occasions in the history of the world have already been listed[13] when events took place which almost all Christians and many who are not Christians would regard as not falling wholly within the bounds of natural law, so that although, in the attempt to explain them, the mechanisms by which they were brought about may be progressively more fully revealed by scientific investigation, there will always remain a mysterious element on which such investigation can throw no light. And the probability thus established is strengthened by an argument from first principles. For we know that God is active and that his activity cannot be reflexive; it must therefore penetrate the eternal order or the temporal order or both. Now in creating the temporal order God must have had a purpose, for God is free,

and the concept of freedom is inseparable from that of purpose[14]; moreover it needs no argument to make the point that, in so far as the ordering of events is under man's control (as is certainly the case to some extent since man is also free), God's purpose is not being constantly aided, indeed in some respects man is actively striving to prevent its fulfilment. But God cannot allow his purpose to be defeated, and he must therefore interfere, either continuously or from time to time, and either directly or indirectly, to set things on the right course. This simple argument points to the fact that God's activity does penetrate the temporal order, and every such penetration is a divine miracle[15].

55. If then it is certain that God can and does perform miracles, why does the matter, for some people, remain in doubt? The reason is that divine miracles do not ordinarily manifest themselves directly in the physical world. Except in rare cases, they are actions by the supra-eternal order on the psychical part of the temporal order, and as we know little about the laws governing the psychical world, breaches of those laws are not recognizable as such and are therefore not accounted as miracles. There can, I think, be no doubt that God does, from time to time, act directly on the physical world, but we learn from the New Testament that his purposes are not to be achieved by spectacular methods; it is probable therefore that his interventions take place at the molecular or the atomic or even the sub-atomic level and accordingly pass unnoticed[16]. This does not rule out the possibility that spectacular action by God on the physical world may sometimes occur, but it seems that such occasions are now rare (although they may at earlier times have been more frequent), and the effects of his intervention are either disbelieved or are attributed to some unknown but wholly natural cause. Moreover, it is, I think, probable that since the creation of man God has increasingly decided to use him as his instrument, exercising his power directly on the eternal being of human souls and thereby influencing indirectly the psychical (and more rarely the physical) constituents of the temporal order. We need not inquire why, if this reading of the facts is correct, God chooses to exercise his miraculous powers chiefly through the agency of man, and otherwise for

the most part by suspending or modifying psychical rather than physical law; we must be satisfied with believing that he can thus most effectively bring about the fulfilment of his purpose in the temporal order.

III. Miracles and Man

56. Since the being of man is partly temporal and partly eternal he has all the equipment necessary for the performance of miracles, and although the arguments by which we deduced that God *does* perform miracles from the fact that he *can* do so cannot be applied to man without a good deal of modification, it is reasonable to suppose that possession of the equipment carries with it the power to use that equipment, that the possession of any power conferred by God imposes a duty to exercise that power, and that as man is not totally disobedient to God he does in fact use the powers with which God has endowed him, including the power to work miracles. Alternatively it may be argued that although man is free his freedom does not extend to enabling him to disregard any part of his divine endowment or to allow any faculty given to him by God to atrophy by complete disuse; from this it would follow that he *cannot avoid* performing miracles. Of these two arguments it seems to me that, although the second may carry some weight, the first has much the greater force; they would of course be clinched if empirical evidence of human miracles could be adduced. This, however, may prove to be impossible, for the reason that we do not fully know the laws of the temporal order, so that any claim that these laws have been overridden can always be met by the assertion that more complete knowledge would disprove the claim, and in such a case neither side can show that the other is wrong. It is more profitable to rely on metaphysical arguments with the object of identifying the spheres, assuming that these exist, in which man's miraculous powers are exercised. It will be seen that these arguments will at the same time go far towards justifying the assumption, so that at the end they have been so strongly reinforced that it would be quite unreasonable to reject them. The arguments

fall under a number of heads which are dealt with in the remaining sections of this chapter and in the following three chapters. It will be found that they do not only increase our understanding of man's miraculous powers and the range of their application, they also enable us to draw out other important consequences of man's place in the hierarchy of being.

IV. The Meaning of Freedom

57. As we have seen[17], the souls of men have eternal being and are therefore free. The word 'freedom', however, as ordinarily used, is imprecise, and we must therefore specify the kind of freedom that man enjoys. In its broadest sense freedom means the absence of constraint; whenever a constraint is imposed there is a loss of freedom. Thus freedom is not an indivisible entity which one may or may not possess; one may have more or less freedom according to the degree to which one is subject to constraint. The constraint may be physical, as when a person is gagged, bound or imprisoned, or it may be mental, as when a man is, or believes that he is, threatened with dire consequences if he acts (or fails to act) in a certain way, or if he is in any way intimidated or overborne by someone with a stronger character, and compelled to do something which he otherwise would not do. The constraints imposed by the laws, orders and regulations made by those on whom we confer the power to govern us are primarily mental constraints, although we invest the administrators of the law with the right to enforce its requirements by also threatening the imposition of physical constraints, where this appears to be necessary to ensure, so far as possible, that its edicts are not disregarded. In general, since the law is a human construct, it can be varied or lifted by the community at will; thus the limitation of freedom inherent in the existence of law is not absolute. Moreover, a primary object of the law is not to limit, but to increase, freedom, for the constraints it imposes are often directed to preventing one individual or group from limiting the freedom of another individual or group. It is for this reason that for the most part

we voluntarily accept the limitations imposed by the law, while remaining on our guard to ensure that the objective of increasing rather than limiting freedom is not forgotten.

58. Since freedom is an attribute of the souls of men which are created by God, we see that it is a gift of God and as such must be an absolute good. From this we learn that it is our duty to aim at creating circumstances in which everyone will enjoy the maximum degree of freedom. In fact, in our attempts to formulate a practical ethical maxim for the guidance of mankind we would be much nearer the truth if in the utilitarian principle that the end to be sought is the greatest happiness of the greatest number (a principle which most democratic governments today regard as axiomatic) we were to replace the word 'happiness' by the word 'freedom'. This of course is not the same as saying that it is our duty, so far as it lies in our power, to grant complete freedom to everybody. It means that we should take as our target a state of the world in which freedom can be gradually but continuously increased without incurring the risk of its being abused. This should be our objective, and it is important that we should clearly understand that it cannot be brought about by passing or repealing laws, but only by the regeneration of human nature[18]. For although law can play its part in aiding the forces of regeneration by providing conditions in which they are not hampered, it cannot supply the necessary continuing impulse, which can arise only in the soul, and will not arise there unless we recognize, in our souls as well as in our minds, that our duty to man is not confined to procuring his physical and mental well-being, it must seek also his spiritual well-being, and that these requirements are not absolutes in themselves but are elements in our duty to God.

59. It might be thought that it does not lie within the power of human beings to increase their own freedom and that of their fellow men otherwise than by lifting the shackles on freedom that they themselves have imposed. It should, however, be clear from what has already been said that the powers of human beings are not thus limited, but extend, to a degree that lies partly within their control, to lifting the shackles imposed by natural law; and it will be my object in the later chapters of

this book to show, not only that this is the case, but also that it is only by using their powers in this way, by diverting, under the guidance of God, the course of events from the path they would follow if the operation of natural law were left untrammelled, that they can discharge their duty to aim at creating conditions in which human limitations on freedom may be eased without the risk of anarchy. As a preliminary to this task we must briefly consider the nature and content of the restrictions imposed by the laws of the temporal order.

60. It is clear that the rule of natural law extends over the whole of the temporal order and over everything whose being is wholly temporal being. Thus not only inanimate nature but also all plants and animals (other than man) are wholly subject to natural law and have no true freedom. It is true that those beings that are endowed with minds, particularly the higher animals, appear to be free, but the freedom we attribute to them is fictitious. Their behaviour is in fact governed by the interplay of physical and psychical law, but we are misled into thinking that it is freely determined because we are almost wholly ignorant of the latter. Thus if a stick is thrown for a dog to fetch it may appear to us that he is free to choose whether to fetch it and bring it back, or to pick it up and then drop it, or not to go after it at all. But this is mere appearance; in fact his action is entirely determined, but because we do not know the laws determining it we ascribe to him a freedom of choice. We are led to do this because we, who have a measure of freedom in the eternal order, by which some of our actions (in the temporal order) are indirectly governed, wrongly attribute this freedom to the temporal part of our being, this being the only part of which we are fully aware and, noting the many similarities between human and animal behaviour, assume that our freedom is also enjoyed by the higher animals.

61. Human beings also, in so far as their being is temporal being, are subject to natural law, and they adapt their lives accordingly. Moreover, as natural law governs the psychical as well as the physical world, the limitations on their freedom it imposes are not wholly external. It is physical law that renders it impossible for a man to leap fifty feet into the air without mechanical aid[19], and it is also because of physical law that if a

man falls and breaks a leg, he is not free to get up and walk. These are both instances of the external action of natural law in limiting his freedom. But this action may also take place internally. Thus it is natural law that decrees that a faulty chromosome may predispose a man to crime; in fact the whole mechanism whereby the mental qualities and, more pertinently, the character, of a human being are determined by his genetic structure (in so far as they *are* so determined) is an instance of the interaction of the physical and psychical worlds in accordance with law. This argument is sometimes adduced in criminal cases; thus if a man is charged with committing a crime of violence and admits the charge, it may be cogently argued in his defence that in his case the urge to violence is innate, that it is the product of his genetic structure and is therefore irrepressible, and that accordingly his freedom to avoid violent action is limited by natural law. This defence must be given weight, for although some of the limitations on freedom resulting from genetic constitution are not absolute and can be offset, the process by which this is done cannot be invoked at a moment's notice, to cause or prevent the commission of a particular act; it is a lengthy process, involving action by the will throughout the course of a lifetime, in which the miraculous powers of man are called into play[20].

62. This brief discussion suffices to show the relation of freedom to temporal being, but it clearly does not touch on the problem of defining the freedom of the soul, for this cannot be described in terms derived from our experience of the temporal order and applicable only to that order. It is, of course, true that the soul is not subject to bodily or mental constraints, and we can therefore properly speak of the soul as being free in the sense that it is not bound by, and is under no compulsion to adapt itself to or even to take note of, the circumstances of the natural world. But these are negative freedoms, whereas the true freedom of the soul is positive, and in order to define its nature we start by reflecting that an essential characteristic of positive freedom is *activity*. (In what follows we shall be speaking only of positive freedom; the qualifying adjective will therefore be generally omitted.) The association of activity with freedom is one of ontological necessity, that is to say, it is not possible for

the latter to *be* in the absence of the former. This statement is axiomatic; any attempt to establish it by reasoning from more fundamental principles would result in nothing more than a restatement in other terms. Its truth is probably most readily seen if it is translated into subjective terms by saying that it is not possible to entertain the idea of freedom independently of that of activity. Briefly, then, we may say that freedom which is inactive and is therefore not exercised is not freedom[21].

63. This paradoxical statement has the merit of driving home the point I wish to make, but the apparent contradiction in it must be resolved, and when this is done a further important point emerges. For we can expand the paradox into the more precise, but less striking statement that if a being is described as being free, or as having any measure of freedom, in a particular sphere, but is totally inactive in that sphere, then the description must be false. Inactivity implies a complete absence of freedom, but this condition may result, not from the imposition of constraints, but from the fact that the being whose freedom is in question has no part in or in relation to the relevant sphere of activity. Thus plants and animals (other than man) are inactive in the eternal order, but this inactivity is not the consequence of imposed constraints but of the fact that no part of their being is eternal being. And in the same way no being, whether temporal or eternal, whether human or angelic, is active in the supra-eternal order, for in this order only God exists and therefore only God is active.

64. We may rule out the possibility that any part of the activity resulting from the exercise of freedom in the eternal order is random[22], for although there may (indeed, as is shown below, there certainly must) be conflict in heaven it is impossible to believe that any measure of chaos prevails there. It follows that the activity of eternal beings is *directed* activity; in other words, that all such beings are motivated by a purpose. This is an absolutely fundamental point; unless all its implications are fully grasped it is impossible to understand the true nature of man and his relationship with God. What has been shown is that it is an inescapable fact, derived by reasoning from undeniable axioms, that purpose is inherent in the structure of eternal reality. It is a fact to which we shall find it necessary

constantly to refer in defining the role of miracle. And it is from this fact also that we draw the important conclusion that heaven is not without conflict, for it is impossible to suppose that its inhabitants – the angels and the souls of men and women who have completed their earthly courses – are all motivated by identical purposes[23], and if there are different purposes the pursuit of one may conflict with the pursuit of another. But it would be wrong to suppose that conflict in heaven is destructive[24], or that it engenders antagonism or ill feeling, for although in the 'linear' temporal world of cause and effect opposing purposes which meet cannot coexist – one must annihilate the other with the consequent impairment of personality – this is not the case in the 'multi-dimensional' world of eternity, where development takes place by metallassis and not by change.

65. The central importance of the conclusion that eternal beings are necessarily motivated by purpose springs from, and is underlined by, the fact that the argument by which it is established can also be applied to God; indeed its application to God has even greater force than its application to eternal beings. For although there is conflict in heaven there can be no conflict in God. Thus, even if it were possible to entertain the notion that God could create the universe wantonly, with no purpose, the argument that freedom implies activity and activity implies purpose would force us to discard it. It follows that the creation of the universe must have been a purposeful activity on the part of God; it must fall into place as part of a gigantic plan, a plan to be worked out in both time and eternity[25]. We cannot possibly hope to grasp the full meaning of this plan, but must be content to try to understand what part we ourselves play in it. That it is (within the bounds of our knowledge) a uniquely important part is obvious for, as we have shown[26], man is a creature in whom God has, in part, expressed himself.

66. From this we deduce that the plan in which man is an active participant is inspired by a purpose objectively inhering in God and not external to him. We can easily conceive, indeed it may possibly be true, that God's purpose in creating the universe is comprised within the limits of birth and death, that

he created it, together with time and space, to endure for a certain time and then come to an end, but we cannot conceive that his purpose for man is thus limited, as such an idea would mean that he was limiting his expression of himself. His purpose for man must therefore be an eternal purpose. The fulfilment of this purpose is what we mean by the word 'salvation'[27], and as man is both an individual and a member of a species, and as he has been placed in a world of space and time, of cause and effect, a world therefore of evolution, it is clear that God's purpose includes both the salvation of every individual and the salvation of the human race. (It may be added that a similar argument can be applied to the angels, who are also in need of salvation, even though they do not have their being in space and time).

67. The conflict in heaven between the purposes held by different eternal beings is contingent; it is possible, however unlikely it may be, to imagine two eternal beings as holding substantially identical purposes. The conflict between these purposes and God's purpose is, by contrast, in part a necessary conflict, though there is also a very important contingent element. The element of necessity arises from the fact that, as God alone is perfect, all created beings must be imperfect. This necessary imperfection has no moral content, it is an imperfection of being, consisting simply in the inferiority of eternal being to supra-eternal Being, although it affects the activity in which eternal beings express their freedom and this, in the case of human beings, often leads to the pronouncement of false moral judgements. The reason is that we are accustomed to applying moral values to the actions to which the activity of human wills give rise, and because of our limited understanding are unable to distinguish between the activities deriving from the necessary and the contingent imperfections of their being[28]. The inferiority of eternal being to supra-eternal Being is most directly displayed in the fact that in the case of the former personality is individualized, with the consequence that the concern of eternal beings is mainly concentrated on what they deem to be most likely to contribute to their individual well-being, whereas supra-eternal Being, though also Personal, is the source of, and inheres and is manifested in, and is

therefore concerned for the well-being of, everything that is. The inferiority is also seen in the failure of eternal beings, through the imperfection of their understanding, to grasp clearly the part assigned to them in the working out of God's plan, with the result that the purposes which they seek to achieve necessarily conflict, in some measure, with the purposes ordained for them by God.

68. We may reasonably suppose that the necessary element in the imperfection of created beings is fully allowed for in God's plan. For this element no repentance is called for and no forgiveness need be sought. In so far as it is a source of conflict between the purposes which eternal beings seek to achieve and God's purpose, he adapts the intermediate stages in the working out of his plan, without modification of the ultimate objective, to reduce the conflict to a minimum. It is, however, clear that, in the case of human beings at any rate (and the same is true in the case of some of the angels[29]), the necessary imperfection is not the only imperfection leading to conflict with God. For human beings not only fail to understand clearly the role they are required to play in the working out of God's plan, they fail also to make it their primary objective to remedy this defect in their understanding, and have so failed since their first appearance on earth; moreover, in so far as they do understand their true role they fail to accommodate their objectives to fit this role. These failures are not attributable to the necessary imperfection of their wills, they are not imposed by irresistible forces inherent in the structure of reality; their origin lies in the free choice of the wills of human beings, in other words, they are contingent failures. It is, of course, not suggested that the purposes which the wills of human beings have freely selected are in all cases directly opposed to the purposes assigned for them by God, as leading to the fulfilment of his plan, but it is certain that some of them are, and it is probable that few, if any, are in full conformity with his will. For this defect in the activity of our wills, which constitutes original sin[30], and for which we ourselves are fully responsible, repentance is needed and forgiveness must be sought; but even if in these respects we fall short of what is required, we may be certain that, as in the case of our necessary imperfection, God

in his mercy is continually adapting the details of his plan to take account of the circumstances to which our failure to comply with it gives rise, without modifying his ultimate objective, which is the salvation of the human race, as a general will adapt his plan of campaign to take account of the varying fortunes of a battle, without losing sight of the fact that his ultimate object is victory.

69. This analysis brings us to the point where we can define the nature of the freedom possessed by eternal beings, and in particular by the souls and wills of human beings. For although all eternal beings hold and seek to achieve the fulfilment of purposes which must diverge in some measure, and in some cases do diverge in much greater measure than is imposed by necessity, from God's purpose, God could impose constraints on their activity, preventing any progress being made towards the realization of their sinful purposes. Presumably he would do so if direct interference were necessary to prevent the irretrievable frustration of his plan, but the conditions prevailing in the world show that, except in such drastic circumstances (and it is questionable whether they could in fact arise), he does not interfere, so far as the plan relates to human beings, leaving it to them to work out their own salvation by the free exercise of their wills[31]. Thus we arrive at the truth that lies at the core of our understanding of the phenomenon of man, the truth that the freedom of the soul, and more particularly of the will which is its active agent, is *freedom from constraint by God*. This freedom of purpose is related to, but must be distinguished from, the freedom of being possessed by all eternal beings[32], since the former, but not the latter, can be abrogated without annihilating the being possessing it[33], and in fact God must obviously reserve the power to abrogate or curtail it, at least momentarily, otherwise it would lie in the power of man not only to diverge from the purpose ordained by God but to override it, and this, of course, God would not permit.

70. The conclusion at which we have now arrived shows that man's true freedom, the freedom of his soul and will, is an attribute of such fundamental significance that the endeavour to understand it must take precedence over any other task that the human intellect can undertake. For this freedom is not

merely the freedom from constraint by natural law, which the soul enjoys by virtue of the nature of its being, it is also freedom from constraint by God, and is consequently a vital factor in man's relationship with God. It confers on man the power to determine issues having eternal value, and is therefore of infinitely greater importance than the power (which is in reality only a derived or commuted power) of individuals to decide how to act in particular circumstances, which is what is ordinarily meant when the expression 'free will' is used.

71. A further point of fundamental importance, already hinted at[34], is that the freedom of the soul is not a mere negative freedom, an absence of restriction, it is a positive asset. This can be seen by noting that as God is the Creator and Author of everything that is, it would be natural to expect that every identifiable thing is under a compulsion to act in accordance with the laws laid down for that thing. If an artifact is constructed by a human being, it is designed to serve a particular end, and it cannot of its own volition behave otherwise than is provided for in its design and construction. (If it fails to serve the end for which it is designed or to operate in the manner intended by its designer this is not because it decides or wills to act improperly but because its construction is faulty or because it is compelled to perform its task in circumstances not envisaged at the time of its construction.) The point is that there is nothing that either the designer or the constructor can do about this; he cannot, either by avoiding the imposition of a constraint or by the positive conferment of a power, enable any machine (even a computer) to determine its own behaviour; every human artifact must, subject to the laws of nature, act in accordance with its design and construction. (These can, of course, be altered, but the artifact then becomes a new thing.) And it might be expected that, by a similar reasoning, every divine construct must act in accordance with its design and construction, and also, where applicable, with the laws of nature, which are themselves divinely ordained. But this expectation is not realized in the case of human beings, and from this it follows that the freedom they enjoy, the freedom from constraint by God, does not lie in the fact (for it is not a fact) that God has failed to impose certain restrictions which he

might have imposed had he wished to do so; the restrictions are already there in the form of the laws, themselves part of the expression of God's essence, by which the whole universe is governed; it lies in the fact that God has, by a positive act, conferred on mankind the power to *override* them.

72. This fact carries with it the important consequence that the conferment of freedom on man is a part of God's stupendous plan for the whole of his creation, and as God cannot be inconsistent with himself it must also be part of his plan that man should exercise his freedom in accordance with that plan. In other words, the statement that the souls of men and women are free from constraint by God is not to be interpreted as meaning that God turns a blind eye to the manner in which they exercise their freedom. He is *concerned* that they should exercise it rightly. Nevertheless, since they are free from constraint, God's concern does not take the form of compulsion, but of *obligation*, a relationship which is *sui generis* and cannot be defined otherwise than in tautological terms, as all ethical philosophers have understood, but which is seen by this reasoning to derive directly and solely from the ontological status of God and man and the relation established between them by the positive gift of freedom.

73. Moreover, the argument by which we have been led to these conclusions can be carried to a further stage. For if we combine the facts that:

> (i) God has established a special relationship with man by conferring on him the positive gift of freedom;
> (ii) he is concerned that men and women should exercise their freedom in conformity with his plan, one element in which is that they should achieve salvation;
> (iii) he is personal and therefore active, and is also the source of all goodness and all power;

it becomes obvious that God is willing to help every individual and also mankind as a whole to play their true roles in working towards the fulfilment of the plan. Now it is a basic doctrine of Christianity that man cannot achieve salvation by his own unaided efforts; for this the help of God is needed[35]. This, however, need occasion no despair, for although God imposes no constraints his help will be freely given provided that it is freely sought. We can therefore be sure that, although he does not impose himself if no approach to him is made, he will respond to any appeal, however small. And on this fact faith must take its stand, so that, even when it appears to men that their condition is desperate and that their problems are insoluble, hope, if rightly directed, need never be abandoned.

74. It is not now difficult to establish the connection between the exercise of freedom and the performance of miracles. For as man's purposes (i.e., the purposes whose achievement is sought by the activity of his free will) are commensurate with God's purpose, a fact which is seen to be true because it is the divergence between these that constitutes man's original sin, their fulfilment must lie in the eternal order. But as God also attaches value to man's behaviour on earth, this cannot be entirely governed by temporal law; it must in part be governed by his free will. It follows that although the ultimate objective of the will must be eternal its activity must also be effective in the temporal order; it must in part govern behaviour. Thus the eternal being of man must, in pursuing its objective in the eternal order, create objectives in the temporal order, and in endeavouring to attain these temporal objectives must act on his temporal being. Every such action must involve a disturbance of the laws of nature, and this, in accordance with the definitions given in paragraphs 48 and 51, means that in every such action a miracle is performed.

V. The Two Classes of Miracle

75. This brings us to our central problem, that of describing how man performs miracles and in what manner the exercise of his power to perform them is displayed. This is not only the central problem, it is also the most difficult, for the reason that the answers to these two questions cannot be deduced from first principles, nor can the occasions on which man's thaumaturgic power is displayed be brought within the scope of empirical

investigation. It is impossible to devise a set of experiments from which it could be established that if certain conditions are set up a miracle will result, for in any such experiment the inevitability of the occurrence of the result whenever the conditions are satisfied would show that the relation between them is not one of miracle but one of law.

76. In these circumstances there is only one course to follow; that is to set out what I hold to be the true theory and to leave this to justify itself by its inherent reasonableness and by the fact that it provides a more comprehensive and more self-consistent explanation of the human phenomenon than any other. The theory will classify man's thaumaturgic powers under three heads – those operating within the individual, those bearing on the evolution of the human race, and those directly affecting the outside world. Miracles falling under the first two heads are essentially of the same kind and will be called *perithaumata* (singular perithauma), those falling under the third head are sufficiently distinct to demand a different description; these may be called *apothaumata*. It is the latter that ordinarily spring to mind when miracles are spoken of, because although they are probably rare they may well be spectacular (e.g., healing miracles). Moreover, apothaumata are important, and may become increasingly so in the future[36]. Nevertheless, it is by means of perithaumata, which occur more or less continuously but are for the most part unobserved, even by the agent, that the characters of individuals and of the human race are built up. The following three chapters will therefore be devoted to describing how man's perithaumatic powers are exercised, leaving the description of apothaumata to be given in Chapter VI.

CHAPTER TWO

NOTES AND REFERENCES

(The numbers in brackets indicate the paragraphs in which the references occur)

1. (44) Compare the definition of Truth as 'agreement with reality'. This is an absolute definition, for it presupposes that 'reality' is absolute reality, not dependent on the opinions of any person. It is true that agreement must be agreement between two things, and that, as one of these is 'reality' the other must be a statement made by, or a thought or idea in the mind of, some intelligent being (not necessarily human – angels may hold opinions), so that the definition implies the existence of such beings; nevertheless it does not suggest that truth is in any way relative to the opinions of those beings. In fact, since the concept of truth implies the existence of beings who perceive it, we may amplify the definition of truth by saying that a person is perceiving truth in regard to a particular matter if his relation (or the relation of his mind or soul) to that matter is in conformity with the relation of God to it. We can indeed go further and say that the perception of truth cannot be defined in any other way; in other words the fact that we recognize that the concept of the perception of truth has a meaning is evidence of the existence of God. If God does not exist, then although we may speak of 'truth' we cannot assign to it any ultimate meaning.
2. (45) Although I shall be arguing that miracles do occur, I do not suggest that such phenomena as these are miraculous. On the contrary, I think it probable that, though unusual, they are entirely natural, being instances of the operation of the laws of psycho-physical interaction (see paragraph 33).
3. (46) It has already been remarked (in paragraph 15) that

randomness cannot prevail in the temporal order. It should be pointed out, however, that what is excluded is absolute randomness, i.e., the real, not merely the apparent, absence of causal control of the sequence of events. (It is, perhaps, relevant to point out that it is by no means easy to define with precision what is meant by 'causal control in the sequence of events', the control that characterizes a deterministic system. An attempt at such a definition is given in Chapter V, Note 10). In everyday speech 'random' or 'chance' is often used to describe the outcome of a set of actions or circumstances in which the operative causes are not supposed to be non-existent, but are extremely complex and, so far as they can be known, apparently free from any factor which might favour one result rather than another. In such circumstances all possible outcomes are held to be equally probable, and prediction of the outcome in a particular case becomes impossible. It is in this sense that 'random' is used when we say that the distribution of the cards when four hands are dealt from a well shuffled pack, or the fall of a tossed coin, is random, but as used here (and in paragraph 15) the word is intended to mean the non-existence of any cause, and not merely that the causes are complex and apparently unrelated to the particular features on which attention happens to be directed.

The exception cited in the text has been included in order to forestall the criticism that Heisenberg's Uncertainty Principle has been ignored. This principle states that in any experiment to determine the position and momentum of sub-atomic particles there is necessarily a margin of error, and that the product of the errors in the specification of these two characteristics is equal to Planck's constant h. This fact would seem to allow for a certain measure of randomness in the movements of these particles, but it seems to me to be certain that randomness cannot prevail macroscopically, and that if it prevails in isolated parcels of space-time then in order to avoid chaos it must be assumed that such isolated parcels have definite boundaries, through which randomness cannot escape, so that each may be treated as a particle, whether of physical or of psychical reality, and that, despite the absolute randomness of the internal structures of these particles, in their interactions between themselves and with other types of particle, they obey definite laws.

It is interesting to note that the principle that randomness must be excluded was recognized as early as the sixth century. Boethius (c. 480-524 AD) in his celebrated *De Consolatione Philosophiae* wrote (V, i): 'If chance be defined as a result produced by random movement without any link of causal connection, I roundly affirm that there is no such thing as chance at all, and consider the word to be altogether without meaning, except as a symbol of the thing designated. What place can be left for random action, when God constraineth all things to order? For "*ex nihilo nihil*" is sound doctrine which none of the ancients gainsaid, although they used it of material substance, not of the efficient principle; this they laid down as a kind of basis for all their reasoning concerning nature. Now if a thing arises without causes, it will appear to have arisen from nothing. But if this cannot be, neither is it possible for there to be chance in accordance with the definition just given.' (English translation by H.R. James, London, Elliot Stock, 62 Paternoster Row, 1897; p. 226).

4. (46) In paragraphs 52, 53.

5. (48) The range of God's power to create systems need not be limited to the universe known to us, but the reference to space and time is necessary, otherwise the concepts of motion, action and reaction would have no meaning.

6. (48) If the reaction took place in accordance with the laws of A then B (or that part of B involved in the action and reaction) would itself form part of A and there would be no miracle. If the elements of B are themselves governed by law, differing from the laws of A, then any reaction in B would take place in accordance with the laws of B.

7. (48) It is clear from this definition that the concept of miracle is, notwithstanding what has been said in paragraphs 43-47, a relative concept, but the relativity inherent in the concept is the relativity of divine creativity and not of human knowledge. It appears that the whole physical universe revealed to our senses is governed by the same laws, and if the boundaries of mind are defined as in paragraph 33 the same is true of the psychical universe. These two taken together

therefore constitute such a system as is referred to in the text, but we have no reason to suppose that God has not created other universes S_1, S_2, and so on, which are governed by laws differing from the laws of nature known to us.
8. (50) In paragraphs 15 and 21.
9. (50) Thus the system A does not include the souls of human beings which, though 'attached to' and influencing temporal beings, themselves have eternal being.
10. (52) Since God is supra-eternal he can (and certainly does) act in the eternal order. But, as we have already seen (paragraph 23), the principle on which the eternal order is governed, i.e., the principle governing metallassis (see paragraph 19), is freedom subject to the overriding power of God. Thus when God acts in the eternal order the effect is to interfere with freedom rather than to abrogate law. It is therefore inappropriate to describe his actions in that order as miracles. The same conclusion follows directly from the definition of miracle given in paragraph 48, as this involves the concepts of space and time, which of course have no relevance to eternity. Moreover, if, as suggested in paragraph 22, eternity proceeds from God, his actions in eternity cannot be miraculous, since he cannot override himself.
11. (52) Although the argument of this paragraph is primarily designed to show that a God who is unable to perform miracles is no more than a demiurge, it also goes far towards showing that such a limitation of divine power is highly improbable. Thus if the existence of a Creator God is admitted the probability that he can perform miracles must also be admitted; conversely, denial that a Supreme Being, if he exists, has the power to perform miracles is very nearly tantamount to denying his existence. Such a stance is, however, unscientific, because the existence of God as at least a demiurge cannot reasonably be doubted by anyone who admits the force of cumulative probability as providing a valid ground for assent. There are indeed several lines of argument, based on metaphysical reasoning, designed to establish the truth that God exists, and although each of these separately might be dismissed as inconclusive, taken together they create a very strong probability that the proposition is true. Of these the best

known are St Anselm's 'ontological proof', the five proofs of St Thomas Aquinas (based on Aristotle), and the argument from design, which Immanuel Kant thought to be the most cogent; to these may be added the proof advanced by René Descartes. We might also cite the fact that many people claim to have had direct experience of God, but the sceptic would dismiss such experiences as having no evidential value, since they cannot be repeated at will and cannot be communicated. The probability of the truth of the proposition is, however, further supported by the fact that, as pointed out in paragraph 47, it is very difficult to account for the appearance of life, the association of mind with matter, or the creation of man, without postulating the existence of a supernatural agency. When all these 'proofs' are superimposed the existence of God becomes a virtual certainty. The God whose existence is thus proved is not, of course, the Personal God of Christianity, but many of the doctrines of Christianity can be deduced if the further assumption is made that the words 'Our Father' are not merely a grammatical expression but contain a profound truth.

12. (53) Note that when Milton, in *Paradise Lost* (vii, 165-171), is describing the Creation, he recognizes that God has not poured the fulness of his essence into the universe, but he does not suggest that he has severed himself from it. He quotes God as saying (to the Son):

> ' . . . ride forth, and bid the deep
> Within appointed bounds be heaven and earth;
> Boundless the deep, because I am who fill
> Infinitude; nor vacuous the space,
> Though I, uncircumscribed myself, retire,
> And put not forth my goodness, which is free
> To act or not; . . . '

13. (54) In paragraph 47.
14. (54) See paragraph 64.
15. (54) Some of the events recorded in the Bible that are ordinarily regarded as miraculous may have been interventions by God in the eternal order, and these, as I have pointed out in Note 10 above, are not miracles, but others, such as the

conversion of water into wine (John ii, 1-11) or the calming of the storm by Jesus (Matthew viii, 24-27 = Mark iv, 37-41 = Luke viii, 23-25), cannot easily be so classified and should therefore be accepted as true miracles, i.e., interventions by God in the temporal order.

16. (55) Great signs and wonders are the mark of *false* Christs and *false* prophets and not of divine action (Matthew xxiv, 24 = Mark xiii, 22); or else they herald the end of time (Luke xxi 8-11 and 25-28). Note also that Jesus referred to signs and wonders, not as illustrations of his power or that of his Father, but as tests of faith (John iv, 48). In the Old Testament also, God speaks, not in the wind that rends the mountains, or in the earthquake, or in the fire, but in a still, small voice (1 Kings xix, 11-13).

17. (57) In paragraph 26.

18. (58) cf. John iii, 1-13.

19. (61) Although it may appear to be a trivial matter it is worth noting that it is not impossible that men may at some future time overcome this disability (or other similar disabilities imposed by physical law) by evolutionary development, although it is unlikely that they will do so, for the simple reason that the necessary incentive is never likely to arise or, if it did arise, to persist for a sufficiently long time. For, as we shall see in Chapter IV, the evolution of man is partly under the control of his will, but the process is necessarily slow. For such purposes as these it is both easier and quicker for man to use his brain to invent an appropriate mechanical device.

20. (61) It is of course more usual, partly because it is very much easier, to cite environmental circumstances as a defence against a criminal charge or as an excuse for antisocial behaviour than to attempt to assess the part played by heredity. Nevertheless, it is the latter that is fundamental. To put the matter briefly if not with absolute precision, the defects of character attributable to environment (in which must be included not only bad housing, broken homes and similar social disadvantages, but also, and even more importantly, the failure of parents and teachers to inculcate true ideas of right and wrong and a realization that antisocial acts resulting from evil motives will ultimately have to be atoned for) can be

remedied if appropriate action is taken by the mind, and this can be stimulated by suitable rewards and punishments, whereas those resulting from genetic causes require action by the will.

21. (62) The fact that freedom implies activity holds in the supra-eternal as well as in the eternal order of being. Thus the statement made in paragraph 9 that God is active is not only an essential element in Christian belief, it must be true absolutely of any god to whom freedom is ascribed. If the activity of God is denied we must also deny his freedom. And as it is probable that the concept of freedom could never have arisen in the human mind unless freedom were inherent in God it may be held that the activity of God can be deduced from the fact that we can formulate the idea of freedom.

The freedom of God is of course not only absolute but is unlimited; its exercise is not confined to any particular sphere. The freedom of the angels and of human souls, on the other hand, is freedom in the eternal order and includes freedom of being, in the sense described in paragraph 23; it also includes freedom from the principle of causality (and therefore from all natural law), but it is certainly not uncontrolled (see the following Note), nor is it absolute or unlimited. It is a gift from God which may be modified or withdrawn at his will.

22. (64) It has already been pointed out (in paragraph 15 and Note 3 above) that randomness cannot prevail in the temporal order. The truth of this proposition is perhaps recognized by intuition rather than established by strict reasoning, but any argument or insight by which it is supported would apply with even greater force in the eternal than in the temporal order. (And it must be immediately obvious that it applies in the supra-eternal order, for nothing appertaining to God can be random).

In interpreting the principle in its application to the eternal order, however, we cannot refer to notions of cause and effect, since these are temporal concepts, having a meaning only in a medium that is linearly ordered. In fact no form of words can be found that will adequately express what the principle means in eternity, because we have no way of visualizing the relation between an occasion in eternity and the 'contiguous' occasions.

The nearest we can get to a formulation of the relation is to say that although eternal beings are free their freedom is exercised within the framework of a 'law of metallassis' ordained by God, as he has also ordained the laws governing change in the temporal order.

23. (64) It is probable – we may even say that it is certain – that human beings enter heaven with the same purposes with which they were motivated on leaving earth, in so far as these purposes are located in the eternal order. It is also possible, or even probable, that they do not immediately discard notions involving the application of those purposes in the temporal order. This is equivalent to saying that the transition at death, whereby temporal being is discarded, is in some respects, in fact in respect of all those matters that are of vital importance, a continuous and not an abrupt transition.

24. (64) This is true of conflict between eternal beings. Conflict with the supra-eternal Being is of course in a different category, because this conflict *must*, in the ultimate, be settled in God's favour. The original conflict with God, the conflict from which all other conflicts spring, is that recorded in Revelation, Chapter xii, where we are told that Satan, having rebelled against God, was cast out from heaven. The consequences of that struggle have certainly involved destruction, antagonism and hatred on an immeasurable scale.

25. (65) cf. 1 Corinthians ii, 7-10, where St Paul says: 'I speak God's hidden wisdom, his secret purpose framed from the very beginning to bring us to our destined glory. None of the powers that rule the world has known that wisdom; if they had, they would not have crucified the Lord of glory. Scripture speaks of "things beyond our seeing, things beyond our hearing, things beyond our imagining, all prepared by God for those who love him"; and these are what God has revealed to us through the Spirit. For the Spirit explores everything, even the depths of God's own nature'. (Revised English Bible version).

26. (65) In paragraph 38.

27. (66) cf. Josef Pieper: 'In history, it is not the past, not "what actually happened", which is of philosophic interest. . . . What really and in the deepest analysis happens in history is salvation and disaster.' *The End of Time*; Faber & Faber Ltd.,

1954, pp. 13 and 22.

28. (67) This reinforces the injunction given in Matthew vii, 1, 'Judge not, that ye be not judged'. For we see that our judgement is impaired, not only by our inability to separate the contributions to a person's behaviour made by his heredity and his environment, or by these and any other factor having a bearing on the formation of his character (and, as we shall see in the following chapter, the determinations of his will are very relevant here), but also by our inability to distinguish between the necessary and the contingent imperfections to which his will is subject, and which affect its determinations. The former difficulty might to some extent be overcome by research, as the issues involved lie in the temporal order, but the latter must for ever lie outside our investigative powers.

29. (68) See paragraph 93.

30. (68) Since this defect is common to all eternal beings it follows that angels also can sin. We have already noted (in paragraph 66) that they, like man, are in need of salvation.

31. (69) But see paragraph 73.

32. (69) See paragraph 23.

33. (69) But see Chapter IV, Note 2.

34. (71) In paragraph 62.

35. (73) The claim that man can achieve salvation by his own unaided efforts is fairly widespread today. It is, however, a false creed deriving from the heresy known as Pelagianism. (Pelagius was a Welsh or Breton monk who lived about the end of the fourth and the beginning of the fifth century, and who put forward a doctrinal system in which the role of the human will was emphasized and the need of divine grace was minimised; in particular he denied the doctrine of original sin, as then understood.) Dr C.B. Moss, in *The Christian Faith* (SPCK, 1954, p. 155) says that Pelagianism 'is very attractive to the ordinary man of independent will and common-sense religion and morals; and particularly to the Englishman. Probably 90 per cent of the English laity (that is, practising members of Christian congregations) are unconscious Pelagians.' Pelagianism, particularly in its modern aspect, results from giving a predominantly moral interpretation to the concept of salvation. The duty of the individual man is to live the good life, and

the duty of mankind is to build a secular utopia; and although God may be called upon from time to time to put matters right when they have gone wrong, both these objectives can be achieved by the right use of the human will and without the need for any mystical food for the soul. It is largely because these false notions have played a prominent part in the thoughts of men since they first appeared on earth that evil is, and always has been, so powerful an influence in human affairs.

36. (76) See paragraphs 219-225.

3

THE CREATION OF CHARACTER

77. A *perithauma* is a miracle performed by a human being in which the direct effect of the miracle takes place within the agent himself. Perithaumata do, of course, affect the outside world, especially other people, but this is because the effect of the perithauma is to change the agent, so that his behaviour towards, or his influence on, other people or things is different from what it would have been if the perithauma had not been performed.

78. The first important function of man's perithaumatic capability is the creation of his own character. As a preliminary to the task of describing how this function is discharged we must first analyse briefly what may be called the springs of human action. This is a matter on which there is a good deal of confusion of thought. The commonly held opinion is that all action, other than reflex action[1], springs either from desire or from will, or from a mixture of the two, and that the analysis cannot be carried further without introducing moral considerations. Thus most people, if asked to define the roles of desire and will, would interpret the question in an ethical context; they would assume that the question to be answered is how these two active forces fit into an ethical system, and to this they would reply that some desires are good and others evil, and that it is the function *and duty* of the will to overcome evil desires, or to strive to do so. Many would add that there is greater merit in overcoming an evil desire by an effort of will than in not having the desire at all. Many would also say, and nearly everyone would have said before modern psychological

theories had obtained so strong a hold over our way of thinking, that we can always exercise will-power to conquer an evil desire if we want to do so.

79. But this common view is easily seen to be unsatisfactory. An obvious objection is that, in the statement that we can use will-power to overcome evil desires if we want to, it is impossible to attach any precise meaning to the word 'want', or to specify in what faculty the experience of wanting resides, i.e., whether it is a desire or an act of will. (Alternatively, the impossibility may be said to be that of defining the word 'we', as an agent independent of desire and will[2]). An even stronger objection is that the common view provides no criterion for distinguishing between the spheres of action of desire and will. As I have said in the preceding paragraph, attempts to define these spheres are usually based on moral considerations rather than on psychological analysis, and are therefore apt to lead to some form either of Puritanism or of Manicheism[3], both of which are distortions of Christian truth[4]. Views deriving from one or other of these false theories are in fact very widely held. Thus a common error deriving from the Puritan outlook is to associate desire with pleasurable activities, whether bodily or mental, which are held to be wrong, while will is regarded as a faculty which under the guidance of conscience impels us to do unpleasant or painful things which are held to be right. The error of Manicheism is closely related to that of Puritanism, it is to suppose that the physical world was created by the Devil (or by some being very much lower than God), and that accordingly the body can only be a vehicle for sin; those who incline to the Manichean view are therefore likely to assign to desire the role of seeking to satisfy (and at the same time to enhance) bodily needs, and to the will the role of opposing these in the interests of psychological or spiritual benefits.

80. The theory that desire and will act at the same level[5] and are to be distinguished by reference to moral considerations is, however, not only open to the objection that the roles of the two faculties cannot be satisfactorily defined, it suffers also from the defect that no useful results can be deduced from it. Moreover, it postulates that man is not a unity but is constantly at war with himself, and although it is certainly true

that the human personality may be a theatre of conflict, this is not waged between two opposing faculties; it is a conflict of allegiances in which the freedom of human beings, in the deep sense in which that concept has been defined in the previous chapter, is involved. The protagonists in the struggle have their being beyond and outside the human personality, and since freedom is a property of the soul (and only of the soul), it is within the soul that the issue is joined[6].

81. Now the being of the soul is eternal being and our description of the forces by which the behaviour of men and women is governed must therefore involve the eternal order and its relation with the temporal order. Moreover, the soul is not only the recipient of God's activity, being free it is itself active[7], and for the discharge of its active functions it needs an organ or faculty; this organ is the will.

82. Thus the distinction between desire and will is not that they occupy different places in the scale of moral values or take opposite sides in the struggle between good and evil; it is a distinction of being (*esse*) and function. It is of course true that one of the scales by reference to which desire and will fall to be judged is a moral scale (others relate to the intensity and the extension, in time or eternity, as the case may be, of the forces they exert), and moral theory also enters by virtue of the fact than an important distinction between desire and will is that the moral scales by reference to which they are to be assessed are not identical, that for desire being the scale of right and wrong, whereas that for will is the scale of good and evil. This particular detail of ethical analysis need not concern us here, but as right and wrong belong to the temporal order, whereas good and evil belong to the eternal order, it serves to emphasize the fact that the distinction between desire and will is ontological, not ethical. Desire is in fact a motivating force residing in the mind, and its being is temporal being; the will on the other hand is the active organ of the soul and its being is eternal being. It follows that while the role of desire must not be underrated, for it is a governing factor in the ordering of our daily affairs, the role of the will is infinitely more important; and in this statement the reference to infinity is to be taken literally, for whereas time is finite, eternity is infinite.

83. With these considerations in mind, the mechanism involved in the determination of action may be readily described. (It should be borne in mind that action is not necessarily overt; thoughts, feelings of pleasure or pain, of benevolence or animosity, and other mental conditions and activities should also be included). The immediate cause of *all* action, other than reflex action[8], is desire; this is true even of actions that are painful or unpleasant. Desire is of course an immensely complex force, it serves both as a repository of mental aspirations and as a source of mental energy; and the ends it seeks to attain may almost be described as infinitely varied. Some desires are relatively weak, others very powerful; some are ephemeral, others persist over a long period, possibly even throughout the greater part of a lifetime. Desires associated with bodily needs, such as hunger and thirst, cease when the need has been met. This is true also of the desire for sexual satisfaction, but this desire is distinctive in that it is not only extremely powerful but is also constantly renewed even when the function which it is designed to perform has been fully discharged. Hunger and thirst are continually renewed because otherwise the body would die, but sexual desire, the biological function of which is to maintain the continuance of the human race, is not extinguished when a sufficient number of offspring have been produced to ensure that this objective has been achieved. This, of course, is in part a consequence of the operation of natural selection, a consequence brought about by the need to ensure that there would always be a sufficient number of units in every generation for the process of selection to eliminate the individuals least fitted for survival in their environment, and thereby to provide for adaptation to a changing environment. But in the case of human beings this purpose has been largely discarded, in fact it is being deliberately frustrated by the actions of human beings themselves, and it might be expected therefore that the power of sexual desire which, even if natural selection were allowed to operate without hindrance, would be far greater than is needed to maintain the species and to provide sufficient variation for adaptation, would begin to diminish. This, however, is not happening, and is extremely unlikely to happen.

84. Other desires, such as the desire to take a holiday, may be indirectly related to physiological needs, but neither these nor the more primitive desires mentioned in the preceding paragraph are of interest from the point of view of our present inquiry, since they do not have any bearing on the power of man to perform miracles.

85. The desires that are germane to this inquiry are those which are not triggered by the need to maintain the life of the individual or of the species, and are unrelated, or only remotely related, to that need. These are seldom ephemeral; indeed they may persist over many years. Examples are the desire to wield power in some sphere of action, whether large or small, the desire to acquire great wealth or to live a life of holy poverty, the desire to become eminent in some branch of learning or in the mastery of some craft or art, the desire to devote oneself to some cause, the desire to be loved or respected, or the desire to conform to the norm and to attract as little attention as possible. Desires of this kind, which may dominate the whole life of an individual, and are the key to much of his character, may be described as parent or ancestor desires, because in order to achieve their purposes they give birth to a large progeny, extending over many 'generations'. Thus, to take a simple example, the desire to become proficient at playing the violin may father the desire to get up early every morning to put in an hour's practice before breakfast, and this in turn fathers the desire to set the alarm clock every night. It is easy to think of other offspring of this parent desire, each of which has its own progeny, extending perhaps over several generations, the last representative being a direct spur to action, e.g., to lay down the novel I am reading and go to my desk to write to a friend inviting him to come with me to a concert. Or again, the parent ambition (or desire) may give birth to the desire to pass a particular examination; this produces the desire to attend certain lectures, and thus to catch a particular bus or train. When this point is reached, desire, having as it were set the machine in motion, hands over to reflex action, which organizes and arranges all the movements necessary to ensure that the lecture hall is reached in time.

86. Whence do these parent desires originate? They are, of

course, in some way connected with the structure of the brain or the physique (or both) of the individual harbouring them, and these features are primarily genetically determined, although the genetic data are also conditioned and modified by the environmental circumstances in which the individual has lived since his birth. Thus the parent desires of any individual are related to his heredity and his environment, but we should greatly misunderstand the nature and undervalue the status of human beings if we were to suppose that the relation is one of cause and effect. Neither heredity nor environment is the origin of those parent desires which mould a person's character and thus largely determine the course of his life, nor can either of these factors, or both together, provide the driving force which is so marked a feature of parent desires, although of course both must be concerned in supplying the physical and psychical energy by which the progeny of the parent desires are expressed in action.

87. The importance of what is here stated cannot be overrated. A clear understanding of the fact that in their most basic and enduring characteristics human beings are *not* the product either of their heredity or their environment alone, although both of these obviously play an important part in determining the manner in which these basic characteristics are manifested, is equivalent to an understanding of a large part of the meaning of the statement that man is made in the image of God[9]. This understanding also points to the source of parent desires. They are peculiar to man and must therefore have their origin in that feature which distinguishes man from all other created beings, namely the possession of a soul.

88. Thus the source of parent desires, at least of those which mould the development of character, and excluding those which are purely biological or instinctual, such as the desire for self-preservation and for reproduction[10], is to be found in the soul, and since it is clear that we are dealing with an activity and not with a power of absorption, we place this origin in the soul's active organ, which is the will.

89. We see then that it is not the function of the will to engage in a contest on equal terms with desire at the level of the latter. Being eternal the will is superior to desire which is temporal.

The soul is, however, 'in contact with' the mind, and at one of the points of contact the will can and does act on and influence desire. It is important to note, however, that the traffic is one-way, for desire has no power in itself to act on or influence the will. The task of the will is to control the whole complex of desires by which the pattern of a person's life is governed and his character is built up and revealed. In the discharge of this task the will is free, but its activity is of course not random or capricious. It formulates and seeks to achieve a purpose or purposes, and although in the final analysis these purposes must lie in the eternal order[11] – they must, in fact, all be variants or aspects of a single purpose, which is nothing less than that of conforming, or failing to conform, to the will of God – during the earthly life of the person concerned (whom we may call the host) they are manifested, at least in part, in temporal activity. The will takes note of the physical and mental features of its host, and determines how these may best be used for the fulfilment of its purpose; and to achieve its ends it exercises its power, as the occasion may require and possibly continuously, on the faculty of desire, creating, annihilating, strengthening or weakening, particular desires, and generally moulding the whole complex of desires, in order to bring about the object it has in view. For the most part it confines its activities to the realm of parent desires, leaving these to breed, through the operation of natural law, such progeny as they may require for the realization of their objectives in action; but occasionally the will may find it necessary to create an 'action desire', that is, a desire which is a direct course of action; when this happens we are apt to make the mistake of ignoring the intermediacy of the created desire and of supposing that it is the will itself that is the direct cause of the action taken. The reason for this error is that whereas normally the operation of the will lies below the level of awareness, on the rare occasions when it creates an action desire it comes so near the surface of awareness that the intellect, which of course knows that the will exists, ascribes to it a more direct role than it actually fulfils.

90. Clearly, in the ultimate, a person must be identified with his soul, since all else is mortal[12]. The soul expresses itself through the will and this expression is an activity, every

element of which involves a transference of energy from the eternal to the temporal order, overriding the laws of the temporal order at the point at which the transfer takes place, and is therefore, in the strict sense of the word, a miracle. Moreover, the purpose of the transfer of energy is to create and control the complex of parent desires, and the will is therefore, to the extent that this purpose is achieved, or is set on the way to being achieved, the architect of character; from this it follows that the will is the supremely important active feature of the personality, and that miracle, which is the means by which the will carries out its functions, is the supremely important mechanism actively affecting our temporal life.

91. It must, however, by recognized that as the expression of the soul through the will is effected through the medium of desire it is conditioned by the bodily and mental features of its host, and also as the will, having created, destroyed or modified desires to achieve its freely chosen ends, hands over to natural law in the expectation that this will lead towards the implementation of those ends, an expectation that may not be fully realized, the revelation of the soul to the outside world, and even to the host himself, may be very imperfect. The condition of the soul, and therefore also of the will, is in fact fully known only to God. It is in this fact that we find the grounds for the duty, imposed on all, of forgiveness and of refraining from judgement[13]. These duties are the more binding in that our inability to see clearly into the condition of our own souls and those of others is not only a fact but is a state of affairs for which we ourselves must bear a large share of responsibility, because, as we shall see in the following chapter, we have guided our evolution, in regard to eternal truths, in such a way as to enhance our appreciation of the temporal manifestation of those truths at the expense of our understanding of the truths themselves.

92. Two further points must be made which, although they add nothing to the cogency of the proof that the ground of individual personality lies in miracle, are necessary to complete our understanding of this analysis of the springs of action and to forestall objections that might be made to it. The first relates to the statement, made earlier[14], that the human personality is

a theatre of conflict or tension. The truth of this statement derives from the fact that the will, having eternal being, must locate its ultimate objective in the eternal order. The will cannot create an objective *ex nihilo* and it must therefore have objectives placed before it between which it can freely choose. Now the will is a characteristic of personality and each of the alternatives before it must have its source in some being of at least equal status, that is to say, a being who is at least a person. It is obvious that one of these must be God who is, of course, greater than any person, being three Persons in one Being; the other cannot be equal to God but must be ontologically greater than human beings; this being must therefore be an angel.

93. From this we derive the Christian doctrine of Satan, a doctrine which is nowadays very much out of favour but is none the less true. We have already seen[15] that the activity of God and his independence of the temporal order implies the existence of created beings in the eternal order. These are the angels and, as angels are imperfect and capable of sin (as has also been shown[16]), it is easy to accept the hypothesis that in one or more of these beings the spirit of self-aggrandizement took root, to the extent that he (or they) rebelled against God and sought to undermine his power. It ought not to be necessary to say that Christian doctrine does not require that the conflict between God and Satan should be thought of as a conflict of physical beings as depicted in *Paradise Lost*, but unfortunately those whose object it is to undermine the Christian faith often employ the device of asserting that it involves the acceptance of propositions that are obviously untrue or even absurd, and equally unfortunately there are too many who allow themselves to be misled by this device. The fact is, of course, that Christian doctrine consists of a set of truths, of which some are historical, some ethical, some soteriological and some metaphysical, and for the teaching of the metaphysical truths allegories must be used, as in the early chapters of Genesis. The sceptics fall into error not only in denying the metaphysical truths (among which must be included the reality of miracles) but also in accusing the Christian of holding to the literal truth of the allegories. No doubt some have done

so, but the truth of a theory is not to be judged by the attitude to that theory of its least learned adherents.

94. We therefore claim that, as the hypothesis that Satan exists is reasonable, is vouched for by Scripture[17], and enables us to give a rational and coherent account of the problem of human behaviour, and in particular the problem of evil, we are justified in asserting that the hypothesis is true. And when this assumption has been made it is easily seen that we may describe the tension in the human soul as arising from the conflict between God and Satan, both of whom are rival claimants for the soul's adherence and loyalty[18]. On the one hand God puts forward the objective of love (*agape*), sacrifice and complete submission to his will; Satan on the other hand offers the objective that he himself has sought to achieve, the object of self-aggrandizement and independence of God[19]. There are probably few, if any, people whose souls have adopted the second alternative in its entirety, that is to say, who have wholly rejected God (and even if there are any such, they are still redeemable), and certainly there are none who have placed themselves in complete submission to God and whose wills have so aligned themselves as to accept as their sole objectives the ends prescribed by God for them as conducing to the fulfilment of his plan for mankind as a whole. Most people divide their allegiance, and this is the underlying cause of all (or nearly all) the psychological and spiritual disorders that afflict mankind. For, as a house divided against itself cannot stand[20], men seek a remedy by trying to reconcile the claims of God and Satan and, with this end in view, by persuading themselves that these opposing claims *can* be reconciled. Alternatively, in order to avoid the traumas resulting from the attempt to reconcile the irreconcilable, men persuade themselves that the objectives devised by Satan are in reality prescribed by God. This persuasion reveals itself in some of the errors of both individual and social ethics that are current today. Nevertheless, we must not lose sight of the fact that although all men have pursued the path of aggrandizement and independence of God, all have also adopted some elements from God's programme, and it is on this fact that our hopes for the future must be grounded[21].

95. The second point requiring special mention relates to the statement made earlier[22] that desire is the direct cause of all action, including actions that are painful or unpleasant. How can desire prompt us to action that we know will cause us pain or discomfort? The answer is that few actions are the direct result of one isolated desire; in almost all cases action is determined by the 'resultant' of a whole complex of desires, and among these are two parent desires which, in appropriate circumstances, can exert an overpowering influence. The first is the desire to act in such a way as to arouse the approval of other people, particularly of those whose opinions we respect. This desire, which is always present, and exerts its influence whenever a relevant issue arises, has probably become a dominant factor as a result of evolution, and to the extent that it has done so without the intervention of the will and simply as conducing to the preservation of the species through natural selection it has little moral content, although it often has valuable practical consequences. (As will appear in the following chapter, however, the development of this desire may in part result from the exercise of the power of will, and to the extent that this is the case it has, of course, moral significance). The other special parent desire, which is equally powerful, is the desire to act in accordance with a code to which the agent himself attaches normative moral value. Of course these two desires often reinforce one another, but the second, which is of immense importance, stems in two ways from man's relation to God and is probably independent of evolution. First, the admission of the existence of a norm — that is to say, of an absolute standard of good and evil — comes about because the will has grasped the fact of God's plan for mankind and his concern for man's salvation, which is what his plan is designed to achieve, and secondly, the existence of the desire shows that the will recognizes the force of obligation[23], that indefinable force by which the will, though free, feels itself urged to submit to the will of God. These two characteristics of the will, which illustrate God's supremacy over Satan, while not denying the latter's power, and which provide the ground for hope of the ultimate salvation both of every individual man and woman and of mankind as a whole, are truly moral, and are not

morally diminished by the fact that the norms to which they give their support are often, through the fallibility of both our intellects and our wills, false norms. To the extent that they are false the advancement of God's plan is of course hindered, but we may be sure that God will not allow the links attaching the wills of men to his own will to be severed, even though, for the purpose of maintaining this attachment, he may sometimes find it necessary to override the freedom he has conferred on mankind.

CHAPTER THREE

NOTES AND REFERENCES

(The numbers in brackets indicate the paragraphs in which the references occur)

1. (78) The expression 'reflex action' is usually restricted to mean those bodily actions which take place without the intervention of the agent's mind, or which he either cannot control at all (e.g., the beating of his heart) or can only control within very narrow limits and by a positive effort of 'will' (e.g., breathing or blinking). This, however, is very imprecise, and throughout the remainder of this book I shall use the expression to mean those actions, i.e., those bodily sequences, in which either the mind is not active at all, or its activity is purely epiphenomenal, that is to say, the mental concomitant of the action is caused by the bodily condition but does not itself act as a cause. (It should be noted that as the latter alternative seems to imply an action without reaction it must be held to be questionable whether any purely epiphenomenal activities take place). Normally, when the word 'action' is used, it will be assumed that reflex actions, as thus defined, are excluded.
2. (79) It may be argued that this objection has little weight, as that element in the common view against which it is directed, namely the statement that we can always overcome wrongful desires by will-power if we want to do so, is no longer widely held. But although this statement, in the form in which it is set out here, is false, many of those who deny its truth do so on the deterministic ground that heredity and environment may compel a certain pattern of behaviour, against which compulsion it is useless for the will to struggle; and the first part of this ground is only partially true and the second certainly false. In fact, as will appear in the course of this chapter, the will plays a

very important part in the control of desire.

3. (79) Mani (or Manichaeus) was a gnostic teacher of the third century(c. 216-276 AD). He founded a dualistic religion of great complexity which, in one or another form, spread through Europe in the Middle Ages and, as stated in the text, colours the beliefs of many people today. Although he regarded himself as a Christian his system is largely based on Zoroastrianism. The fundamental idea is that reality is governed by two principles, Light and Darkness (cf. Ormuzd and Ahriman), and as in the case of all such dualistic religions its followers easily fall into the error of identifying these with the mental or spiritual world and the physical world respectively. A fascinating account of the spread of the Dualist heresy will be found in *The Medieval Manichee*, by Sir Steven Runciman (Cambridge University Press, 1947). It should be pointed out, as against what is said above, that Sir Steven considers that this particular error has not survived. 'The Christian heresy of Dualism,' he says, 'the Tradition that found its origin in the days of Cerdon and Valentine, died without issue, before the sword of the Turks and the fire of the Dominicans.' This is no doubt true, so far as any institutionalised form of the heresy is concerned, but it seems to me that the modes of thought that characterize the heresy have at all times, including the present, found ready acceptance in the minds of those who are not aware of the full implications of Christian doctrine.

4. (79) In order to avoid misunderstanding, which may easily arise because so many people identify Christianity with its ethical code, or with the observance of that code, it must be emphasized that in saying that Puritanism and Manicheism are distortions of Christian truth, it is neither stated nor implied that the adherents of these ways of thought are worse, or have less love for their fellow men, than other people. In fact most people base the conduct of their lives on the code which they learned in childhood, supplemented by the social ethics of the group to which they belong, rather than on theological considerations. It should be added that Puritanism is a much less dangerous error than Manicheism. For the former is not incompatible with the greater part of Christian doctrine, it is only in its interpretation of the Christian ethic that divergence

manifests itself, whereas the latter, by regarding matter as evil, must deny either the goodness of God or the doctrine of the Creation, which declares that everything that God has created is good (Genesis i, 31) or, alternatively, must hold that the world was created by some lesser being than God. It may also be added that a dose of Puritan ethics may be needed to remedy the present ills of society deriving from the opposite creed that the pursuit of individual pleasure (sometimes disguised as 'doing one's own thing') is always justified, or from the corresponding communal ethic of utilitarianism.

5. (80) This supposition is clearly implied in what I have described as 'the common view', and reveals an even more subtle objection to that view. This is that the hypothesis leads either to an infinite regress or to an absurdity. The argument whereby this is established may be briefly stated as follows:- It is obvious that desire accounts for a very large number of those of our actions which are not merely reflex. (In fact, reflex mechanisms and the mechanism of desire almost continuously interact, and jointly determine action.) If then the will is to be invoked as a third determining factor, operating on the same level as the other two, some principle must be postulated to provide the criterion by which the will determines to intervene, and this principle must be accorded absolute status within the will, else there would have to be a further faculty to provide the means of determining when this principle should be applied. This faculty would also have to operate according to some principle, which itself would have to be absolute, else a still deeper faculty would have to be postulated. Thus if the principle by which the intervention of the will is determined is not held to be absolute, we are led into an infinite regress, and we deduce that the principle must operate absolutely. For example, if the criterion for intervention is that of pleasure and pain, so that desire is held to account for the performance of those actions in which pleasure predominates over pain, and the will for those in which pain predominates over pleasure, then it would have to be supposed that the will *always* supports the cause of unpleasantness. Similarly, if the criterion applied by the will is that of good and evil, it would have to be supposed that the will *always* supports the cause of good. Since

any such supposition is absurd, the statement that the will cannot act on the same level as desire follows.
6. (80) See paragraph 94.
7. (81) See paragraph 62.
8. (83) See Note 1 above.
9. (87) Genesis i, 26, 27.
10. (88) But although the reproductive instinct and the desires to which it gives rise are biological in origin and therefore belong to the temporal order, the intensity and persistence of sexual desire beyond what is necessary for the preservation and development of the human race are the result of the activity of the communal will. See Chapter IV, Note 28.
11. (89) See paragraph 74.
12. (90) But, as will be shown in Chapter V, part of man's temporal being can be transformed into eternal being and thus made immortal.
13. (91) Matthew vi, 14, 15; vii, 1.
14. (92) Paragraph 80.
15. (93) In paragraph 10.
16. (93) See Chapter II, Note 30.
17. (94) Jesus was in no doubt that Satan existed and could act on the souls of men. See, for example, Matthew iv, 1-11; xii, 26; xvi, 23; Luke x, 18; xiii, 16; xxii, 31; John xii, 31; xiv, 30, xvi, 11. Note that in John Satan is referred to as the prince of this world.
18. (94) This is the conflict of allegiances referred to in paragraph 80.
19. (94) cf. Genesis iii, 4, 5. See also Chapter II, Note 35.
20. (94) Mark iii, 25.
21. (94) cf. the statement made at the end of paragraph 40 that God cannot forget man, nor can man forget God.
22. (95) In paragraph 83.
23. (95) See paragraph 72.

4

THE MASTERY OF EVOLUTION

96. The conclusions we have reached so far may be summarized and clarified as follows:

> (i) God, when creating man, laid down a plan for his salvation.
> (ii) In bringing about the fulfilment of God's plan, every human being has a part to play[1].
> (iii) The means adopted by God to achieve his purpose has been to implant in every human being a soul and in every soul a will by means of which the soul can act.
> (iv) The being of the soul and the will is eternal being; this means that it can only be annihilated by a positive act on the part of God, whereas temporal beings, which include the bodies and minds of human beings, require unceasing positive action by God to maintain their continuance in being.
> (v) The eternal being of the soul and the will also implies their freedom. This freedom is freedom from constraint by God and is subject only to the condition that it will be withdrawn if withdrawal is necessary to forestall the irretrievable frustration of God's plan[2].
> (vi) The will of every human being can receive the messages which God the Holy Spirit sends to it; and can respond to those messages. Thus the will recognizes the existence of good as an absolute emanating

from God and experiences the force of obligation, the knowledge that it has a duty to further God's plan.

(vii) The will is also aware of the fact that by a continuous act of submission it can learn at all times how it should align itself in order to conform to God's plan.

(viii) The part to be played by each human being in the plan is adjusted by God to suit the physical and psychical abilities and limitations of that human being, as determined by his heredity and his environment.

(xi) The will, however, selects its own objectives which since man is not perfect are bound to differ in some measure, and because he is sinful certainly do differ markedly, from those which would be dictated by complete submission to God's will, being in fact in part objectives which Satan has offered as having greater attractions.

(x) Since during their earthly lives human beings express themselves in action, the determinations of their wills have to be translated into desires which are the direct cause of action. The translation is usually effected by the creation, annihilation and modification of parent desires which govern action through their progeny.

(xi) Since the control of desire by the will constitutes an interference with the operation of temporal law by an entity having eternal being, it is, in the strict and only meaningful sense of the word, a miracle.

(xii) The overriding power of God is revealed in the fact that one of the most powerful parent desires in the minds of all people is the desire to act in accordance with a moral code to which normative status is given. The existence of this desire, which cannot have arisen by the laws of evolution alone, shows that, knowingly or unknowingly, all people acknowledge the existence of a standard of good and evil deriving from a source outside human beings and outside the temporal order, and its significance is in no way diminished by the fact that the code to which adherence is given is often, because of the wrongful orientation of the human will and the fallibility of the human mind, a faulty one.

97. It is not difficult to see, however, that while this summary sets out the relation of every man's will to the achievement of his own salvation, it does not contain a full description of the functions of his will. For God has created man in a temporal world which is necessarily a world of change; he has, moreover, created him a living being subject to the laws by which the processes of life can accommodate change. In the case of all living creatures in the temporal world other than man, the adaptation of life to change is governed by temporal forces – the laws of natural selection and of the hereditability of mutational but not of acquired characteristics – but as God has a plan for mankind it is clear that the evolution of man cannot be wholly subject to these impersonal forces, which can take no note of the plan. Moreover, God does not impose his plan dictatorially, as this would abrogate man's freedom; it follows that man must be able in some measure to guide and control his own evolution. In one sense of the word 'evolution' he is able to effect this control by recording and learning from the past, thereby building up an edifice of knowledge and experience, by virtue of which all the temporal features of his life, including not only the external trappings but also the furniture of his mind and the available activities on which his mind can exercise itself and in which it can find delight and enjoyment, have been enormously developed and expanded, with the consequence that his life has been enlarged and enriched in ways that primitive man could never have envisaged. But although the word 'evolution' is often used in this sense, as when people speak of social, political or economic evolution, or of intellectual or aesthetic evolution, it is a sense which throws no light on the fundamental power of development by which man is distinguished from all other living temporal creatures.

98. We can establish the existence of this power either by observation or by an argument *a priori*, and the two arguments not only lead to the same conclusion but are closely related,

and both indicate the source of the power and the manner in which it is exercised. The *a priori* argument proceeds directly from the considerations of the preceding paragraph. For it is clear that the substance of God's evolutionary plan cannot be limited to the production of ever more elaborate artifacts, whether these are ends in themselves or are the means of providing for the enlargement of mental experience (e.g., works of literature or art). For even though such artifacts may be the expression of some eternal truths, and may, by modifying the structure and content of the minds of those by whom they have been constructed, provide for their souls a source from which they can draw further inspiration; even though they may be the means of disseminating to others besides their originators some insight into the reality of God, they remain, in the last analysis, temporal constructs; and to suppose that God would create a being only a little lower than the angels[3] and would prescribe for this being a plan whose content could be expressed solely in terms of artifacts having only temporal reality would be blasphemy, since it would liken God to a man who spent his life in constructing ever more intricate jigsaw puzzles, only to throw them away when he had completed them. The evolutionary plan for mankind must therefore be a plan for the evolution of man himself, and not merely of the products of his muscle and brain, however elaborate or abstract these may be, and however much they may derive their inspiration from eternal or supra-eternal sources.

99. St Paul has expressed this truth in the great eulogy of charity, which he included in his first letter to the Corinthians[4]. For he tells us there that 'whether there be prophecies they shall fail; whether there be tongues, they shall cease; whether there be knowledge, it shall vanish away', and it is easy to see that what he here pronounces to be doomed to ultimate extinction are the temporal products of men's brains, including even those which draw their inspiration from above, i.e., from the higher orders[5]. Charity alone does not fail, and the reason is that charity is not temporal but eternal. It affects the eternal being both of him who gives and of him who receives. But this is not all. For charity does not consist merely in social or political effort on behalf of others, or even in subordinating one's own

well-being to that of others; it consists in seeking wholeheartedly to promote the well-being, both now and for all future time, of the whole of God's creation that lies within man's reach, and this can only be accomplished by the sincere self-abnegating effort to place one's will in submission to that of God and, so far as possible, to identify its objectives with those assigned by God for the evolution of mankind and of the world, and thereby to promote the coming of his kingdom. It follows from this that the realization of the essence of charity demands an effort of the communal will as well as of the individual will, whose duty it is, first to align itself rightly, and then to help the wills of others to place themselves equally under the domination of God[6].

100. For the second argument showing that man must be endowed with a power to supplement the evolutionary forces implanted in nature we note that it is not only the content of men's minds that has increased (a fact which would suffice to account for intellectual or social evolution), their capacity has been enlarged and the subtlety of their working has become ever more intricate. This increase in the capacity and ingenuity of the human mind has to be accounted for, and it cannot be denied, except by the most inflexible determinists, that the ordinary processes of evolution by natural selection are insufficient for this purpose. No doubt these processes provide a satisfactory explanation of the increase in the size and complexity of men's brains and also, by the interaction between the physical and psychical realms, in the greater capacity of their minds to formulate and work with abstract ideas as well as with practical or utilitarian matters, but it is impossible to attribute to those processes all the highly complex mental capacities and abilities displayed by (for example) the Greeks of the time of Plato, Aristotle and Euclid, the medieval theologians, the Renaissance artists or the scientists of the seventeenth century and after. Many of the mental achievements of men such as these have no relevance to survival, and from this we infer that a force other than those of temporal evolution has been at work.

101. The effect of this additional force is seen, and therefore evidence for it is found, in the fact that from his earliest

beginnings man has acquired and has continually developed a set of basic desires directed towards the future, desires to increase the range and penetration of his mind, to increase also its power to grasp abstract ideas and to analyse and synthesise the relations between them, to expand the range of aesthetic experience, to understand the principles of his own being and of its relation to its Author, to deduce from those principles the origin and nature of the moral law, and to relate the objects of all these desires to the status of mankind as a whole in the hierarchy of being and his role in the scheme of the universe; in short to understand what he is and why he is here. It is the acquisition of this complex set of desires and the fact that, having been acquired, its constituents have increased and are still increasing in strength and range, indicating the existence of a master desire to bring about this increase, that show the insufficiency of evolution in the temporal order as the sole cause of man's development. For, as stated above, these desires are directed towards the future, whereas the essence of all evolutionary theories, whether Darwinian or Lamarckian, is that evolution proceeds by the application of natural law to the situation as it is, without regard to the future. Nature did not plan the evolution of the various genera and species that have appeared on the earth; nature did not envisage in advance the anatomical, physiological and psychological structures of lions, eagles and dolphins, or the beauty and utility of oak trees, or the functions of bacteria, bacilli and viruses, and adapt the evolutionary processes to ensure the fulfilment of this preconceived plan; these, and all other living creatures except man, have come into being by the operation of natural law, at every moment of time, on the circumstances prevailing at that moment. But although man, while on earth, cannot escape from those laws, the fact that his development has been oriented in the light of a vision of the future shows that its course has been in part governed by additional forces which in their temporal manifestation take the form of desires, acting mainly at the level of the unconscious, of the kind listed above. These desires have come into being, not by the abrogation of natural law, but by the action of forces supplementing and (as a logical consequence) apparently overriding it[7].

102. Clearly the desires governing the evolution of mankind are parent desires, and as they do not arise from natural law (although this plays its full part once the desires have been created) we must seek their origin elsewhere. Equally clearly, once the question has been posed, the answer becomes obvious. For we have seen that parent desires can be created by the will, and as the desires we are now considering are, above all others, oriented towards the future and as the will is the only human faculty which can freely select objectives, it is to the activities of the wills of men and women that these desires, which have the power to guide the evolution of the race, must be ascribed.

103. We see then that man can control the evolution of the human race by the exercise of his will, and that one of the elements in this control is the creation of parent desires. Since desires can be communicated those people or groups of people who are motivated by like desires can act in harmony and thus bring about social evolution but, as I have already pointed out[8], social evolution alone is insufficient to account for the observed facts of man's past development and to provide the impetus for his future development, particularly in so far as this will promote, or impede, the fulfilment of God's plan for mankind; we must therefore postulate some further activity and some additional mechanism to account for those facets of the evolution of man himself (as distinct from the products of his brain) which are not attributable to natural causes. Since this activity must make use of the principles by which natural evolutionary processes are governed the only possibility is that either the will itself or a parent desire created by the will acts directly on the reproductive cells in such a way as to give rise to mutations whereby the next generation will have characteristics more nearly in accordance, even though only marginally so, with the will's objectives. If the will acts directly on the reproductive cells it is this action that constitutes the miraculous element in the control of evolution, but where the mutations are caused by parent desires it is the creation of these desires that constitutes the miraculous element. In the latter case it is for the scientist rather than the theologian or the metaphysician to discover the means whereby the desires are translated into genetic change.

104. The fact that, whether the influence of the will on the genes is direct or indirect, a miraculous element is involved needs to be stressed, because it is natural, in an age when it is taken for granted that all phenomena can be explained in terms of the motions and mutual relations of physical particles or wave structures, to seek in these terms an explanation of the process whereby the wills of human beings initiate genetic change. It is clear, however, that no such explanation can be given. The reason is that, as the will has its being in the eternal order, where the laws of linear cause and effect do not apply, the manner in which it carries out its selected tasks is not amenable to discovery by scientific investigation. What can be said with certainty is that the end result of the will's activity is the creation of mutations, and that while some of these may be directly created, in other cases the will, having selected a particular line of development, creates a desire, probably unconscious, for that development and then withdraws, leaving it to the interaction between the mind and the body to transform this desire into the appropriate mutation. It is possible that future research will reveal how this final transformation, which takes place within the causal realm, is effected but the action of the will, being miraculous, must always remain a mystery.

105. I have said that the realization of the essence of charity, which is the same as the promotion of the coming of the kingdom of God on earth, requires an effort of the communal will, and it is now easy to see how such an effort can influence the evolution of the race. For if a large number of people in an intermarrying community share similar objectives, (whether charitable or otherwise), the wills of those people will give rise to similar mutations, and development along the lines dictated by the objectives will be furthered. Where on the other hand, the objectives sought by the members of the population are widely different, the mutations created will tend to cancel out, and no development in any marked direction will result. Clearly the operation of these communal efforts of will must be distinguished from the laws of natural selection. For in the case of the latter the mutations are random[9], and those which do not aid survival are eliminated, whereas in the case of the

former the mutations are not random but directed, and it is the numerical preponderance of like mutations engendered by widely shared objectives that brings about the willed evolutionary development.

106. Obviously the manner in which man has used the immense power thus conferred on him is of supreme importance, and it is therefore our duty to consider whether it has been used for good or for ill. This question has been answered by the Christian doctrines of original sin and redemption. It does not fall within the province of a book on the power of miracle to examine these doctrines in detail or to attempt to elicit their full meaning, but some exposition is necessary, as both these doctrines have something to say about man's thaumaturgic powers.

107. A brief reference to the doctrine of original sin has already been made[10], but for our present purpose a fuller explanation is needed. When man was first created [11] he was, and was seen by God to be, good[12]. This does not mean that he lived in a state of bliss, or that his environment was utopian, or that his behaviour was in all respects irreproachable. Man was then, as he still is, an animal, even though the description of him as such leaves out his most important feature, and he behaved as other animals behave, fighting as necessary for a mate, or to secure food for himself and his family, but otherwise reasonably peacefully; no doubt he was of uncertain temper and quick to become aggressive on suspicion of attack or if his instinctive needs were unsatisfied. The statement that man was created good is only very indirectly connected with his behaviour, and the idea that before the Fall he lived an idyllic life in idyllic surroundings is a travesty of the truth. The story of the Garden of Eden and of the temptation and Fall of man is certainly not to be dismissed as meaningless or even as unimportant; if treated as an allegory it will be found to embody and express some of the most profound truths about the status and condition of man[13]. But obviously it is not to be taken literally, and the story of the seduction of our earliest ancestors by the false promises of the serpent and their consequent expulsion from the garden is not to be interpreted as recording a sudden or dramatic deterioration in their behaviour or their environ-

ment. For the statement that man was created good but is now fallen and in a state of original sin is not a statement about his behaviour, or even about his instincts or his desires, it is a statement about his will. It asserts that, although the wills of all men are now wrongly oriented, when man was first created his will was not directed to any objective conflicting with the will of God. In fact it was at first probably not directed to any objective at all. It was an entirely new faculty, an organ of the soul, having eternal being, endowed by God with internal energy and the power of directing itself, but lacking the means of discerning such guidance as was available to it, implanted in an animal which, in all other respects, was wholly temporal.

108. Thus it is reasonable to suppose that these newly created wills at first made little or no attempt to direct themselves. Time was needed for them to take stock of the faculties of the beings in whom they were implanted and of their environment, to become aware of their powers and to understand their functions and duties. Gradually, over thousands or even hundreds of thousands of years, they came to grasp dimly the concept of obligation, and to realize that their task is primarily to guide the evolution of mankind along the lines prescribed by God and secondarily, as a specific task for each individual will and as part of the means of discharging the primary task, to mould the desires of their hosts and thereby to create their characters. As part of this task they implanted in the minds of their hosts the concept of duty, thereby enabling those minds to develop the idea of a moral law distinct from, superior to and entirely overriding that deriving from the operation of natural law. Since they were open to the influence of the supra-eternal order they learned that their creation, which was also the creation of man, was (as it continues to be) a purposeful activity on the part of God, that the necessary implication of their having been implanted in a being having a temporal element was that this purpose included a plan for man's development in time, and that they had the power and were under an obligation to guide man along the path leading to its fulfilment, and finally, that this path is a narrow one, from which any divergence must involve a conflict with the will of God[14]. But as they were also open to influences from the

eternal order they encountered the enticements of Satan who, seizing the opportunity provided by the appearance of these newly created beings, stressed the advantages of development along other lines. What remains to be said is very simple. The wills of men tried to steer a middle course, and have continued to do so throughout the whole history of mankind; they have divided their allegiance between God and Satan, and have sought to enjoy the expected benefits of following the path pointed out by Satan, with its promise of both immediate and long-term satisfactions, while not losing sight of the path ordained by God.

109. It is sometimes said that everything that happens is in accordance with the will of God. But this is true only in the sense that God has willed that man should be free to work out his own salvation[15]. He is ever ready to help so long as man's efforts are rightly directed, but does not interfere where they are wrongly directed, save in extreme cases, or when his help is actively sought. But the fact that God stands aside except where his aid is invoked does not mean that events conform to his will. The manifold evils of the world show that this is not the case, that man in his evolution has not followed God's plan, and that his will and consequently also his desires and actions often conflict with God's will. Clearly the grounds for man's divergence from the true path cannot be attributed to God, nor can they be attributed to the forces of evolution acting through natural law, for these are God's creation and being unfree cannot, by themselves, make for evil. They must therefore be sought in man himself. Now man, like all created beings, is imperfect[16], but he is also free and therefore capable of sin. This would not in itself be a fault, nor would it have evil consequences, but man is not only capable of sin, he is actually sinful; more pertinently he has fallen into original sin by selecting, through the agency of his will, the wrong objectives for his evolution. (As Dr Johnson has succinctly said: 'We fail of being happy because we determine to obtain happiness by means different from those which God appointed'). We cannot avoid being imperfect, but imperfection in relation to infinity allows for infinite evolutionary development without reaching perfection. The plan for mankind is therefore not merely a plan

whereby each individual, knowing himself to be imperfect and sinful, is under a duty to seek his own salvation, it is a plan whereby the whole human race, though steeped in original sin, is under a duty to evolve along a pre-ordained path, leading towards a state in which, though imperfection must remain, original sin is replaced by submission to God's will, and progress is towards the realization of God's kingdom. It therefore envisages a change in human nature itself – not merely a superficial change such as might be brought about by a modification of the environment (e.g., better housing or a more effective educational system) but a change at the most fundamental level of all, a change in the quality and aspirations of the souls of men and women, in short, the regeneration of the human race[17].

110. It must be borne in mind that man has never been able to foresee the ultimate results of the determinations of his will. God has not revealed to man the nature of his kingdom; he has only laid down the principles and rules by which men must govern themselves if their efforts to build the kingdom, which can never be entirely abandoned[18], are to be successful. We know indeed that much will be revealed to those whose souls are open to receive the Holy Spirit[19], and we may be sure that, if men had not left the true path, each successive step along the line of development would have been made clear as soon as the previous step had been taken and its consequences assimilated[20]. Moreover, we may reasonably suppose that men's vision would progressively have penetrated further and further into the future as they advanced along the path. But at the beginning the distant prospect was not made clear, nor were any immediate delights offered; on the contrary the way forwards was shown to be a way of self-denial[21], although it would have been found to be a way of joy and deep satisfaction[22]. And to us, who are already far from the true path and are the inheritors of characteristics created by the wills of our forefathers, the vision we might have had has become almost totally obscured[23]. Satan likewise conceals from us the ultimate consequences of following his lead; indeed he persuades us that by so doing we shall build utopia, but does not reveal that what he presents to us as utopia is very different

from the kingdom of God. Moreover, it seems certain that the temporal and eternal realms have been so constructed by God that departure from the true path impairs our judgement and our power to penetrate the screen set up by Satan to deceive us, and as with the passage of time we wander further from the path, this disability increases and the task of remedying it becomes more difficult.

111. It is thus between these two claimants for our allegiance[24] that the battle has been waged, and it is clear that, although the final outcome must be either the victory of God or the eternal destruction of the human race, man has, since the time of his creation, been ambivalent in the choice of his objectives. Three victories for each side may be mentioned as being of particular significance in the course of man's evolution. The first victory for Satan is that men have rejected the concept of submission as being an unworthy ideal and have sought instead the ideal of self-aggrandizement. As a result of this pursuit they have ceased, in their relations with nature, to rely on the natural superiority over the temporal creation which they hold by virtue of their dual ontological status, and have developed instead an attitude of arrogance, exemplified by an insistence on temporal superiority. This has led them to look on the natural world, not as a gift for which they are responsible as trustees, and which may be degraded by their Fall and uplifted by their collaboration with God, but as something to be subdued and forced to serve their ends, whether noble or ignoble.

112. The second victory for Satan is closely allied to the first but involves an even greater evil and must ultimately prove to be even more disastrous. For whereas the first victory leads man to regard the temporal order as a proper field for exploitation and is therefore an offence against God's creation, the second is a direct affront to God himself. It consists in the development of the idea that man is or can become independent of God, and of the establishment of this idea of independence as an ideal to be pursued by the wills of men. The motto of this objective is 'Glory to man in the highest, for man is the master of things'[25]. It is this false ideal that inspires the heresy of Pelagianism, a heresy which, as already noted[26], is wide

spread today, even though it may not be known by that name. It leads also to the dethronement of God, to the notion that God is not an objective Being whose ontological status is immeasurably higher than that of any part of his creation, but is the name given to man's spiritual, or at least his 'highest', experiences and aspirations. It leads, in fact, to the reduction of theology to anthropology[27], and is a heresy to which many churchmen and theologians, as well as many laymen, would today give their assent. It is a wholly false and dangerous line of thought which, if persisted in, must increase man's estrangement from God, and thereby render his return to the true path the more difficult.

113. The third victory for Satan, although less fundamental than the second, has perhaps had equally serious practical consequences. It consists in the fact that the wills of men have pursued the objective of maximising pleasure; they have sought, not only to multiply the occasions by which pleasure can be obtained, but also to increase without limit the capacity of their hosts to experience pleasure. As a result desires have increased in both number and intensity, and a master or parent desire to push this increase to the uttermost limit has been created[28]. The consequences of this activity of the wills of men are for the most part too obvious to need mention, but there is one consequence which affects the whole human race and is of immense importance, and which must be attributed to this cause, although at first sight this attribution seems impossible, since it is a consequence appearing to be the direct opposite of any effect to which this cause could give rise. This consequence is the enormous capacity of men and women to experience pain. Pain is, logically, inevitable in the finite world containing sentient beings (it is, in the last analysis, a desire[29], the desire that circumstances should be other than they are, and like other desires, it can vary over a wide range), but in extreme cases its intensity is far greater than is necessary for the preservation of life or the maintenance of the species[30]. Why should this be so? Clearly some factor other than natural evolutionary forces must have been at work. In animals the capacity to experience pain is almost certainly limited to what evolution has ordained, and the exceptional capacity of human

beings must be attributed to the one characteristic which essentially distinguishes such beings from all others, namely the possession of a soul and a will. Thus, strange as it may seem to be, the capacity to experience pain in the high degree to which it has risen in human beings has actually been *willed* by mankind. Not, of course, consciously willed, but nevertheless willed. The only possible explanation of this extraordinary phenomenon is that the capacity to experience pleasure is inseparable from the capacity to experience pain, and that the two capacities increase in roughly the same ratio. We conclude therefore that what has been communally willed is the maximisation of the capacity to experience pleasure, and that the capacity to experience pain to the harrowing degree that is characteristic of human beings has been an unwanted but unavoidable concomitant of that willed development.

114. The three victories for God are, as might be expected, related to the eternal verities, namely truth, beauty and goodness, and in each case (as has also happened in regard to the victories of Satan), the activities of the communal will have not been limited to creating desires whereby its objectives may be approached, but have also created a master desire to increase these particularized desires to the maximum.

115. The first victory relates to the search for knowledge of the physical and psychical worlds and of the laws by which they are governed. No doubt the natural laws of evolution have contributed to the creation of these intellectual desires, as enabling the members of the human species to adapt themselves to their environment and to modify their environment to promote their own survival, but clearly the craving for fuller understanding of the created universe is far more powerful and far more extensive than is necessary for the preservation of the species. It must therefore be a product of the communal will.

116. The second victory relates to the realm of artistic production and appreciation. Here again natural law has played its part. For clearly the recognition of ideals and their promulgation by means of the written word, by pictures, sculpture and music, have aided the survival of the species. But the bearing of marginally different levels of aesthetic talent on individual or tribal survival can never have been very great, and even if we

find the origin of aesthetic delight in the pride of craftsmanship and assess the survival value of craftsmanship at its maximum, we still have to account for the facts that the greatest artists, writers and musicians have devoted their talents to revealing, to the best of their ability, the essence of God, and that some have felt that in so doing they were discharging an inescapable duty. This is true whether the work of an artist is representational or abstract, whether that of a writer is philosophical, historical, biographical or fictional, or that of a musician is intended for sacred or profane performance. It is true also whether the producer of the work is or is not aware of the fact that his object has been the revelation of God; it may be true even in the case of someone who has persuaded himself that God does not exist, or who would claim that, in so far as the concept of duty applies to the manner in which he exercises his talent, it can have no more than a secular meaning. The driving force behind this orientation of their artistic urges cannot be found in natural law and must therefore reside in the wills, not only of the artists themselves, but also of the community in which they have lived and worked, and which, by a long and slow evolutionary process, has come to value and enjoy works having no measurable survival value. We are driven to the conclusion, therefore, that all really significant artistic productions are the expression of the communal will which, in the exercise of its power miraculously to control the evolutionary process, has used the talents of those members of society who are appropriately gifted to embody its objectives in temporal forms in which they can be apprehended by the senses, and which thereby influence, in a greater or lesser degree, the minds of all to whom they are addressed or on whom they impinge. It is probable that the influence thus exerted by artistic productions cannot be wholly avoided or resisted, even though the response to it may be (and may often rightly be) one of rejection; and from this it follows that the responsibility resting on artists of all kinds is a very heavy one. We conclude also that the greatest artistic productions are those in which the primary objective to which they give expression is the revelation of the essence of God, or of some further step towards the realization of his plan for mankind.

117. For the third victory for God we point to the fact that the virtue of benevolence, the desire to promote the well-being of others, which is the essence of charity, has increased in range so that now, in those parts of the world that are adequately equipped, it is extended to almost the whole population. In this case also we must make due allowance for the operation of natural law, for it is obvious that benevolent concern, expressing itself in efforts to promote peace, to eradicate disease and to spread knowledge must make for the survival of the human race. Indeed most species of animals display some measure of benevolence towards the members of their own species. But the efforts of man to help others extend far beyond those of any other species, and while increased knowledge, by providing information about where help is needed and the means to extend benevolence widely, must be acknowledged as making its due contribution, it does not suffice to account for the desire, now active over a large part of the human race, to aid the development of millions of people whom they have never seen, and who, or whose descendants, may become competitors with their benefactors for inadequate supplies of food and dwindling reserves of raw materials and other natural products which have become increasingly essential to the preservation of life. For this excess of benevolence over what nature, with the stimulus provided by knowledge, would ordain as necessary to survival, we must seek the explanation in the power of the human will which, in submission to the will of God, has created in so large a part of the human race the desire to serve its fellow men.

118. These and other characteristics show that human beings have advanced in a direction not wholly divergent from the true path, that they have progressed – some would say have made marked progress – towards the goal assigned for evolution, which is the salvation of the human race, and which may otherwise be described as the building of the kingdom of God. But they have not kept strictly to this path. Their condition may be likened to that of a group of people who have set themselves the task of climbing a mountain. The peak is not visible and there is only one path by which it can be reached. The climbers have wandered far from this path, but they know

that their efforts must be directed upwards, and that this constitutes a duty which they have in some degree tried to discharge. Thus although they have made some progress towards the peak they find themselves in rough ground where the way forward is far from clear, and conflicting voices urge them to follow different paths, or even to abandon the struggle to advance further. This analogy illustrates the conflict of objectives that is the root cause of the confusion that is and always has been so characteristic of men's approach to the problems of life. The urge to build the Tower of Babel[31], which was frustrated by the multiplicity of conflicting voices to which it inevitably (i.e., by God's decree) gave rise, has always been present within the wills, and consequently also within the minds, of men. The result is that, even when an evolutionary goal has coincided with the will of God, its pursuit has been contaminated and marred by the presence within the communal will of opposing urges.

119. The effects of this contamination can be readily seen in regard to the three victories for God described in the preceding paragraphs. Thus the pursuit of knowledge, good in itself[32], has been largely rendered a force for evil by the fact that in a number of different fields the ends sought to be achieved, towards which the acquisition of knowledge is directed, are prescribed by Satan, whose objective is the ultimate destruction of the human race and thus of one of God's great experiments in freedom. One example of this is in the use of knowledge of the structure of matter and of biochemistry to construct weapons which have the power of crippling a whole nation or even of annihilating the entire human race. Of course, Satan does not make the elementary mistake of trying to implant in men's minds a desire to destroy their fellow men for no particular reason; instead he persuades them that their neighbours are dangerous, that the source of the danger is in their ideology, that conflicting ideologies cannot come to terms with one another, and that, in the last resort, false ideologies can only be eradicated by the annihilation of those holding them. Thus men come to believe that the prospect of universal destruction can be justified on moral grounds[33]. However, Satan is well aware that God will not allow his experiment in

freedom to be thus abruptly terminated, and he therefore supplements these by more subtle persuasions[34], such as by implanting in men's minds the idea that the solution of the world's problems can be achieved (and can only be achieved) by the increase of wealth and by guiding their pursuit of knowledge towards this end, by encouraging men to wallow in luxury and to seek it as a prime good, by leading men to believe that they can safely, or even beneficially, usurp the functions of God or of God's natural creation by adopting schemes of genetic engineering and by directing research accordingly, and finally, by infecting men's reasoning powers with plausible but superficial notions, based (though falsely based) on the knowledge they have acquired, which lead them to conclude that neither he nor God exists.

120. The aesthetic sense of human beings, which is the ability to perceive and understand reality through the medium of artistic productions, is likewise good in itself, and has, throughout the history of mankind, been used primarily for good purposes. It has thus been the means whereby the purest emotional experiences have been obtained. But this sense is also susceptible of being perverted by Satan, who is ever ready to divert men's highest faculties to serve ignoble ends. He seeks to do this both by debasing public taste and by infecting the minds of artists in all media, persuading them to use their talents to express his own aspirations rather than, as is their duty, to reveal the essence of God. Where he thinks it will be helpful to his cause he even leads them to believe that in aiming at the former they are achieving the latter. The growing secularization of thought that has been so marked a feature of the twentieth century has led to a significant development in this perversion of the talents of artists, writers and all who aspire to point the way to the future. It finds expression also in the field of entertainment which, like art, can influence profoundly the minds of men and women, and particularly of the young. It reveals itself also in the use of such slogans as 'the duty of the artist is to reveal his own subconscious mind', or 'to display the world as it really is', or even of the pointless phrase 'art for art's sake'. None of these slogans is wholly false, but all express, and express in a distorted form, only a small part of the

truth. Their use therefore provides an excellent opportunity for Satan to exert his evil influence. On the other hand no harm can result from taking them as a partial guide, provided that those who do so are motivated, at the level of their wills, by the search for God.

121. And finally, even the increase in benevolence has been diverted from its true end. For if the desire to promote the wellbeing of mankind is to serve the purposes of God two conditions must be satisfied. The first is that the concept of well-being must be applied to all three of the elements of which man is composed, namely, to his soul, his mind and his body. And the second is that those who are exercising benevolence must do so with humility, not only in relation to those whom they seek to help but, much more importantly, in relation to God. For benevolence which is not directed to serving the true end of man may be, in the eyes of God, more harmful than indifference, and will certainly fail to bring satisfaction in the long run to those receiving it.

122. It is easily seen that these two conditions are interrelated and that the effort to satisfy one will contribute to the satisfaction of the other. A full analysis and development of the meaning of the expression 'good will towards men' is beyond the scope of this book, but as our examination of the miraculous powers of the will has led us to consider the objectives sought by mankind and the bearing of the Fall on those objectives, three points must be made to clarify the issues involved, and to show that neither of the two conditions specified above has been wholly satisfied.

123. The first is that in our interpretation of the concept of well-being we have often reversed the true order of its constituents. Primarily we should seek to promote spiritual well-being, our second concern should be for psychological well-being and our last for physical well-being. The true order is spirit, mind and body, but it is usually taken to be body, mind, spirit; and the danger inherent in this reversal is that the service of the bodily needs of those to whom good will is directed may be held to be the only objective. Provided that this danger is avoided the attitude of mind of those who give the body priority can, of course, be defended. For it is certainly true that where there are

bodily needs these must be given first attention. A hungry man or a man who is afflicted with disease is in no condition to appreciate the spiritual value of Christian teaching (which, because of our own faulty understanding, has in the past often been misdirected) or the spiritual meaning of the highest artistic productions, nor do we help a man's soul in its search for God by allowing him to starve to death. But while the effort to conquer hunger and disease must be given temporal priority, particularly in view of the rapid increase of population which has greatly extended the range and magnified the intensity of these evils, this effort, if it is held to be the final objective, must ultimately fail. We must unceasingly remind ourselves that the ultimate objective is the building of the kingdom of God and that this requires that the target of our benevolence should be the complete well-being, in the right order of priority, of those whom we try to serve, so that, although circumstances may compel us to concentrate first on their bodily needs, we never lose sight of the fact that the satisfaction of these is only a step towards providing them with a fuller opportunity to know and to implement the will of God, and towards a fuller realization of our part and of how we also, who are taking the initiative, can implement his will.

124. In illustration of the error that must in some way inhere in our concept of well-being we may point to the fact that some of the problems our help is directed to solving are actually increased in difficulty and complexity by the efforts made to solve them. For the eradication of hunger and the conquest of disease in those parts of the world where those evils are most prevalent has led to such an increase of population that the extent of malnutrition, with all the suffering to which it gives rise, has almost certainly not been diminished and may even be increasing both in range and in degree[35]. It is axiomatic that if our ultimate objectives were truly in conformity with the will of God the pursuit of those objectives could not lead to inconsistency, and we must therefore conclude either that our objectives are wrong or that the manner in which we are seeking to achieve them is faulty. In either case the only escape from the dilemma in which we find ourselves is to cease to rely on our own unaided judgements and to try in humility to learn what is

the true will of God.

125. The second point to be made about the exercise of benevolence is that we take it for granted that well-being is promoted by, and only by, the creation of wealth. We assume that the problems afflicting the nations of the world, both developed and developing, are primarily economic and that if the solution to the economic problem can be found the physical, psychological and moral problems will become less acute and may even vanish altogether. The very fact that we describe those nations which we regard as being in need of aid as 'developing' is indicative of our false understanding, for we associate development with industrialization or at least with the exploitation of natural resources. But the notion that men's true satisfaction will, or even can, be attained by such means is as great an error when applied to others as when we apply it to ourselves. It reverses the order of priorities laid down by Jesus in the commandment 'Seek ye first the kingdom of God, and his righteousness; and all these things shall be added unto you'[36].

126. The third point to be noted is that we commonly assume that benevolence (or charity) is a one-way traffic. This is obviously a corollary of our emphasis on wealth as a necessary and sufficient condition of well-being, for this assumption implies that benevolence necessarily flows from the wealthy to the poor nations. But since the assumption is false we ought certainly to examine the validity of the conclusion, and when we do so we very easily see that the conclusion is wrong. It is of course obvious that if the concept of benevolence is limited to its physical aspect the poor nations can contribute nothing to the wealthy nations except by way of exchange, but with a wider understanding of well-being it will be found that the benefits to be distributed are by no means moving in one direction only. There is of course an important difference between the application of benevolence to meet physical needs and its application to meet psychological and spiritual needs. Physical deprivation is plain for all to see and is readily admitted by those who suffer it; there is therefore usually no difficulty in persuading them to accept the offer of help. But people are generally unwilling to admit that they are in

psychological or spiritual need, and benevolence must remain ineffective if it is rejected by those who might most benefit from it. The practice of benevolence in the realms of the mind and the spirit thus demands a degree of mutual understanding far beyond that needed for the offer and acceptance of physical aid.

127. From this it follows that we in the Western world must be ready to reach out for and accept what those of different and in some cases more ancient cultures have to offer. It must be emphasized, however, that I am not advocating eclecticism or some form of syncretic religion. Christianity, if it were fully understood, would be found to contain everything that is necessary for the salvation of the individual and the evolutionary salvation of the human race[37], but it is not, and being infinite can never be, fully understood. The Christian nations have therefore a contribution of priceless value to make to those who know nothing of or who have rejected Christianity (although in their efforts to make this contribution they must adopt a far more humble attitude of mind than they have sometimes adopted in the past if they are to avoid misrepresenting what they are trying to teach, and must remember that misleading the innocent, in so far as it is the product of a sinful will, carries with it a special punishment[38]). The Western nations, therefore, which profess Christianity, are in a very privileged position to promote the well-being of others in all three of its aspects; but they must also learn that they may be receivers as well as givers, and that what they can receive relates particularly to the first of those three aspects, namely the spiritual aspect. We must not hesitate to study what other religions have to offer in regard to the understanding of God, of man's place in the hierarchy of being and of the purpose of his creation; and also in regard to techniques of attuning the mind to respond more readily to the promptings of the will and of severing its links with the body, thereby aiding the transformation of being which provides the furniture that we may take with us into eternal life[39]. But all these things must be done with a proper alignment of the will, so that they are truly part of the effort to obtain a fuller understanding of Christianity and its relevance to contemporary circumstances, as being the

only religion which is wholly true and contains all truth.

128. It is clear from what has been said that the Fall has been, and continues to be, a major factor in human evolution. It is a perpetual defect inhering in the wills of men, expressing itself in two ways: first, in the creation of desires which are opposed to the will of God, and secondly, in the contamination of those desires which are broadly in conformity with the will of God, so that these seldom result in actions that are wholly good. We might conclude from this that the condition of man is desperate and that progress towards the establishment of the kingdom of God is impossible. But this conclusion would be false, for in drawing it we ignore the fact that although man is fallen, he is also redeemed. The meaning of this, as of all Christian doctrines, is infinite; we are, however, concerned here not to expound its full meaning, or even its full application to contemporary man, but only to draw out its relevance to the miraculous power of the human will to mould individual character and to guide the evolution of the race.

129. It is part of Christian belief that mankind has been redeemed by the sacrifice of Christ on the Cross and his resurrection from the dead, and that all men and women are thereby assured of eternal life[40]. This would seem to involve a contradiction, as it might suggest that redemption was a specific event whereby the condition of man was, in an instant, fundamentally changed, so that those whose lives preceded that event could not be affected by it. But although the Crucifixion and Resurrection of Jesus took place at definite moments in time, they were much more than events in time; being acts of God they were significant occasions in all three orders of reality. Thus they were and are operative in eternity as well as in time, and as the eternal order is 'in contact with' the whole of space-time its influence cannot be limited to any particular point in space or any particular moment of time. The redemption effected by the sacrifice of Christ is an eternal and therefore also an everlasting sacrifice, applicable to the whole eternal order and to the whole created universe. The fact that it broke through into the temporal order in tangible and visible form at a particular place and time is no doubt meaningful, and it is our duty to try to learn what truths it may

contain, but it in no way impairs its significance and power as a guarantee of salvation for the angels (including even Satan) as well as for all mankind, and indeed for the whole world of living and non-living matter, which is involved with mankind in his Fall.

130. At the individual level the doctrine is an assurance that although the objectives towards which any particular person's will is directed, whereby within the framework provided by his heredity and environment his character has been developed, may diverge widely from those ordained by God, whether specifically for him or generally for all mankind, he will never be rejected by God. He has only to repent, that is to say, to acknowledge, as an act of will, the falsity of these goals, so that his will seeks to realign itself more nearly in accordance with the will of God, to be assured of having the full backing of God in the pursuit of new goals.

131. But the fact that redemption is not localized either in space or in time is proof that it has an evolutionary as well as an individual application. And its meaning in the wider field is substantially the same as in the narrower. Redemption is not only redemption of the individual man or woman, or even of all men and all women, it is redemption of the human race. Its meaning is that, however far men may have wandered from the true path, they will be given the invincible aid of God in returning towards that path, provided that they repent. And in this context repentance means group repentance, acknowledgement by a portion of the human race forming a roughly homogeneous whole, a group sharing a broadly common cultural outlook and sufficiently closely integrated to be able to exercise communal will-power, that the course of its evolution has diverged widely from that ordained by God. The acknowledgement of error must apply not only to the initial assignment of objectives to be aimed at, in so far as these conflict with those assigned by God for the human race as a whole and for the particular group in question, but also, with the same qualification, to the assignment of subsidiary objectives, as the occasion for determining such objectives has arisen. The acknowledgement of error must also be accompanied by a sincere effort by the communal will, not only to renounce its error, but

also, in humility, to seek the guidance of God for its own reorientation, and for the enlightenment of the communal vision, so that the group may be shown how to set about remedying the evils brought about by the pursuit of false goals, and may also be given a glimpse of God's ultimate goal, so that a return towards the true path of evolution may be begun.

132. It will be clear from what has been said in this and the previous chapter that the miraculous power of the human will to create the individual character and, acting communally, to create the character and determine the evolution of mankind, is not to be interpreted in any narrow or superficial sense. Nor should it be supposed that the action of the will is sudden or dramatic. In both cases the process, though immensely powerful, is gradual and almost unobservable over a short period. In the case of the individual it extends over the whole course of his life, including his life beyond the grave, and in the case of mankind it extends over the whole era during which man has lived on earth, and will continue until the end of time, and even beyond. The conclusions we have reached are not to be taken as implying that a man who is cruel, avaricious or dissolute can, by a simple act of will, become kindly, generous or chaste overnight, or that the human race can, by a simple exercise of the communal will, quickly eradicate all the undesirable tendencies that give rise to all the manifest evils in the world. We are in both cases dealing with the operation of a faculty lying below the level of overt behaviour, a faculty whose activities reach to the deepest level of our being, since it is a function of our eternal being, whereas behaviour, however lasting its effects may be, is a feature of the temporal order.

133. It will, I hope, also be clear that the condition of man, though grievous, is most certainly not hopeless. Repentance, in the broad sense in which it has been defined above, is all that is needed to secure his regeneration. But it must be true repentance. It is not sufficient for the individual to feel regret for having committed particular sins, or for a nation or a larger group to admit the errors recorded in its history. Repentance requires unqualified acceptance and acknowledgement of the fact that we are not, either as individuals or as a race, the sort of people that God intended us to be. Once we recognize this fact,

and also the fact that the only way in which we can become more nearly what we ought to be is by wholly submitting our judgements to the guidance of God, we shall find that the solution to the problem of regenerating the world and ourselves will be slowly but quite surely revealed. This assurance is powerfully given by Christ himself, who is Alpha and Omega, the first and the last, the beginning and the end, in the message delivered to the church of the Laodiceans: 'Be zealous therefore, and repent; behold I stand at the door and knock; if any man hear my voice, and open the door, I will come in to him, and will sup with him, and he with me. To him that overcometh will I grant to sit with me in my throne, even as I also overcame, and am set down with my Father in his throne. He that hath an ear, let him hear what the Spirit saith'[41].

CHAPTER FOUR

NOTES AND REFERENCES

(The numbers in brackets indicate the paragraphs in which the references occur)

1. (96) It may be asked what part can be played by an infant who dies within a few hours, or even within a few months, of birth, or by a foetus which, though it may have been the dwelling place of a living soul for nine months in its mother's womb, is stillborn. The answer to this question is, probably no part at all during the period of earthly embodiment of that soul; but as the soul, once created, has eternal being, it makes its contribution by metallassis in the eternal order. For our earthly life is not the only occasion available for working out our salvation, or for making our contribution to the salvation of mankind.

2. (96) It is possible that withdrawal of the freedom of the will would also be annihilation of the soul. If this is the case we must conclude that God would adopt other means than the withdrawal of freedom to secure the fulfilment of his purpose. For we may reasonably suppose that freedom would be withdrawn only from those souls that have irreversibly rejected God, and we must, I think, dismiss the idea that any soul has ever *completely* rejected God or will ever do so. The idea that God, whose unimpaired goodness is axiomatic (or rather is tautological, since 'goodness' cannot be defined otherwise that in terms of God) would or even could create a soul which, though endowed with complete freedom, could irreversibly reject its creator, would seem to involve a contradiction. Even Satan is bound to recognize the existence of God, and must be aware that his efforts to thwart God's plan are evil, and also that they must ultimately fail.

3. (98) Psalm viii, 5; Hebrews ii, 7.
4. (99) 1 Corinthians xiii.
5. (99) But some of the temporal products of men's wills can be endowed with eternal being and thereby preserved. See Chapter V.
6. (99) It should be noted that this does not necessarily (or even probably) mean persuading others to accept one's own judgements and opinions. The will of God for one person does not necessarily coincide with his will for another. No man may aim at forcing others to subordinate their wills to his will, however rightly this may be aligned; his duty is to induce others to seek God's will for themselves.
7. (101) See paragraph 49.
8. (103) In paragraph 97.
9. (105) Mutations are not, of course, absolutely random; that is to say, they are not indeterminate or uncaused (see Chapter II, Note 3). If we eliminate the action of the will, mutations are the inescapable effect of all the causes acting, but are described as random because these causes are so numerous, so complex and so inaccessible, as to be beyond the reach of analysis. The point of the principle of natural selection is not that mutations are strictly random, but that they are random with respect to survival; they are not, in fact, directed to any particular end, not even the end of the preservation of the species, but are widely varied. Certain mutations happen to be more beneficial in regard to survival than others, and it is these that are transmitted to the next generation.
10. (107) In paragraph 68.
11. (107) The fact that man has an eternal element whereas other animals do not justifies our speaking of the creation of man.
12. (107) Genesis i, 31.
13. (107) Paul Tillich, writing as an existentialist, has said: 'The story of Genesis, chapters i to iii, if taken as a myth, can guide our transition from essential to existential being. It is the profoundest and richest expression of man's awareness of his existential estrangement and provides the scheme in which the transition from essence to existence can be treated. It points, first, to the possibility of the Fall; second, to its motives; third,

to the event itself; and fourth, to its consequences.' (Tillich; *Systematic Theology*, Vol. II; James Nisbet & Co. Ltd., 1957, p. 35). And again, 'Perhaps no text in literature has received so many interpretations as the third chapter of Genesis. This is partly due to its uniqueness – even in biblical literature – partly to its psychological profundity, and partly to its religious power.' (Ibid. p. 42).

Although Tillich speaks of the uniqueness of the Genesis story it is, in fact, parallelled by myths in other cultures (see, e.g., John S Dunne: *The City of the Gods*; The Sheldon Press, 1974; pp. 6 and 9). This fact in no way detracts from the significance of the story; rather it reinforces it, for it shows that the concept of the Fall, the recognition that the problems confronting mankind arise from his having aimed at becoming as a god, knowing good and evil, and that in this process a supernatural agency has acted as instigator, are, though not universal, at least fairly widespread.

14. (108) Matthew vii, 13, 14; Luke xiii, 24.
15. (109) This statement is not to be read as implying that man can achieve salvation by his own unaided efforts. See Chapter II Note 35.
16. (109) Paragraph 67.
17. (109) cf. John iii, 1-13.
18. (110) cf. the statement at the end of paragraph 40 that God and man are so closely interrelated that neither can forget the other.
19. (110) 1 Corinthians ii, 9, 10.
20. (110) Matthew x, 26; John xvi, 13. But although the Spirit is willing to lead us into all truth, our readiness and ability to receive it are, and always have been, limited. Our vision is blinkered (1 Corinthians xiii, 12), and at different times the blinkers obscure different revelations of truth. Thus in the twentieth century much of the truth revealed before the advent of the scientific revolution is rejected by all but a few. But there are hopeful signs that our willingness to be guided by the Spirit into a wider vision of truth is growing and may grow further during the coming century.
21. (110) Matthew x, 34-39; xvi, 24-26; Mark x, 21.
22. (110) Matthew xi, 29,30.

23. (110) 1 Corinthians xiii, 12.
24. (111) See paragraph 80.
25. (112) Algernon Swinburne: *Hymn of Man.*
26. (112) In Chapter II, Note 35.
27. (112) Rudolf Bultmann, in reply to a challenge from Karl Barth, who had accused him of this error, said: 'I would heartily agree: I *am* trying to substitute anthropology for theology, for I am interpreting theological affirmations as assertions about human life'. (*Kerygma and Myth*, vol. i, p. 107; quoted by John A.T. Robinson: *Honest to God*, SCM paperback, 1963, p.50). Dr Robinson comes close to agreeing with Bultmann, for he says, in the passage in which the above quotation appears, 'This is very close to the position we have been taking'. But the inevitable result of reducing theology to anthropology is the reduction of anthropology to zoology. If God is no more than the hypostatization of man's 'highest' aspirations, then the word 'highest' becomes indefinable, except in temporal terms, so that man, and therefore also God, is no more than an animal. In other words, the number of orders of reality is either three or one. If the supra-eternal order does not exist, then neither does the eternal order.
28. (113) This fact is clearly illustrated in the case of sexual desire, which human evolution has increased in intensity and persistence to a point far beyond what is necessary for the procreation of the species, and greatly exceeds the corresponding urge in other species. Of course many species of living creatures produce young or seeds or spores vastly in excess of what is required for their own continuation; it seems that the ordinary processes of evolution have brought about this prolificity in order to provide adequately for the hazards of a competitive ecology and for adaptation by natural selection to a changing environment. But in the case of man the situation is entirely different. Human beings do not produce vast numbers of offspring which are then left to fend for themselves in an environment that is largely hostile; in fact reproduction is not seen as the sole or even the primary reason for sexual activity. This is a difficult matter to discuss because, however carefully one chooses one's words, misunderstanding is hardly avoidable, for the reason that people tend to adopt very rigid and

prejudiced attitudes to sex, and to suspect that anyone who differs from them, even though only marginally, belongs to the extreme wing of the opposing school of thought. I must emphasize, therefore, that in citing this unparalleled level of sexual desire as an example of the third victory for Satan, I am not to be taken as implying that the existence of sexual urges, or indulgence in their satisfaction, is in any way evil. I have already pointed out (in paragraph 79) that the principle underlying the Puritan outlook, the principle that pleasure is inherently evil, is heretical, and this applies to sexual as well as to other pleasures. Nor do I intend to imply any criticism of the so-called 'permissive society' of today, which is only a very silly though rather tragic (but probably only temporary) manifestation of a proclivity which has been growing for many hundreds of thousands of years. I am doing no more than to point out that the intensity and continual recrudescence of sexual desire (which must be distinguished from, though it is associated with, sexual love) as experienced by human beings, is the result of a willed development, and that the activities of will by which they have been engendered, are certainly not fully in accord with the will of God. This is easily seen to be the case when we reflect that it is as a consequence of these activities that we are now faced with the problems of (*inter alia*) birth control and abortion, both of which practices must, in present circumstances be regarded as unavoidable and therefore, in appropriate cases, justifiable and *right*, although neither can be regarded as *good*. If there were no conflict with the will of God the temporal standard of 'right' and the eternal standard 'good' would necessarily coincide. (cf. paragraph 82).
29. (113) This shows that there can be no pain (as we understand the word) in eternity, for desire is essentially a phenomenon of the temporal order. It is this that distinguishes it from will. Thus in eternity (and therefore also, for human beings, in life after death) pain is replaced by an experience of the will, an experience of which the soul is *aware*, urging towards a resolution of any situation in which the soul feels frustrated or distressed. The urge may, of course, be rightly or wrongly directed. Thus we must expect to find, in eternity, that

the activity of the will by which the soul seeks to improve its condition may in some cases render that condition even more unsatisfactory. Only by submission in humility to the will of God can the right course be found.

30. (113) A similar point has been made by F.R. Tennant in his Hulsean Lectures for 1901, published as *The Origin and Propagation of Sin*, (Cambridge University Press, 1902): 'It would be maddening to some minds to believe that many of the more awful kinds of human agony are the direct expressions of the will of God. The heaviest burden which distresses human thought is not the existence of evil, of pains and temptations, but their goading intensity and their chaotic distribution.' (p. 133).

31. (118) Genesis xi, 1-9. Note that the Tower of Babel is the symbolic expression of man's urge towards self-aggrandizement; it was because of the sinful nature of this urge that God destroyed the Tower.

32. (119) All knowledge must be either (i) direct knowledge of God; or (ii) indirect knowledge of God through knowledge of his creation; or (iii) knowledge of what is opposed to God and has entered the minds of men by the exercise of the freedom of will conferred on angels and on human beings. Of these the first two are obviously good. And although the third may be used for evil purposes and may thus have evil consequences, it is not in itself evil. The evil lies in the purposes which direct how the knowledge is applied.

As regards the second, which includes the whole range of knowledge obtained by the methods of science, no argument is needed to make the point that this, although good, can also be wrongly used, for the fact that it often is so used is plain for all to see. A particular danger inherent in the use of scientific knowledge is that, through the defect of our wills, the potential evil latent in purposes appearing to be good is often not perceived (see paragraph 110), so that unexpected ills arise from well-intentioned investigations. The distinction between what is good and what is right is here clearly illustrated; thus although all knowledge of nature (including human nature) is good it may often be right to forego it in some particular field.

The ultimate question is whether the knowledge is sought in order to increase our knowledge of God, but the analysis of motives presents such enormous difficulties that it is seldom easy to answer this question, or to say, when this motive is clearly present, to what extent it is contaminated by other less worthy motives. One test (which, however, is not applicable to all cases) is whether the investigation involves actions which are obviously wrong (e.g., cruelty). For if the *sole* ultimate objective is the glory of God, no evil can inhere in the methods required to achieve it.

The first branch of knowledge – direct knowledge of God – is not open to abuse in the same way as the second and the third, for if a man genuinely seeks it his objectives must be pure, and if God truly grants enlightenment as to his essential nature, whether to one man or to the whole world, and if that enlightenment is fully grasped and clearly understood, it must tend towards the perfection of its recipients, although of course the impetus to action it gives may be resisted. But this is not to say that in the case of direct knowledge of God original sin is powerless or even inactive. On the contrary, such knowledge provides particularly fertile ground for Satan who, since our wills have allowed themselves to be corrupted by him, finds it easy to sow the seeds of misunderstanding and schism. This is evidenced by the almost universal misunderstanding, both spiritual and moral, of the revelation of God in Jesus Christ, and by the tragic conflicts to which it has given rise. Satan is aided in promoting and fostering this misunderstanding by the fact that to fallen man truth is usually disturbing and often unpalatable, the divine reality too searing a vision to be accepted except in a diluted and distorted form. As an example of the misunderstanding and consequent distortion of reality we may cite the error referred to in paragraph 91 (a further instance will appear in paragraph 123), namely, that of ignoring all but the temporal manifestations of eternal (or supra-eternal) truth or, what is even worse since it is in effect a form of idolatry, that of substituting for the essence of such truth a temporal object or experience which, though it may in part embody and even express some aspect of that essence, can do so only very imperfectly, and at a lower ontological level. These two errors are respectively illustrated by two features of contemporary thought which, though distinct, are alike in that they both involve the constriction of Christianity into a very narrow field; the first by identifying it with its ethical code to the exclusion of its many other aspects, and the second by confining it to some form of personal experience which, though in rare cases it may be truly spiritual, is as often as not merely psychological. The subjective aspects of religion have of course their proper place, but those who cultivate them to the exclusion of its outward-looking aspects are likely to end by denying the transcendence of God. It is against such overemphasis on personal experience that the warning that 'whosoever shall seek to save his life shall lose it' (Luke xvii, 33) is in part directed. A further danger, inhering in both these errors, is that they may very easily lead to the replacement of theology by anthropology and of Christianity by a mere ethical humanism (see Note 27 above).

33. (119) It will be understood that in putting forward these considerations I am not arguing in favour of unilateral disarmament. Any such interpretation would betray a complete misunderstanding of what I have said. The construction of weapons of defence is in fact an instance of the application of scientific knowledge to purposes which, though evil, are contingently justifiable because, as a consequence of the original sin of our forefathers from which we cannot now escape, we have developed a communal character and have constructed an environment and a set of mutual relationships which render the holding in reserve of such weapons, and even in extreme cases their use, inevitable.

34. (119) cf. Genesis iii, 1.

35. (124) The time left for solving the population problem is short. The total land area of the world (excluding Antarctica) is 135 million square kilometres. Omitting mountain ranges and deserts the total habitable area might be taken to be about 100 million square kilometres. The density of population in Europe (excluding the USSR) is about 103 per square kilometre and it is reasonable to suppose that the maximum

average density that the world can comfortably support is not greater than 100 per square kilometre. This assumption leads to the conclusion that the maximum supportable population of the world is 10,000 million people. The present (1988) population is over 5,000 million and this is increasing at the rate of about 1.5 per cent per annum. If this rate is continued the maximum supportable population will be reached in the year 2034. Obviously steps must be taken to control population growth long before that date. It may also be pointed out that if the expectation of life (at birth) is to be raised throughout the world to seventy years (as most people would probably consider to be desirable) the birth rate throughout the world must be reduced to 14.3 per 1,000 per annum, because in a stable population the expectation of life at birth multiplied by the birth rate equals unity.

36. (125) Matthew vi, 33.
37. (127) John xiv, 6.
38. (127) Matthew xviii, 6 (= Mark ix, 42 = Luke xvii, 1, 2).
39. (127) See Chapter V.
40. (129) We know that every human being, by virtue of his being human, possesses eternal *being*, and it might be thought that, because of this fact, he must also possess eternal *life*. It is of course true that the soul can never die, but in Christian thought life means much more than not being dead. Life is a dynamic concept, of which an inescapable characteristic is change (in time) or metallassis (in eternity), and this development must be in the direction of either greater harmony or greater disharmony with God. For we have already seen (paragraph 64) that purpose is inseparable from eternal being, and in eternity the only alternatives are to be for or against God (Matthew xii, 30). Moreover, in living beings consciousness is most highly organized and therefore most nearly complete (see Chapter V), and we may therefore describe eternal life as the conscious activity of the soul in eternity. Now God is the ultimate end of organization, for, as he is self-consistent, in him there are no disruptive forces, and it follows that, if eternal life is positive (and if it is not it ceases to be life), it cannot finally resist the pull towards God. Thus we arrive at the conclusion that eternal life is progress towards unity with

God. This illustrates the point of Christ's remark: 'I am come that they might have life, and that they might have it more abundantly'. (John x, 10).
41. (133) Revelation i, 8; xxi, 6; iii, 19-22. See also John vi, 37: 'him that cometh to me I will in no wise cast out.'

5

THE TRANSFORMATION OF BEING

I. The Meaning of Resurrection

134. The supreme importance of the miraculous powers of the will and of the objectives which, by the exercise of those powers, the wills of human beings seek to attain, both for themselves as individuals and for mankind as a whole, needs no further proof or emphasis, but it is clear that these are not the only tasks for which those powers must be invoked. For although the activity of the will in creating and shaping the desires of each individual and thereby building up his true character is of overriding importance during his lifetime (since, subject to his heredity and his environment, it is these desires that determine how his earthly life is lived), the effects of the will's activity would come to an end, so far as the individual himself is concerned, when he dies, if the will did not take further action. But the will, being eternal, cannot be satisfied with achieving results which are confined to the temporal order and perish with the death of its host. It is of course true that a man's achievements during his lifetime may be preserved and may influence the lives of generations long after his death, and that in this way the effect of his will in shaping his individual characteristics may be of great help to those who come after him, and may thus contribute to the social evolution of mankind. It is true also that his will may contribute to the genetic evolution of mankind by initiating mutations which affect his own offspring and, through them, future generations. All these are important, but even though they may last to the

end of time they are still temporal, and therefore cannot satisfy the soul, whose fulfilment can only be achieved in the eternal order.

135. Moreover, 'some there be, which have no memorial; who are perished, as though they had never been[1];' and who have not, by an act of will, initiated any mutation. And yet each of these is as important in the sight of God as a man who has left imperishable works behind him. Of course the soul (and therefore also the will) of every human being is immortal, in that its being is eternal being, and it is therefore the vehicle of eternal life, but this fact cannot exhaust the meaning of immortality or the significance of the soul's importance in the sight of God. For God has so ordained the course of events that for a period of time, which may be no more than a few minutes or may be as long as a hundred years, the soul of every individual human being is harnessed to a temporal being, and even though God may have played no positive part in determining how long that period should be he must be concerned with the manner in which the soul has exercised its freedom during the time of its association with a body and a mind. If this were not so it would be impossible to attach any meaning to life on earth, which would be no more than a meaningless incident, without purpose or effect, in the eternal life of the soul. And this is an impossible supposition, for the soul, though its being is eternal being and is therefore created into eternity, is projected into time. Its association with the temporal being of the body and the mind is a deliberate act by God, and nothing that God does is capricious or meaningless.

136. It follows that the effects of the activity of every human will during the earthly life of its host, however apparently insignificant and however humble they may be, must in some way be immortalized. This cannot be by a reaction on the soul of the will's psychological creations, for the temporal order cannot causally affect the eternal order[2]. In all relations between the two orders it must be the element which has eternal being that takes the initiative and supplies the energy, and the only possibility, therefore, is that the will, reaching out from its habitation in the soul, selects certain features from the body and the mind of its host, and transforms their being from

temporal to eternal being. And this act is of course a miracle.
137. The reference to the body in this statement suggests that we shall find here the true meaning of the expression 'the resurrection of the body'[3]. It is a belief widely held among Christians and universally among Muslims that the immortality which human beings enjoy, or must be prepared to meet, is something much more positive than the preservation of the soul in being; it is in some sense a resurrection of the body. The concept of resurrection, as distinct from that of immortality, pervades the whole of the New Testament, and it is noteworthy that when Jesus spoke of resurrection the word he used, as recorded by the evangelists, has the very definite connotation, not of a persistence in being or of a preservation of life, but of a renewal, of rising again or of causing to stand or rise again[4]. It is perhaps not surprising that some Christians have in past times interpreted the idea of resurrection as meaning that a physical body, peculiar to each individual, will be provided at the Day of Judgement, which they hold will take place at the end of the world (i.e., when time and space cease to be), but there can be very few who would today proclaim this as their belief, and it is easy to see that such a fundamentalist interpretation must be rejected, since it contradicts the principle (implicit in the concept of the eternal and temporal orders as media for distinct modes of being) that matter is linked with space-time in such a way that the existence of either implies the existence of the other. Moreover, the notion that the resurrected body is physical is contrary to the teaching of St Paul, who makes it abundantly clear that it is a spiritual body[5]. He does not describe this spiritual body, but he gives us a clue to its genesis when he says that 'this corruptible must put on incorruption, and this mortal must put on immortality'[6]. Thus St Paul confirms the conclusion reached in the preceding paragraph, for his words can only mean that some entity associated with human beings, an entity having temporal being, is endowed, by a specific act, with eternal being; and we may reasonably attribute the power by which this transformation of being is effected to the will, which is the only element of the human structure which is able to make a positive impact on man's temporal being. The choice of the entity (or entities)

whose being is to be so transformed rests with the soul. (It might be thought that the transformation would be effected by an act of God, and it is of course true that God supplies the power by which the will causes the miracle to take place; moreover, he is ready and willing to help the soul to make the right choice if his aid is sought, but he in no way compels the choice. This must be so because otherwise God would be interfering with the freedom of the soul on a critical occasion, perhaps the most critical in its career. Thus the soul is the arbiter, and its active organ, the will, gives effect to its decisions).

138. This is, however, still very imprecise, but we can add a measure of substance to the rather elusive notion of a transformation of being by adapting certain ideas of the Jesuit thinker Pierre Teilhard de Chardin, and applying them to the concept of man as set out in the earlier chapters of this book. Teilhard de Chardin was not only a member of a highly intellectual religious order and a mystic, he was also a scientist, specializing in palaeontology, and his scientific work nurtured a passionate interest in the problem of evolution, which he rightly saw as directed, and which he strove to assimilate to the comprehensive truth revealed in Christianity. His ideas in their most mature form are set out in his book *The Phenomenon of Man*[7], in which he traces the working out of the evolutionary process from the earliest stages of the earth, through the advent and expansion of life, to the birth and development of the power of thought, culminating in the emergence of man, in whom this power is enlarged into the power of *reflective* thought, the power 'not merely to know, but to know oneself; no longer merely to know, but to know that one knows'[8].

139. Teilhard seeks to discover the principle lying at the base of this directed property of evolution, and he finds it in the Law of Complexity and Consciousness[9]. This law rests on four pillars, four concepts which pervade the whole of Teilhard's thought, namely, atomicity, structure, consciousness and directedness. He recognizes that the whole of temporal reality, that is to say, not only the physical world but also the psychical world, is atomic[10], and he sees clearly that the difference between the multitudinous variety of things of which these two worlds are

composed lies in their structure. (Thus the nature of an atom depends on the number and structure of the protons and neutrons in its nucleus, the nature of a molecule on the number and structure of the various kinds of atoms it contains, and so on. Likewise the nature of a thought, a feeling, an emotion or a desire, depends on the number and structure of the psychical particles it contains.) So far as the physical world is concerned there is nothing novel in these ideas; the originality of Teilhard's thought lies in his extension of them to the psychical world and in his application to them of the concepts of consciousness and directedness to build a model of the course of evolution from the beginning to the end of time. It would be impossible to summarize this imaginative and prophetic vision of the world in a few paragraphs, but fortunately it is not necessary to attempt such a task; for our present purpose all that is needed is to extract those parts of the system that will help us to give substance to the meaning of resurrection.

140. For Teilhard the basis of phenomenal reality is consciousness[11]. He holds that every fundamental physical particle and every fundamental psychical particle is endowed with a quantum of consciousness. (The word 'particle' is to be understood here in a generalized sense, as including wave structures or other elemental forms). Moreover, consciousness is associated not only with atomicity, but also with structure or organization. We may, for convenience, think of organization and consciousness as being atomic, and we must associate with every 'unit' of organization (or, to use the word preferred by Teilhard, complexity) a quantum of consciousness. Thus if two or more physical particles or two or more psychical particles come together to form a more complex organized unit, or if one or more physical particles and one or more psychical particles unite to form a more complex organization, the total consciousness of the new unit exceeds the sum of the quanta of consciousness of its physical and psychical constituents. Thus, speaking of the power of human beings to engage in reflective thought, Teilhard says, 'Here as elsewhere in the universe, the whole shows itself to be greater than the simple sum of the elements of which it is formed'[12]. The additional consciousness thus appearing may be called 'organization consciousness'.

141. Finally, Teilhard holds that in order to account for the phenomena of the world, and in particular for the phenomena of life and thought, we must add the principle of directedness. He insists that the world is not static but is constantly evolving. This is of course obvious enough, and is implicit in the concept of a temporal order, but it is possible to hold that change is inseparable from time and at the same time to hold that the universe is essentially static, that although there is continual change there is no development. Teilhard would regard such a universe as meaningless. To give meaning to reality we must believe that, however chaotic change may appear to be, there is, underlying all change and therefore all evolution, a principle whereby the universe is being urged towards the fulfilment of a purpose[13]. He drives this home by insisting (quite rightly, since the point he makes is obviously true), that nothing can be fully understood except in relation to its end, and to the status of this end in relation to the overall guiding purpose. Thus he says, 'Not a single thing in our changing world is really understandable except in so far as it has reached its terminus'[14]. In its application to structural reality he holds that this inbuilt principle of change and evolution acts as a force on the physical and psychical elements of which the universe is composed, urging them to form ever more complex structures, thereby leading to an ever increasing quantity of consciousness in the universe[15]. Thus the evolution of living creatures starting from primitive forms and developing ultimately to produce the mammals is not fully accounted for by the application of the laws of nature as revealed by science; there is in addition a driving force producing a movement towards greater complexity and an increase of consciousness. The culminating point of this development is, of course, Man, in whom the growth of consciousness has reached its peak[16].

142. The drive towards greater organization in living matter is in direct opposition to the second law of thermodynamics[17], and to account for it we must postulate that the passage from pre-life to life can take place only as the result of a specific act of the Creator, whereby there is implanted into matter of appropriately complex structure a new principle of orientation, a principle superimposed on natural law, by virtue of which in

living beings an increase of organized complexity, and therefore of consciousness, becomes a pre-ordained feature of evolution. This principle may be called the *telos*. Clearly the first implantation of the telos into nature involved an interference with nature's laws, and was therefore a divine miracle, and the same may be true of its subsequent activity. We need not however inquire, and it is probably impossible to say, whether God acts directly and continuously through the telos to disturb natural law or whether, having pointed the telos in the right direction, he has endowed it with power to discharge its function without further aid from him, other than that of maintaining it in being[18] and supplying it with the necessary energy; but it is important to stress that, in either case, the power exercisable by the telos is not in any way comparable with the miraculous powers of human beings, who are certainly not merely instruments for the transmission of divine power[19], but are endowed with power which they can exercise freely.

143. One further point needs to be made before we can define more precisely the nature of the miracle performed by the will in what I have called the transformation of being. This is that Teilhard recognized that there are different levels of consciousness. Thus in relation to the world before the advent of life he speaks of pre-consciousness[20], and in relation to the condition of man in the distant future he speaks of super-consciousness[21]. It is true that he appears to regard the transition from one level of consciousness to the next higher level as being continuous, but on this point he is ambiguous, for he also speaks (and insists on the importance) of *critical points*, 'involving a change of state'[22] and among these critical points he instances the genesis of life[23], the birth of thought in the primates[24], and the first appearance of man[25]. All these instances have occurred within the sphere of temporal reality (for although he sees that the appearance of man and of reflective thought marked a critical point in evolution he does not, so far as I can discover, link it with the appearance on earth of an entirely new mode of *being*, i.e., of eternal being in association with temporal being. This, however, may be because, as he himself makes clear, his concern is with phenomenal reality only, and not with metaphysics[26]). Nevertheless I do not think he would deny,

and in one passage at least he goes some way towards admitting[27], that in addition to the distinction between the different levels of temporal consciousness, account must also be taken of the even more important distinction between temporal consciousness, at all its levels, and eternal consciousness, and between both of these and the supra-eternal or divine consciousness of God. For we certainly cannot deny to the higher levels of being an element, essential to its being, that infuses all temporal being. We shall therefore assume that everything that has eternal being is possessed of consciousness, and that the consciousness of eternal beings is of a different, and higher, order from that of temporal beings; and to mark the difference we shall use the phrase 'spiritual consciousness' to describe the former.

144. We are now in a position to apply these ideas to give a meaning to the phrase 'the resurrection of the body'. As already indicated[28] this must mean that the being of some human feature, characteristic or entity, whose being, during the earthly life of its host, is temporal being, is miraculously transformed by the action of the will into eternal being. Now we have seen in the preceding two chapters that the will of every human being, having freely selected its objectives, which in most cases relate to the development of the individual himself, but may also embody factors governing the evolution of the race, seeks to mould the whole body-mind complex in such a manner as will favour the achievement of those objectives. In pursuing this end the will must of course make use of the physical and psychical material at its disposal; it also relies, so far as is consonant with its aims, on the telos and on the laws of the natural world, including, in the case of evolutionary ends, the laws of heredity and natural selection, but where necessary it implants a quantum of energy[29] in order to ensure that development will take place in the willed direction. Its efforts may not be wholly successful, but every successful or even partially successful act of will increases the organized complexity of the mind and may also increase the organized complexity of the body and of the body-mind linkages. Every such increase in complexity increases the organization consciousness of the individual, and it is reasonable to suppose that

in so far as the added consciousness is due solely to the action of the will it is spiritual consciousness, but in so far as it is due to natural causes (even though these may have been originally set in motion by the will) or to the action of the telos, the added consciousness is temporal consciousness. The spiritual consciousness is created by the will *ex nihilo*, a fact which demonstrates clearly that the action of the will is miraculous, but the temporal consciousness is drawn from the totality of organization consciousness in the universe, thereby increasing the external disorganization in accordance with the second law of thermodynamics.

145. Thus every specific act of the will adds to the spiritual consciousness of its host; and as the being of spiritual consciousness is eternal being this may be equally well expressed by saying that every act of will makes its contribution to the growth of the soul, and that the growth of the soul is a growth of consciousness[30]. This is obviously an important conclusion, but it is clearly also insufficient, since the only relevant inference we can draw from it is that (as we already know from more basic considerations) what is created directly by the will is immortal, and if the powers of the will were thus limited it would mean that, so far as its achievements are dependent on the telos or on natural law, they are lost to eternity, and such a loss would certainly not satisfy the soul. We must therefore make the further claim that the will can and does act on the temporal organization consciousness associated with the increase of complexity of the body and mind of its host and of their mutual relations and interactions and transforms the being of this consciousness (in so far as the complexity is consistent with the will's objectives) from temporal to eternal being. This activity of the will is probably continuous throughout the whole of the earthly life of the host. It is obviously a miracle, and equally obviously it constitutes a true resurrection, since the temporal being of the organization consciousness is destroyed and the consciousness is 'reborn' or resurrected as an eternal entity.

146. The significance of the miraculous activity of the will in relation to resurrection can be more clearly grasped if we fix our attention on the human being as a whole. The totality of

the consciousness of a human being, which is made up of the individual 'atoms' of consciousness of the physical and psychical particles of which his body and his mind are composed, together with the organization consciousness (or complexity consciousness) associated with the grouping and mutual relations of all these particles by virtue of which that person is individualized, all these together make up a distinct unit of consciousness – the characteristic consciousness of that person; separate and clearly distinguishable from the characteristic consciousness of all other persons. Parts of this characteristic consciousness are continually being shed and replaced by other atoms of consciousness, as the atomic or molecular particles of his body and his mind are shed and replaced, and with these the soul has no concern. But other parts, particularly of the organization consciousness, are seized on by the soul, which instructs its active organ, the will, to adopt them and to transform their being to eternal being, uniting them with those parts which, having been *created* by the will, already enjoy such being. The created elements enter on eternal life at the moment of their creation, and the transformed elements, which from now on will be referred to as the *resurrected* elements, at the moment when their being is transformed. They play their part in the soul's activity during the remainder of the earthly life of the host, during which time that activity is of course conditioned by the limitations of his bodily and mental powers, and at his death enter on untrammelled eternal existence. It should, however, be added that, since the being of both the created and the resurrected elements is created by the will, it may also be annihilated by the will, either during the lifetime of its host or after his death, if they appear to the soul to be no longer of use to it; it may also, of course, be annihilated by God either with or without the agreement of the will.

147. This description of the creative activity of the will leads to the conclusion (which at first sight may seem remarkable but on reflection will be seen to be at least reasonable if not actually axiomatic) that death and resurrection are not confined to a particular moment but are processes continuing throughout the whole of life. This is of course a commonplace in regard to the physical constituents of living creatures. The cells of the

body, which may be held to be the smallest parts that can be said to have life (or, as we may say, in which the telos is active), are continually being cast off and replaced; the cast-off cells die and the telos transfers its directing power to the new cells as they are built up and take the place of the discarded cells. It has, in fact, been said that we start to die as soon as we are born, but we should qualify this aphorism by adding that we are also continually being reborn so long as we are physically alive[31]. Further, although the 'particles' of the minds of living creatures are not identifiable (or at any rate have not yet been identified), and we do not know how they are organized into 'psychical cells', it is reasonable to suppose that they also are continually being discarded and replaced. But in order to account for memory we must suppose that some psychical cells, possibly those having a particular structure, are retained throughout life[32], and it is probable that the organization consciousness of these memory cells are among those selected by the soul for the transforming activity of the will, except where they appear to the soul to have no relevance to, or to be such that their immortalization would tend to frustrate, the achievement of its objectives.

148. But although death and resurrection are continuous and inescapable features of our life on earth it is also probable that the moment of the final death of the body is special. For the soul cannot fail to realize that this is the moment when its attachment to the body and the mind ceases to limit its development, and also that this moment is the final opportunity for it to select those features of the physico-psychic complex that it wishes to take over by resurrection (as defined above) into the realm of eternity. It is by reference to these considerations that we can give meaning to the despised expression 'death-bed repentance', and can attach positive value to the activity it inadequately describes.

II. Recognition and Communication

149. This analysis of the meaning of resurrection leads inevitably to two questions on which everyone who can think at all

must have pondered, namely, whether we shall be consciously ourselves in the life after death, and whether we shall 'meet' and recognize those whom we have known, and particularly those whom we have loved, on earth. Obviously anything that can be said on these issues can be no more than speculation, but on a matter of such vital importance and universal interest speculation is justified; and if we consider the questions in the light of the description of man on which the argument of this book is based, I think it may be claimed that the conclusions drawn in the following paragraphs command a high degree of probability.

150. Clearly an affirmative answer to either of these two questions is conditional on the preservation of the faculty of awareness through the barrier of death. This condition, however, is one which we may be certain is satisfied. For awareness (which must, as we have already seen[33], be distinguished from consciousness) is a faculty enjoyed only by human beings. A wild animal may know its way through the jungle, a dog may recognize its master, but no animal is aware of its instinctive or other mental powers. Awareness must therefore be a function of that element in human beings that distinguishes them from animals, that is to say, their souls. It is true that awareness seems to be a mental phenomenon, and this is not entirely an illusion, because all experience, whether arising from a condition of the body, or from the stimulus of some external source, or from the activity of the mind itself, is mental experience, and the experience of awareness is no exception to this. But the *experience* of awareness and awareness itself are not the same thing. Because it appears exclusively in human beings awareness must reside in the soul[34], but the soul projects this aspect of its being on to the mind, where it is experienced, and where it infuses the cognitive faculty in such a way that awareness and knowledge of awareness seemingly become identified. In other words, awareness, as experienced, is self-recognizing. It follows that awareness has eternal being and is therefore unaffected by death, although the experience of awareness in eternity may be very different from, and will probably be more intimate than, it is during our earthly life, since self-realization will be direct and not, as now, achieved by projection on the temporal screen

of the mind[35].

151. A particular feature of awareness is self-consciousness or awareness of being oneself, and indeed self-consciousness and awareness, though not identical, are so closely associated that all beings who possess the one also possess the other. Self-consciousness is indefinable, but being universal among human beings, and of so intimate a nature, no definition is necessary. All that need be said is that, because of its association with awareness, its origin is in the soul, and that consequently it is immortal. We can be certain therefore that in the after-life every individual human being will be fully aware of the continuance of his or her being through the experience by which the links with the temporal order are finally broken. Thus we can safely say that Socrates knows himself to be the same Socrates who questioned and taught the youth of Athens in the fifth century BC, and what is true of Socrates is true of every human being, including even those who die in infancy who, though they may be aware of nothing else, are at least aware of being themselves[36].

152. But although we may be assured that everyone will be aware of his or her own identity in the life after death, the question whether we shall readily recognize ourselves and others remains to be answered. For the two issues are quite distinct and an affirmative answer to the question of recognition (even of self-recognition) cannot be inferred from the certainty that identity is preserved. In fact I have no doubt that the answer, in both cases, is 'yes', subject, however, to the qualification that recognition, whether of oneself or of others, may at first[37] be tentative and partial. This need occasion no surprise. Suppose, for example, that an old man were to be shown a film of some forgotten incident in his life as a boy. The film might recall the incident vaguely to his mind, but he might nevertheless say, 'Yes, I can see that the characters are myself and my friends as youngsters, but I would never have recognized them from their behaviour. Of course I know that I have changed over the years, but from this record it would seem that I have changed almost out of all recognition'. Now if such failure of recognition can occur with the passage of time in regard to behaviour, it is even more likely to occur with the

transition from partly temporal to wholly eternal being in regard to the most deep-seated features of our personalities.

153. This illustration is of course not exact, but it serves to bring out the point that one of the difficulties in clarifying our ideas lies in the fact that the problem confronting us is that of describing conditions in eternity, whereas cognition (and recognition), as ordinarily understood, take place in the mind and are therefore essentially temporal phenomena. And this is true whether the word 'cognition' is being used to denote the acceptance of a fact as true, as when we say 'I know that two and two make four', or to express the fact that a certain place, sound, situation or person is one with which we are familiar. This difficulty, however, is very easily resolved; to do so we have only to assume that the soul has its own 'faculty' of cognition and that it absorbs into the ambit of this faculty by the process of resurrection all those items of knowledge acquired by the mind (including the self-cognizing experience of awareness) which it deems to be of service to it in the pursuit of its objectives. Both these assumptions are at once seen to be reasonable, indeed they are obviously true, for it is inconceivable that the information collected by and stored in the mind at the instance of desires created by the will should be discarded simply because the body dies. The mind, in association with the brain, is of course the repository of a vast amount of factual information which is valueless to the soul, because every sense impression received during life has its physical and psychical effect and may be stored in the memory, but the soul is continually exercising its power of selection and resurrects only those impressions which will serve its purpose.

154. Thus both awareness and cognition are seen to be functions of the soul, although both are also experienced in the mind. It is not to be supposed, however, that the problems inherent in the reality and the interpretation of immortality and resurrection are to be solved by simply postulating that every faculty of the mind is parallelled by a corresponding faculty in the soul. The existence of some like faculties must indeed be admitted, but the order of priority and of causation is the reverse of that which our earthly experience would lead us to suggest. The reason for this inversion of truth is that we

are aware of much that goes on in our minds but have only a very slight knowledge of the structure of, and of what takes place in, our souls[38]. We therefore tend to look on our minds as primary and to assume that if the soul is found to have a faculty similar to one of our mental faculties it is the latter that is original and the former a mere copy. The truth, however, is the exact opposite. It is the soul which takes the initiative. Possessing in its structure all the faculties needed to enable it to select and assign its objectives and to pursue them in the eternal order, it seeks to create the means of pursuing them in the temporal surroundings in which it finds itself during the earthly life of its host. It is of course obvious (both from the nature of the task and from our knowledge of ourselves) that this requires action over a long period; the process does not run its full course in the life of each individual, but is spread over the whole of time since the first appearance of man on earth, and therefore involves the evolutionary powers of the will. Thus wherever a parallel can be drawn between the structure of the mind and that of the soul we should seek the cause in the action of the communal will which, by initiating mutations giving rise to heritable characteristics, has created and developed in the minds of men faculties similar in function to (though differing in the nature of their being from) those already existing in the soul.

155. This discussion removes at least some of the doubts that might be felt about the subjective aspects of the problem of recognition, but the objective aspects remain for examination. For what has been shown is that we shall certainly possess the necessary faculties (though in a form not easily intelligible to our temporal minds) for recognizing ourselves and others, but we still have to ask whether what is immortalized, either by direct creation or by resurrection, will be recognizable. It is not difficult to see, however, that so far as self-recognition is concerned this question is not distinguishable from the subjective question, for in asking it the word 'recognizable' must be taken to refer to recognition by the soul, or what may be called 'spiritual recognition', and as this is also what the soul 'experiences', what it is spiritually aware of, during earthly life, and as the soul passes unaltered through the barrier of death[39], there

is no discontinuity to give rise to a failure of recognition. In asking whether we shall recognize ourselves in eternity, therefore, we can see that the question is largely without substance.
156. But not entirely. For, as I have remarked above[40], recognition is likely, at first, to be tentative and partial, and the reason for this is not far to seek. For although spiritual recognition by the soul is continuous from earthly into heavenly life, a great deal is necessarily discarded at (or before) the moment of death. This is most easily seen by an illustration. Suppose that the driving passion by which a man is motivated during his earthly life is the urge to dominate his fellow men. This is clearly a parent desire having its origin in the will and, being independent of the temporal order, can be carried over into eternity. It will, however, give rise to a large progeny, some of which may be wholly temporal and therefore not transferable or transformable. Thus he may decide that his ambition to exercise power will best be served by the acquisition of great wealth, and this will then be a major objective; it may indeed appear to many observers to be *the* major objective, although in fact it is subsidiary to his will to dominate. Clearly, however, it cannot be carried over into eternity, where there is neither money nor any other kind of material wealth. It follows that, although this desire is indirectly created by the will and is in full accord with one of his soul's primary objectives, it is beyond the power of the will to transform its being into eternal being, and accordingly when the man dies and enters into eternal life free from all temporal bonds the desire to acquire wealth has to be discarded. From this example we can see that the eternal personality may appear very different from the same personality encrusted with all its temporal characteristics, and this difference may well cause confusion. The soul is indeed almost certain to experience some bewilderment at finding itself released from the bonds of space and time, even though its true home is in the eternal order. Moreover, the facts that it has been linked with temporal being and that it carries with it those temporal features which it has selected as being worthy of the conferment of eternal being are likely to impede its realization that time is no longer a dominant factor, and it is for this reason that we are entitled to speak of an *initial period* of

confusion and bewilderment[41]. It is, however, certain that these will be quickly submerged in and overcome by the awareness of the continuance of personal identity.

157. The question of the recognition of other people raises more complex issues. We know that we shall recognize ourselves because we enter eternal life in the same spiritual condition and with the same spiritual aspirations as we leave the present life. The cognitive faculties of our minds are not involved and the fact that they may be in error in their estimate of the state of our souls is therefore irrelevant. It would seem however, that our knowledge and understanding of other people is not similarly direct, nor is there the same spiritual experience of continued identity of being to offset other impediments to recognition. Our knowledge of others involves the mediation of our minds; it is obtained by observation of what they say and how they act, and our interpretation of these observed characteristics may be very inaccurate. If the overpowering influence of the things of this world on our minds prevents our having any clear vision of the state of our own souls, is it not likely that we shall be even more in error in our reading of the souls of other people? And if so, what is the likelihood that we shall recognize those whom we have known on earth when the trammels of temporal being are discarded and soul is directly confronted with soul, even when allowance is made for the fact that each soul carries with it the created and resurrected consciousness of much that expressed itself in action and was therefore observable during life on earth?

158. Obviously no firm answer can be given to these questions, but it is worth while to detail some of the factors that are likely to affect the degree of completeness and immediacy of our recognition of friends and acquaintances, and more particularly those whom we have known intimately and loved, when we meet them in eternity.

159. The first is that, in general, our recognition of people will to some extent depend on how well we have known them during life on earth. This is so obvious that it needs no elaboration.

160. The second is that recognition will depend more – much more – on whether we have sincerely, honestly and sympathetically tried to know a person than on whether our meetings on

earth have been frequent. For even if circumstances require us to associate frequently and intimately with him we may take very little trouble to understand him. It is in any event not easy (during life on earth) to distinguish between a person's non-essential characteristics – those resulting from heredity or environment, or from the action of the telos – and his essential characteristics – those that are the creations of his will and therefore embody his true nature, and if there is a lack of interest we shall make little or no effort to overcome the difficulty. In such a case it is to be expected that in eternity, where the meeting of two persons is an encounter between beings displaying, respectively, the essential characteristics of each, together with those non-essential characteristics that reinforce them and are therefore resurrected, there may be no immediate recognition.

161. The lack of interest that mars our understanding of others may spring from active dislike, for most of us make little effort to understand the essential natures of those to whom we are antipathetic; but it may also characterize our relations with our closest friends, in which case the root cause is, as often as not, a lack of charity, springing from, and manifesting itself as, self-centredness, a preoccupation with our own affairs. Of course we all tend, to some extent, to assess and interpret events in general and the actions of other people in particular, by reference to their effect on ourselves rather than (in the latter case) as providing data for the analysis and understanding of their essential natures, but it is a matter of common observation that this tendency to make false judgements, false because they are inward rather than outward looking, is more marked in some people than in others. It is obviously a breach of the commandment to love our neighbour as ourselves and is a serious fault since it impairs all our personal relationships, and not only those with mere acquaintances. Even in eternity we cannot be expected to like everyone, at any rate until our development has proceeded much further than is possible in temporal circumstances, but if our attitude towards those whom we do like is at first marred by self-centredness we shall have to undergo a painful process of re-adjustment.

162. The third factor giving rise to misjudgement during

earthly life and therefore impeding recognition in eternity is that we tend to interpret the actions of others in such a way as to flatter ourselves. It is a matter of common experience that we can usually find some worthy motive for our own actions but are prone to denigrate the motives of others. We like to think that, if placed in circumstances similar to theirs, our reactions would not only be different but would be more meritoriously motivated, and even if we admit that something we have done springs from an ignoble trait, we attribute that trait to heredity or environment rather than to any defect in our essential nature. Of course self-esteem is not necessarily a vice; if it were entirely absent we would be unable to do any useful work in this world; and the man who is constantly bewailing his sinfulness or his weakness of character is by no means to be admired, for his attitude is usually based, not on any genuine recognition of innate sinfulness, but on a desire to call attention to the virtue of his ready acknowledgement of sin. But we have to be on our guard against allowing the virtue of self-esteem to degenerate into the vice of applying different principles and standards of judgement to the actions of others from those which we apply to ourselves, and if we are honest we are bound to confess that we do not always avoid this error. The attitude of the Pharisee in the parable[42] is not exceptional; it reflects a state of mind from which few can claim to be exempt and which infects our judgements more often and more deeply than we like to admit. This warning against dual standards may seem to be platitudinous in relation to our daily life, but the point is that, if it is ignored, our recognition in heaven of those whom we have known on earth will be rendered more difficult.

163. Although the consequences in eternity of yielding to this temptation to apply more lenient standards of judgement to ourselves than to others are similar to those of self-centredness, the two faults have different origins and are not equally reprehensible. For the former often springs from the praise-worthy desire to assure ourselves that we are complying with a self-chosen moral code[43], and it may be found in people whose concern with the impact on themselves of events and the actions of others is usually well-balanced. Moreover, it enables

us, in one respect, to form a truer estimate of other people than we have of ourselves, for we are under no temptation to gloss over their faults, as we certainly are in regard to our own. But its distorting effect is not negligible. It leads us not only to misjudge the motives of others but also to generalize from an analysis of motive to an assessment of character, and thus to attribute to people characteristics which they do not possess, or which are less (or more) powerful than we suppose them to be. We also tend to mistake the source of those characteristics which we rightly attribute to them, supposing them to be due to heredity or environment when in fact they are the products of the will, and *vice versa*. All such errors impair our knowledge of people as they really are and as they will be revealed in eternity. It is probably impossible to avoid them entirely, but they can best be minimized by a constant and searching course of self-analysis coupled with what in theological terms is called repentance[44], so that we may be more fully aware of our own failings, both of action and of judgement.

164. All these factors are important, but their effect should not be exaggerated, and they certainly should not be regarded as justifying a fear of isolation or loneliness in eternity. For none of them imposes an absolute barrier and all may operate in greater or lesser degree. They must certainly hamper our recognition in eternity of those whom we have known, including even those whom we have liked or loved, in temporal life, and must consequently impose on us the necessity of revising our opinions, but they will not, save in exceptional cases, preclude recognition entirely. Generally speaking, the closer the association between two people, and the more intimate, understanding, loving and charitable their relationship on earth, the easier and fuller will be their recognition in eternity. And this principle can be extended. For as human beings have an eternal dimension it must be possible for them to communicate in that dimension while still on earth. It may be, indeed it is probable, that such spiritual communication is incomplete, and it is unlikely to take place between mere acquaintances, or even between two people who have been intimate, if the bond between them is wholly physical, but the way to it is opened by a meeting of minds, in so far as this reflects a parallelism of

wills, and where there is a relationship of true Christian love or charity (*agape*) a spiritual link is forged, so that soul speaks directly to soul, and each builds up a true knowledge of the other's essential nature, knowledge which, being carried over into eternity, must supersede and negate the factors making for non-recognition. We can confidently state, therefore, that true love between two people is a guarantee of recognition in eternity; and we can also be certain that, even if their talents on earth have been widely different, the similarity of the objectives sought by their wills will ensure that they will have the opportunity to develop together by metallassis in their future life.

165. It may be asked, however, whether recognition will not be difficult or even impossible in a case where, of two people who have been closely associated on earth, one dies many years before the other. It is a matter of common experience that if people who have known one another very well in childhood are separated for the greater part of their lives they may fail to recognize each other if they meet again in old age, and this failure of recognition may apply not only to their physical appearance but also to their mental characteristics and other traits of personality. It might be thought, on this analogy, that the separation of death would likewise lead to such a divergence that recognition would be improbable; indeed the divergence might be expected to be very much greater than would be likely to result from mere earthly separation, as the first to die would have experienced the untrammelled development by metallassis that is characteristic of eternity. But this conclusion would be false because it is reached by applying to eternity a form of reasoning applicable only to time. The very great differences apparent in someone whom we have not seen for many years are likely to be only in small measure differences in his essential character; they will for the most part be differences in behaviour, resulting from the environment and other temporal circumstances in which his life has been spent. The condition of his soul may also have changed but as I have pointed out earlier[45] this is not so readily seen. Thus changes in non-essential characteristics may be very prominent in the case of earthly separation and may inhibit recognition, but

these do not arise in the case where development of one of the two people has taken place in eternity. On the other hand development in the essential characteristics of both people will certainly have taken place, and it is probable that the initiative in recognition will rest with the first to be relieved of the restrictions of the temporal order, since he will have the opportunity of deciding how much of his progress should be held in reserve.

166. We can, I believe, carry the argument further and assert, with reasonable assurance, that where souls have pursued similar objectives, or where they have been embodied in hosts whose minds have been endowed with similar talents, there is likely to be immediate recognition, even though the two people have never met on earth, and may have lived in different centuries. Thus Monteverdi and Mozart, or Homer and Shakespeare, or Caesar and Churchill, may be firm 'friends' in eternity. Nor will recognition take place only between those who have been prominent in some particular field of human endeavour. It is a recognition of souls and is independent of the possession of marked talent.

167. Recognition is, however, a passive condition; we may recognize someone in the street without making any gesture, such as a smile, or a wave of the hand, or a spoken greeting, to convey to the other person that we have recognized him. But one of the essential characteristics of eternal being is activity[46], and from this it follows that in eternity we shall not only recognize our friends but will communicate with them. Thus it is certain that, although each eternal being is distinct from and possesses its being independently of all other eternal beings, and although the means of communication with which we are familiar in the temporal order are not available in heaven, influences can be transmitted from one eternal being to another. It would be pointless to inquire by what 'medium' this transmission takes place, or what means of communication are adopted; it is sufficient for us to know that eternal beings do not spend eternity in communication only with God and in isolation from each other. If this were not the case eternity would be unendurable, for it must be remembered that we enter heaven as we leave earth 'with all our imperfections on

our heads' and will need help and guidance for our further pilgrimage. We may therefore also be certain that communication in eternity is not only between the souls of human beings, together with their resurrected 'bodies', but also between these and the angels, whose tasks include, as their name implies, that of acting as intermediaries between God and man.

168. This naturally leads to our asking whether communication is possible between the dead and the living and whether, if so, it does in fact take place. I have no doubt that an affirmative answer must be given to both these questions, although we may not always recognize the source of a communication when it comes to us. It is of course true that the links binding every human being to the temporal order are severed at death, but this severance does not cut him off from those whom he has left behind. For each of us has, while still on earth, his quota of eternal being, and as the eternal order must be a consistent whole, a whole without 'parts'[47], it follows that if we believe, as we must, that the angels and the souls of those who have already passed through the barrier of death can communicate among themselves, we must also believe that communication is possible between the eternal being of those who have cast off their temporal trappings and the eternal being of those who are still bound to the temporal order. And further, we can argue that if communication is possible it must take place, for God does not create possibilities that are never actualized. It is probable, however, that the initiative in this actualization rests with those who are already in heaven, as they are more fully aware of the possibility of communication, and of the means of putting it into effect.

169. It remains therefore only to ask whether examples can be given of circumstances in which communication between the dead and the living has clearly taken place. We may discount the claims of mediums to transmit messages from those who have 'passed over', assuring their relatives and friends that they are very happy; a few of these may be genuine but it is probable that most are no more than psychical experiences occurring within the range of action of natural law. We must also ignore those cases in which someone has had a vision of God, or some other experience indescribable in ordinary

language, an experience for which he can give no rational account and which he therefore attributes to a divine source, a direct impact of God on his soul and mind. We pass over these cases, not because they are not genuine, for many of them no doubt are, but because they are not instances of communication between eternal beings in different orders, but are due to the activity of the supra-eternal Supreme Being.

170. However, instances of the kind of communication with which we are here concerned are not far to seek. For almost everyone must either have experienced, or have heard of someone who has experienced, a conviction that a decision to adopt, or to refrain from adopting, some course of action has not been reached by his own unaided reasoning powers, but has been prompted by a relative or friend from beyond the grave, who has sounded a note of encouragement or warning. Of course not all such cases can be accepted as evidence of genuine communication; psychical experiences can very easily be misinterpreted and may be wrongly attributed to activity in the eternal order, but it would be carrying scepticism and cynicism to improper lengths to dismiss all claims of this kind as spurious. It would indeed be unscientific, for the business of science is to accept all the evidence and to try to account for it rationally, but not to confine rationality within pre-assigned bounds.

171. Other instances of communication on purely personal matters could no doubt also be cited, but much more important for mankind as a whole are the cases in which those who have been released from the restrictions imposed by their temporal natures reveal to those still on earth the higher wisdom to which they have access. It seems to me to be not only probable but certain that it is by this means that new interpretations of knowledge, new philosophical insights, new revelations of reality through the medium of art, music and poetry, are made available to mankind. It would, of course, be absurd to suppose that everyone receives messages of this kind from the dead. Such communication is probably rare, for those who have access to the higher wisdom of the eternal order are no doubt careful to avoid communicating it to anyone whose temporal mental equipment would debar him from under-

standing it and of transmitting it without undue distortion. Some distortion is inevitable owing to the defects, both temporal and eternal, common to all human beings, but no doubt the departed select as the recipients those who are least likely to misrepresent them. Their choice must also be restricted to those who are willing to act as transmitters of this kind of eternal wisdom, and these are likely to be few, for it is certain that the majority of people would resist an attempt to burden them with messages of such spiritual weight. This resistance is not necessarily a fault, for it may be no more than a recognition that the truth revealed in the communication would be beyond the compass of the recipient's mind.

172. It is, in any case, not for us to apportion praise or blame, but we are not debarred from seeking to analyse and understand, and we must recognize that, besides those who shrink from taking on a task which they know to be beyond their powers, there are others who, though well equipped, both bodily and mentally, to transmit messages from the eternal order, are reluctant to face heavenly truths, and refuse to act as intermediaries for the benefit of mankind. If this reluctance is the reflection of a disoriented will it may well be ranked as a fault (though only a negative fault), and we should therefore all be ready, so far as lies in our power, to receive and pass on, either by the example of our lives or by such other means as our gifts enable us to adopt, such eternal truths as are vouchsafed to us, provided that we are satisfied that they *are* truths and that they come from a source that is concerned to assist mankind in the struggle to fulfil the will of God.

173. This proviso is necessary. For messages from eternity may be sent, not only by human beings who have left behind the constraints of temporal being, but also by the angels, *including the fallen angels*, whose objective is to hamper the progress of man towards his assigned end, and who are constantly seeking to use the talents of the most gifted individuals to alienate the wills of men from God by perverting their intellects and their aesthetic responses. The danger here is immense. Our duty demands, not that it shall be avoided, for that is impossible, but that it shall be constantly attacked, and this requires first that it shall be recognized. This is the most difficult and most pressing

task of mankind. It is particularly pressing at a time, such as that through which we are now passing, when the advance of scientific knowledge encourages the growth of hubris, and the rapid changes in social structures, both national and international, promote the belief that nothing is stable, that intellectual convictions, the canons of aesthetic judgement, and the content of the moral code, are all relative to ephemeral circumstances. Opinions may differ on the degree of success of the Christian communities in discharging the duty of opposing these tendencies, but the fact that a large number of highly intelligent people would claim that the tendencies are not evil and should be encouraged rather than discouraged is in itself evidence of their widespread diffusion and their power.

174. We know that Satan and those who have followed him in rejecting God and in trying to usurp his place are constantly tempting men and women to follow their lead, and it is obvious that one of the most powerful weapons they can use is to present to them false and distorted images of the meaning of truth, of what lies behind observable reality, of the road to utopia, of scientific integrity, of aesthetic excellence and of the basis of ethics and the necessity and true content of a moral code. But it is not only those eternal beings who are inspired by evil who may thus mislead mankind; those whose wills are rightly directed may also do so inadvertently, for it must be remembered that they, whether they be angels or the souls of departed men and women, are still in a state of development, and can therefore be no more than imperfect transmitters of truth, beauty and goodness, though we must believe that they have a clearer and fuller vision of these verities than any human being whose soul is not completely open to the revelation of God himself can possibly have. From this it follows that all those who aspire to lead mankind forward bear a very heavy responsibility; they must learn to submit their judgements to the divine judgement; for we are told that for those who are endowed with the talents and skills to guide the thought and aspirations of mankind but who do not aim at aligning their wills with the will of God and who therefore mislead those whom they are sent, or whom they claim, to lead, a very special punishment is reserved[48]. And a similar though perhaps less

onerous obligation rests on all mankind, for we cannot learn to distinguish false from true guidance unless we first learn the art of Christian humility, which lies at the opposite pole to hubris. The difficulty of meeting this requirement lies in the fact that humility, being an art rather than an intellectual discipline or a code of behaviour (though these are also involved in its practice) demands the activity of the will as well as of the mind. Indeed it is only by the activity of the will that the necessary state of mind can be engendered.

III. The Metaphysics of Consciousness

175. I have spoken, loosely, of the recognition in eternity of the characteristics of those whom we have known on earth but, as we have already seen, what in fact is preserved for recognition, whether by resurrection or otherwise, is the organization consciousness either created or transformed in being by the will and selected by the soul as being germane to its aspirations. Obviously, therefore, whatever the nature and content of the mental state selected for immortality, the organization consciousness associated with the complexity (or increase in complexity) by which that state is brought into and maintained in being must contain its whole essence, that is to say, it must contain all that determines that that state is what it is. This fact suggests that consciousness should be identified with substance, in the medieval sense of that word[49], and the validity of this identification would seem to be reinforced by the fact that Teilhard de Chardin regards consciousness as a fundamental constituent of all reality.
176. On the other hand, he nowhere identifies it with substance, but although this objection must be given some weight, it is not conclusive, for he makes it clear that his approach is wholly phenomenological[50], and he would therefore not have regarded it as relevant to his thesis even to consider the question. He does not claim to provide a metaphysical interpretation of reality but is concerned only with reality as it presents itself as a phenomenon. Thus for him consciousness is not the metaphysical groundform on which the accidents, i.e.,

the physical and psychical properties, are built, or in which they inhere; if he had applied his mind to the matter (and had accepted the categories of substance and accident as valid for the description of reality) he would probably have classified it as an accident, differing, however, from most other accidents in that it is a property of all substance and of every individual substance, (as mass or energy is a property of all physical substance and the capacity to experience is a property of all psychical substance). The fact is, however, that, apart from his insistence on the universality and fundamental status of consciousness, his ideas on how it should be regarded in relation to the other properties of matter and mind are obscure. Thus in one passage he describes it as a kind of primordial 'spiritual' fluid from which the physical particles of which the universe is made have condensed[51]; elsewhere he regards it as an entity which is atomic or 'monadic'[52] in structure and which, though not measurable by any means known to us, has the property of magnitude or intensity. His definition of consciousness as including every form of psychism has already been given[53], but this does not answer the question whether he held it to be ontologically prior to matter and mind.

177. A more powerful objection to identifying consciousness (in its Teilhardian sense) with substance is that the medieval philosophers, do not all agree on the precise meaning of the words 'substance' and 'accident' or on how differences in phenomena should be allocated to one or the other category. Moreover the modes of analysis which lead to the formulation of the categories and give them importance are unfamiliar to the modern mind, but this should be attributed to a defect in contemporary philosophic thought rather than to greater enlightenment. The problem of what precisely is preserved unchanged when (for example) an acorn becomes an oak remains to be given philosophic recognition and expression, and this is most easily and effectively done by adopting a theory which draws a distinction between that in which the essence of a thing resides and the mutable and ephemeral appearances by which that thing is made known to our senses. Clearly also such a theory should, in accordance with Occam's Principle[54], avoid the duplication of terms whose meanings

nearly coincide, or which are designed to express the same thing but may be differently interpreted in their application to the natural world. On the other hand, if a link between the thought of Teilhard de Chardin, extended as in the present chapter to include the idea of resurrection, and the thought of the medieval philosophers is to be forged, the theory must provide for a distinction to be drawn between Teilhardian consciousness in its widest sense and organization (or complexity) consciousness, since the latter can be transformed in being by the will whereas the former can not. A further point is that, although the modern mind is in error in rejecting outright the categories of substance and accident, its insistence on reducing the number of fundamental entities to a minimum and on describing the observable differences between things so far as possible in terms of structure alone cannot be faulted; consequently the basic importance of structure must be fully allowed for in the theory.

178. Clearly, therefore, we cannot identify Teilhardian consciousness with Scholastic substance *simpliciter*, without specifying the particular sense in which the word 'substance' is used and without distinguishing between consciousness and organization consciousness. By combining the ideas underlying these categories, however, we can arrive at a simple description of reality, both physical and psychical. We define 'substance' as the immaterial, i.e., non-physical, and possibly also non-psychical, substratum which contains the whole essence of a thing, and serves as a home for all the properties whereby that thing is revealed to our senses. We also postulate that at the basis of everything in the temporal world, both physical and psychical, lies Teilhardian consciousness. This is undifferentiated and is not apprehensible by either the soul or the mind. Its being is temporal being, and this is not transformable into eternal being by human agency (although no doubt it is so transformable by God). In order to give recognizable being to a thing we have to add form or structure, and this involves the addition of organization consciousness. The essence of that thing lies in its organization consciousness, which must therefore be equated with its substance, as defined above[55]. Organization consciousness is apprehensible by the soul, although its

being may be either temporal or eternal; it is eternal if the consciousness has been created directly by the will but is otherwise temporal. In the latter case, however, it has the potentiality of being transformed by the will into eternal being.

179. The point of this analysis is that, by equating organization consciousness with substance, it is made clear that the miracle performed by the will in transforming the being of consciousness from temporal to eternal being is a miracle of transubstantiation. It is thus akin to the miracle of Transubstantiation which those who accept that doctrine believe takes place in the sacrifice of the Mass. The two miracles are alike but of course are not identical, the difference being that whereas the transubstantiation effected by the will is a human miracle, in which temporal being is transformed into eternal being, the Transubstantiation of the Mass is a divine miracle, in which the temporal being of the substance of the elements is transformed into supra-eternal being. In both cases, it is perhaps hardly necessary to add, the accidents remain unchanged.

CHAPTER FIVE

NOTES AND REFERENCES

(The numbers in brackets indicate the paragraphs in which the references occur)

1. (135) Ecclesiasticus xliv, 9.
2. (136) This is because eternity is not conditioned by time (see paragraph 18). Moreover, it is implied in the whole concept of miracle that influences can pass from a higher to a lower order, but not *vice versa*. See Chapter I, Note 21 and paragraph 51.
3. (137) This phrase occurs in very early creeds, going back to the fourth century (see Henry Bettenson, *Documents of the Christian Church*, The World's Classics, Oxford University Press, 1943; pp. 33, 34). It is embodied in the Apostles' Creed, which is constantly repeated by Christians in church services throughout the world. It does not appear in the Nicene Creed, the present form of which (as used in the Western Church) was fixed at the Council of Chalcedon in 451 AD, but the notion of resurrection, as distinct from immortality, is preserved. The wording of the Nicene Creed is '*et exspecto resurrectionem mortuorum*', 'and I look for the resurrection of the dead'.
4. (137) The word most frequently used is *anastasis*, which means 'raising up', or 'making to stand up again'. It is this word that the evangelist John uses to record Jesus' saying 'I am the resurrection and the life' (John xi, 25), and he uses the corresponding verb to record the assurance given by Jesus a few moments earlier to Martha that her brother Lazarus would rise again (John xi, 24). Other instances of the use of this word will be found in Matthew xxii, 29-32 (= Mark xii, 24-27 = Luke xx, 34-38), where Jesus told the Sadducees that at the resurrection they neither marry nor are given in marriage; and in Luke xiv, 14 and John v, 29, where Jesus promises rewards

to the righteous at the resurrection; (this promise is also given in the Lucan version of the reply to the Sadducees). Sometimes the word *egeirein*, to waken, or rouse up, is used, as when Jesus spoke of his own resurrection in Matthew xvi, 21; xx, 19; John ii, 19, 22.
5. (137) 1 Corinthians xv, 42-44. The meaning of this incredibly profound and obviously inspired chapter in St Paul's letter to the Corinthians will probably never be exhausted; new interpretations and understandings will be discovered as man's spiritual awareness is further developed.
6. (137) 1 Corinthians xv, 53.
7. (138) Pierre Teilhard de Chardin: *Le Phénoméne Humain*, written 1938-1940 (Paris, Seuil, 1955); translated into English by Bernard Wall under the title *The Phenomenon of Man* (Collins, 1959). In the following Notes this book is referred to as *PM*.
8. (138) *PM*, p. 165.
9. (139) References to the law of complexity and consciousness appear in most of Teilhard's works, but the fullest exposition is given in *PM*, the whole of which is devoted to the development and interpretation of the law, although nowhere in the book (or elsewhere, so far as I am aware) does he state it explicitly, preferring to allow it to unfold as a general principle of evolution governing the whole of reality, or at least of phenomenal reality, and to draw out its implications, which he shows to be both extensive and profound. His thought is saturated with the ideas of the unity of diversity and the inevitability of evolution towards a pre-assigned end, not as a consequence of the determinism of cause and effect, but arising from the fact that God is Alpha and Omega, the origin of all that is and the end in which all that is must ultimately be fulfilled. Although Teilhard is not a Hegelian – he nowhere makes use of the dialectic method – he would agree with Hegel that 'philosophy is concerned with the true and the true is the whole', and 'The Absolute is the process of its own becoming, the circle which presupposes its end as its purpose and has its end as its beginning' (see Frederick Copleston, SJ; *A History of Philosophy*, Vol VII, Burns & Oates Ltd., 1963; p. 170). For Teilhard also the universe can only be properly seen as a whole – 'the stuff of

the universe, woven in a single piece according to one and the same system (which we shall call later on "the Law of Consciousness and Complexity"), but never repeating itself from one point to another, represents a single figure. Structurally, it forms a Whole' (*PM*, p. 45). The whole is 'granular' (p. 49), it is made up of individual particles, and the outward properties of these can be studied by science. But as the particles are all concerned in the working out of the grand evolutionary process, which transcends the analytical aims and methods of science, the outward properties do not exhaust their full nature. *There is in every particle a germ of consciousness.* Thus, again speaking of 'the stuff of the universe' he says, 'there is necessarily a *double aspect to its structure . . . co-extensive with their Without, there is a Within to things. . . .* Primitive matter is something more than the particulate swarming so marvellously analysed by modern physics. Beneath this mechanical layer we must think of a "biological" layer that is attenuated to the uttermost, but yet is absolutely necessary to explain the cosmos in succeeding ages. The *within, consciousness* and then *spontaneity* – three expressions for the same thing.' (*PM*, pp. 56, 57). And later, 'We are seeking a qualitative law of development that from sphere to sphere should be capable of explaining, first of all the invisibility, then the appearance, and then the gradual dominance of the *within* in comparison to the *without* of things. This law reveals itself once the universe is thought of as passing from *State A*, characterized by a very large number of very simple material elements (that is to say, with a very poor *within*), to *State B* defined by a smaller number of very complex groupings (that is to say, with a much richer *within*).' (p. 61). A more nearly explicit statement of the law is given later in the book in the words 'the universe . . . is . . . in process of organic *involution* upon itself (from the extremely simple to the extremely complex) – and, moreover, this particular involution "of complexity" is experimentally bound up with a correlative increase in interiorisation, in the psyche or consciousness' (p. 301). A simpler, but incomplete, statement is given in *The Future of Man* (Collins, 1964) on page 111: 'the higher the degree of complexity in a living creature, the higher its consciousness; and vice versa.', but this statement leaves out the vital element that the increase of complexity is (for him) itself a law of evolution. In this directed property of evolution there is again an echo of Hegel, for whom 'The Absolute is the totality, the universe. And this totality is a teleological process, the actualization of self-thinking Thought.' (Copleston, *op. cit.*, p. 197). Christopher F. Mooney, SJ, in *Teilhard de Chardin and the Mystery of Christ* (Collins, 1966) quotes the law in the words: 'the law of complexity-consciousness ... means that a more developed consciousness will always correspond experimentally to a more complex organic structure of greater internal unity and concentration.' (p. 39). But this definition also embodies only the descriptive aspect of the law, omitting the essential element that (in living beings) there is an irresistible movement towards greater complexity (see paragraph 141).

10. (139) 'Atomicity is a common property of the Within and the Without of things.' (*PM*, p. 59). 'After the grain of matter, the grain of life; and now at last we see constituted the *grain of thought*' (p. 173). These ideas, if expressed with precision and supplemented by further assumptions which, though possibly unprovable, are probably true, enable us to define the expression 'a system subject to deterministic law'. We can, of course, describe a deterministic system in simple terms as one whose behaviour is, in theory, predictable. But this is no more than a description, and is too imprecise to be of any value. Unless it is amplified the definition of miracle in Chapter II (paragraph 48) is incomplete.

The further assumptions required are:

> (i) The system is composed of physical and psychical entities. (This may be held to be an axiom rather than an assumption, as we know of no observable system of which it is not true).
> (ii) Among the physical entities it is possible to select a set, the members of which are fundamental in the sense that all others can be expressed, directly or indirectly, in terms of them. We shall call the members of this set *physicons*, and in our present state of knowledge we may identify the physicons with the quarks and other sub-atomic particles or wave struc-

tures that have been revealed or may be revealed in particle accelerators.

(iii) The properties of the physical entities we directly observe and the differences between them lie in the number of physicons comprising them and the manner in which the physicons are structurally arranged.

(iv) The condition of each physicon is completely definable by reference to certain characteristics, expressible in numerical terms. These include (there may be others) mass (or energy), position, velocity, spin, electric charge, measure and probability of existence, consciousness (in the Teilhardian sense), and degree of animation by the telos (see paragraph 142).

(v) Likewise the pyschical entities comprised in the system – perception, sensation, thought, knowledge, desire, emotion (love, hate, sympathy, antipathy, anger, fear, etc.) – are distinguished from one another by the number and structural arrangement of a finite (possibly quite small) number of fundamental psychical particles, which we shall call *psychons*.

(vi) Associated with each psychon are certain characteristics, among which we may specify measure and probability of existence, intensity, consciousness, degree of animation by the telos, and orientation, all of which are expressible in numerical terms. The last named characteristic, orientation, must be included because most psychical activity is directed; a thought is a thought *of something*, desire is desire *for something*, and so on.

(vii) In order to allow for the Principle of Uncertainty (see Chapter II, Note 3), we must further assume that, if any of the characteristics of the physicons or psychons is not precisely measurable, the degree of imprecision is contained, i.e., some mathematical function (e.g. the product) of the uncertainties in the specification of two or more of the characteristics is a constant.

(viii) The measure of existence of a physicon or psychon is either one or zero, that is to say, the physicon or psychon either exists or does not exist. If this measure is subject to a probability, then that probability is invariable. In the case of the physicons this assumption is required to account for the phenomenon of radio-activity, in which certain fundamental particles spontaneously cease to exist and are replaced by others. In the case of the psychons it is required to account for the apparently ephemeral nature of certain mental experiences, and also for memory (assuming that in the system there are beings in whom these psychical phenomena occur).

(ix) As the physical and psychical entities in the system interact, we must further postulate the existence of particles (or wave structures) by means of which the interaction takes place. We shall call these interaction particles *hermeons* (from Hermes, the messenger), and we must suppose that these also are specifiable by certain measurable characteristics.

(x) And finally, we must assume that the structure of time is also atomic, each atom of time, which we shall call a *chronon*, being, except as regards its position in the unfolding of time, identical with every other chronon. A chronon is of very short duration, but it is not infinitesimal. (It might, for example, be the time required for a ray of light to traverse the diameter of an electron, say 10^{-23} seconds). The processes of the system must then be thought of as revealing themselves in the form of a succession of still pictures, each lasting for one chronon and, of course, remaining unchanged during that chronon (which otherwise would not be the smallest unit).

If we now call the measured values of all the physicons, psychons and hermeons in the system at any particular chronon the *parameters* of that chronon, then the system is deterministic if it is one in which, if the parameters of any one chronon are known, the parameters of the succeeding chronon are, in theory, predictable. It would then follow that the parameters of all succeeding chronons are also predictable. The assumption made throughout this book is that the whole of the temporal order, including the temporal beings dwelling in it, is such a system. The angels and the souls and wills of human beings, and also of all other beings on whom God has conferred eternal being, and therefore also freedom, are of course excluded from the system.

11. (140) Teilhard defined consciousness as meaning 'every type of psychism, from the most rudimentary forms of interior perception imaginable to the human phenomenon of reflective thought' (*PM*, p. 57). Consciousness, in the Teilhardian sense, must not be confused with awareness; the consciousness of a human being is in no way diminished when he is asleep or anaesthetized; moreover inanimate matter and the primitive forms of living matter have their proper quotas of consciousness, but the faculty of awareness does not appear until we reach the higher forms of animal life.

12. (140) *PM*, p. 178.

13. (141) This is illustrated by the number of words ending in '– genesis' – cosmogenesis, noogenesis, anthropogenesis, and Christogenesis – that are scattered throughout his works.

14. (141) Quoted by Mooney, *op. cit.*, p. 72. The original is in Teilhard de Chardin: *Panthéisme et Christianisme*, Paris 1923; p. 8.

15. (141) At any rate after the appearance of life. But it would seem that Teilhard held that life itself is a product of the law of complexity-consciousness.

16. (141) But man is still evolving. Looking into the future Teilhard sees both a growth and a further concentration of consciousness until a state of super-consciousness is reached. The thinking layer of the earth, (which Teilhard calls the noosphere) converges on itself in such a way that 'myriads of grains of thought' become 'enclosed in a single thinking envelope so as to form, functionally, no more than a single vast grain of thought on the siderial scale, the plurality of individual reflections grouping themselves together and reinforcing one another in the act of a single unanimous reflection.' (*PM*, p. 251). And this convergence does not annihilate personality,

rather it enhances it. 'To be fully ourselves it is ... in the direction of convergence with all the rest, that we must advance – towards the "other".' (p. 263). The ultimate end of the evolutionary process is a concentration in 'a *distinct Centre radiating at the core of a system of centres*; a grouping in which personalization of the All and personalizations of the elements reach their maximum, simultaneously and without merging, under the influence of a supremely autonomous focus of union.' (pp. 262, 263). To this centre Teilhard gives the name Omega, and he regards it as the point at which mankind makes its nearest approach on earth to the transcendent God (pp. 294, 298). It should be added that Teilhard rightly sees that the ideals of social, political and even aesthetic evolution are quite inadequate to reflect the true value of the phenomenon of man (cf. paragraphs 97 and 103). He admits the phyletic value of human achievement but says that in making 'these contributions to the collectivity, far from transmitting the most precious (part), we are bequeathing, at the utmost, only the shadow of ourselves', and asks, 'what is the worth of human works if not to establish, in and by means of each one of us, an absolutely original centre in which the universe reflects itself in a unique and inimitable way? ... The very centre of our consciousness ... is the essence which Omega ... must reclaim.' (p. 261).

17. (142) Teilhard was of course fully aware of the second law of thermodynamics and of the fact that energy is continually being degraded until finally it becomes unavailable. He accepts that the earth must finally undergo a 'heat death', but insists that before this occurs, since man is unique (on this earth) he is irreplaceable, and that accordingly he must infallibly reach his goal. (*PM*, pp. 51, 274-276).

18. (142) It is clear that the telos is a *temporal* entity, since its function is that of guiding development in time, but we cannot rule out the possibility (rather we should regard it as probable) that a corresponding principle exists in eternity.

19. (142) Although not *merely* instruments for the transmission of divine power, they certainly are such instruments (cf. paragraph 55), but the activity of God in this way is probably effected by the creation of souls which are suitable for his purpose; once they have been created he does not interfere

with their freedom, although he will of course respond to any request by them for his help, in so far as their wills accord with his will.

20. (143) *PM*, p.88.
21. (143) *PM*, p. 251.
22. (143) *PM*, pp. 78, 89; see also Mooney, *op. cit.* p. 39.
23. (143) *PM*, pp. 96-102.
24. (143) *PM*, pp. 159, 160.
25. (143) *PM*, p. 171.
26. (143) see paragraph 176.
27. (143) Teilhard de Chardin: *Christianity and Evolution* (Collins, 1971), p. 61.
28. (144) In paragraphs 136, 137.
29. (144) The word 'quantum' has been used in paragraph 140 in the non-technical sense of a quantity measurable in whole numbers of units. In physics a quantum is a unit of *action* or *angular momentum* (i.e., energy multiplied by time) but it is often applied loosely to energy, particularly to the energy of wave motion where the frequency is known. It seems to me reasonable to suppose that the miraculous activity of the will as described in this and the earlier chapters of this book involves the implantation of (newly created) energy, and that this is transferred to the physico-psychic system in units or quanta.
30. (145) It must, I think, be held to be certain that in the long run growth must be in the direction of greater conformity with the will of God, and therefore towards the conquest of Evil by Good. The alternative to this is that God must decide to abandon the human experiment and allow man to destroy himself. But we must also bear in mind that, whatever the ultimate end of mankind may be, in the short term evil must continue to play a major part in human evolution. For, as we have seen in Chapter IV, the communal will of mankind is very far from being aligned to the will of God, and consequently the evolution of man and the growth of consciousness are by no means necessarily proceeding in the right direction. Teilhard de Chardin is usually thought of as an optimist, but in spite of his generally hopeful prognosis he admits the possibility that 'obeying a law from which nothing in the past has ever been exempt, evil may go on growing alongside good, and it too may

attain its paroxysm at the end in some specifically new form.' (*PM*, p. 288). And his final conclusion is that 'In one manner or another it still remains true that ... the human epic resembles nothing so much as a way of the Cross.' (p. 313).

31. (147) cf. 2 Corinthians iv, 16: 'though our outward man perish, yet the inward man is renewed day by day.' St Paul is, of course, speaking of the continuous renewal by God of the souls or spirits of those who seek his aid, but the parallel with the activity of the will in recreating the temporal constituents of the mind is sufficiently close to be worthy of notice.

32. (147) This in no way prejudices any physical theory of memory (e.g., on the lines of the 'memory' of a computer) that may be constructed. Whatever the physical basis of memory may be there is clearly also a mental counterpart.

33. (150) See Note 11 above. Awareness, though closely allied to, is not identical with, the power of reflective thought which Teilhard held to be the characteristic mark of the human species (*PM*, pp. 165 *et seq*).

34. (150) Admittedly this is not a logical deduction, but the close relationship between human beings and their nearest relations in the animal kingdom suggests that any faculty that does not reside or have its origin in the soul will appear at least in rudimentary form in other higher species.

35. (150) It is probable that, in so far as awareness is a construct of the mind rather than a function of the soul, the will is continually transforming its being into eternal being.

36. (151) It is also true of those who, as a result of some physical or mental lesion, seem to have dual personalities. It may be noted here that language is deficient in not distinguishing between the use of the word 'personality' to denote 'the fact or quality of being a person' and its use to describe the characteristics displayed by a person. Using the word in its first sense we may properly say that every human being has personality, but we cannot say this of any animal, for although an animal is an individual it is not a person. The expressions 'X is a person', 'X has personality', 'X is a human being' are identical in meaning; they all state that X is compounded of temporal and eternal being, and that his participation in eternal being consists in his possessing a soul, the essential characteristics of

which are (as shown in Chapter II) freedom, purpose and the power to respond to God. We use the word 'personality' in its second sense when we say of someone that he has a strong or a lovable personality; here we do not simply mean that he is a human being, we are describing the characteristics by which he reveals himself to the outside world. It is of course in this second sense that the word is used when we are describing the symptoms of schizophrenia; and it is salutary to remember that, as we have seen in paragraph 91, the revealed characteristics do not fully reflect the true essence of the person; indeed they may markedly disguise it.

37. (152) See paragraph 156.
38. (154) cf. paragraph 91. Our preoccupation with the affairs of this world is the source of a constant temptation to invert the true order of priority of the relevant factors in all situations transcending the temporal order. An example is our understanding of the relation of fatherhood, discussed in paragraph 36.
39. (155) See Chapter II, Note 23.
40. (156) In paragraph 152.
41. (156) It is not to be supposed that beings in eternity are unaware of the passage of time. So long as time (and space) are part of the structure of total reality their existence must be recognized even by those beings who are not bound by them. The difference between the status of eternal beings and temporal beings in relation to time is that the latter, at any moment of time, exist only at that moment. It is true that those beings which are endowed with memory can recall past moments, and that future experiences can sometimes be anticipated, but the memory is not experienced at the past time nor the anticipation at the future time. The experience takes place at the moment at which it is experienced and not at any other time. In the case of beings in eternity these limitations are wholly lifted in regard to past time and partly lifted in regard to future time. Thus an eternal being has a conspectus of the whole of past time, and can translate itself to that past time, provided, of course, that in so doing it does not contradict its own nature and that it is permitted to do so by God. It can also, although only in a very limited way, project itself into the future, but the

structure of the future becomes increasingly vague as its distance from the present increases, since it is conditioned by the free wills of human beings, and the determinations of those wills cannot be foreseen by eternal beings. Of course *all possible futures* (though not the actual future) can be foreseen by God.
42. (162) Luke xviii, 9-14.
43. (163) See paragraph 95.
44. (163) See paragraphs 128-131.
45. (165) In paragraphs 91 and 154.
46. (167) See paragraphs 20, 21, 62.
47. (168) If the eternal order had parts they would be distinguishable and this would require that a criterion more fundamental than the eternal order itself would have to be postulated, by reference to which the distinction could be 'observed' and defined. The uniformity of the eternal order does not, of course, conflict with the individuality of the eternal beings which inhabit it. This can be seen to be reasonable by noting that in the parallel case of space and time (the temporal order) the uniformity of the order does not conflict with the fact that the objects which have their being in it are distinguishable from one another.
48. (174) Matthew xviii, 6 (= Mark ix, 42 = Luke xvii, 2).
49. (175) See paragraph 41.
50. (176) *PM*, p. 29.
51. (176) 'Before physical and chemical conditions on earth made possible the birth of organic life, the universe either had no existence in itself, or had already constituted a nebula of consciousness.' (*Science and Christ*, p. 47).
52. (176) As I have already pointed out (paragraph 139), the idea of atomicity is central to Teilhard's thought. But he also sees reality in terms of concentrations of atoms and psychical elements, imbued with consciousness, which (borrowing a term from Leibniz) he calls Monads. 'Every unity of the world, provided it be a natural unity, is a monad'. (*Science and Christ*, p. 47). See also Mooney, *op. cit.* p. 232. Teilhard even speaks of Christ as the Higher Monad (*Science and Christ*, p. 57).
53. (176) See Note 11 above.
54. (177) See Chapter I, Note 3.
55. (178) There is a close parallelism here with the philosophy

of St Thomas Aquinas who, following Aristotle, held that the basis of physical reality is that which is not substance but has the possibility of becoming substance; this he calls 'prime matter'. Substance is obtained by an act which gives *form* to prime matter. Thus, so far at any rate as the physical world is concerned, we may equate Teilhardian consciousness with St Thomas's prime matter, form with structure (or complexity) and organization consciousness (or complexity-consciousness) with substance. (See Etienne Gilson: *The Christian Philosophy of St Thomas Aquinas*, Victor Gollancz, Ltd., 1957, pp. 176, 177).

6

APOTHAUMATA

I. Definition

180. An *apothauma* has been defined[1] as a miracle directly affecting the outside world. This definition, though adequate as a reminder of the essential feature of apothaumata, obviously lacks precision, but before we attempt to frame a fuller definition it will be helpful to remind ourselves of certain general features characteristic of all miracles.

181. In every miracle there is an agent and an object affected, and in all cases the mode of being of the agent is either supra-eternal or eternal being. Thus the agent is either God, or an angel, or the will of a human being, living or dead, and from this it follows that the act performed is purposeful[2]. In all cases the mode of being of the object affected is temporal being, thus the object affected must be either a being inhabiting the temporal order or the temporal order itself[3].

182. In the case of miracles performed by human beings during their life on earth, each of whom combines eternal being and temporal being in one personality, the agent is the human will, which has eternal being. The object affected may, however, be either the temporal being of the person whose will is the agent or that of some other inhabitant of the temporal order, wholly distinct from the agent[4], or the temporal order itself. In the former case the miracle is a perithauma, in the latter an apothauma. The object affected in an apothauma need not, of course, be inanimate; it may be a plant or an animal, or the temporal being of a person other than the person whose will is the agent. Clearly the distinction between perithaumata and

apothaumata arises only in the case where a miracle is performed by a human being during his life on earth – in fact the word 'perithauma' cannot have any meaning in relation to other miracles. Clearly also all the miracles discussed in Chapters III, IV and V are perithaumata.
183. In the light of these considerations the formal definition of an apothauma can now be given:

> An apothauma is a purposeful act performed by an agent whose being is wholly supra-eternal being, or is wholly or partly eternal being, directly affecting the temporal order or an entity or entities, animate or inanimate, inhabiting the temporal order, whose being is therefore wholly or partly temporal being, and satisfying the following conditions:
> (i) the act suspends or modifies, momentarily or otherwise, the laws of the temporal order in relation to the entity or entities affected, including the laws of interaction between the temporal order and those entities;
> (ii) there is no reaction on any being in the superior order in which the agent has his whole or partial being, except as may be ordained by the agent (or another being in the eternal order) or by God;
> (iii) in the case where the agent, in addition to possessing eternal being, also possesses a measure of temporal being, the temporal being of the agent and that of the object affected cannot be regarded as belonging to the same individual.

184. It may be noted that in this definition the first two conditions are, strictly speaking, redundant, because (i) it is not possible for beings in an inferior order to act on beings in a superior order except as the latter may ordain[5]; and (ii) it is a consequence of the structure of the temporal order and its relation to the two higher orders that *all* influences emanating from either of those orders and affecting the temporal order must involve some interference with the operation of the laws

of that order[6]. Moreover, and in particular, the words 'momentarily or otherwise' clearly add nothing to the meaning of the definition; their inclusion however serves the useful purpose of avoiding misunderstanding and of driving home the point that the impact of an apothaumata is not necessarily extended in time. It may also be noted that apothaumata are not necessarily spectacular[7]; indeed the effect of most apothaumata is the suspension of temporal law in the psychical rather than in the physical realm, and in either case may take place at atomic or sub-atomic level and so pass unnoticed at the time.

II. The Range of Apothaumatic Power

185. It follows from the definition that all miracles performed by God are apothaumata, for the being of God, which is supraeternal being, is necessarily distinct from all other types of being[8]. And as it has already been shown that if God exists, he must perform miracles[9], it follows that the class of apothaumata is not entirely empty. In fact the power of God to perform apothaumata is both absolute and unlimited[10]. It is absolute because no other being can interfere with it in any way, and it is unlimited because all things are ultimately under his control.
186. God is of course also capable of acting, and certainly does act, on beings inhabiting the eternal order, and although such actions do not qualify to be classed as apothaumata, or even as miracles[11], they decisively affect both development in eternity and, indirectly, the course of events in time. Their importance therefore must not be underrated. The three classes of being whose development may thus be influenced by God are the angels, the souls of men and women whose earthly course has been completed and the souls of men and women now living. It would obviously be pointless to speculate on the manner in which God influences the first two classes, but there is no reason to suppose that the principles underlying such action differ from those governing his involvement with the members of the third class. These, as has repeatedly been stressed in the foregoing chapters of this book, are – (i) to respond instantly and fully to any appeal for help and guidance in achieving the

objectives willed by the souls of men and women in so far as they are consistent with and will tend to promote his plan for mankind, which is ultimately to bring about the salvation of the whole human race and, individually, to bring every human soul into unity with himself; (ii) to allow men and women the maximum degree of freedom to pursue their chosen objectives, including those that are not fully consistent with, or are even in conflict with but are not such as finally to frustrate, the fulfilment of that plan; and (iii) to intervene directly and decisively, contrary to the wills of men and women, if their objectives fall outside those categories.

187. All miracles performed by agents whose being is wholly eternal being are also apothaumata, but the power of eternal beings to perform miracles, unlike that of God, is neither absolute nor unlimited. The activity of eternal beings is not entirely free, since it is confined within the structure of eternity, is exercisable only in eternity and time, and is always ultimately subject to control by God. Nevertheless their range of activity and their freedom to act are very great. For freedom is not only an essential characteristic of eternal being, it also implicitly involves the concept of duty, and as eternal beings, like human beings, are imperfect and subject to sin, they are under a constant duty to aim at overcoming this subjection by rejecting the false promises of Satan and thereby seeking redemption. Thus the duty imposed on eternal beings, including both the angels and the souls and transformed minds[12] of those who have entered into eternal life involves their giving help and guidance to one another. This argument gives additional support to the conclusion reached in the preceding chapter[13] that eternal beings recognize and can communicate with one another. Nor can it be denied that both of these types of eternal being communicate with and influence the souls of those still living, for, as I have already suggested[14], it is from these sources that those who by scientific experiment and theorizing advance our knowledge of the temporal world, or who through the medium of music, art or poetry increase our understanding of God and of the eternal world, obtain their motivation.

188. These activities of eternal beings are, however, not

miraculous as they take place entirely within the eternal order. But the inspiration of scientists, writers and artists does involve miraculous activity, for although the inhabitants of the heavenly sphere may influence the souls and wills of living human beings the effect of such activity can be no more than to create, or possibly only to enhance, the *desire* to produce original work, to advance the boundaries of knowledge or to seek new insights into truth, beauty or goodness. The actual knowledge or insight, the new revelation of the essence of God (or, regrettably, of Satan) must be conveyed directly to the *minds* of those who seek to give expression to the desire, and since this process involves the action of eternal being on temporal being it constitutes a true miracle.

189. The question whether apothaumatic power is possessed by human beings is more difficult. For it can be argued that, although the fact that men can perform miracles is undeniable, all human miracles, including even those apparently involving 'action at a distance' are perithaumata. The argument rests on the fact, based on sufficient observational data to be accepted by everyone other than the diminishing band of those who hold that all the mysteries of nature have been uncovered and all her secrets revealed, that there exist forces or means of transmission of energy which have so far not been reduced to measurement and mathematical analysis, and over which we therefore have little or no control, but which, from time to time, are displayed to a wondering and largely sceptical world. These manifestations may take the form of telepathy (including both the transference of thought and the transference of emotion), psychokinesis, the power to 'see' words or diagrams through an opaque covering, levitation and other paranormal phenomena. As I have already suggested[15], these are instances of the operation of physico-psychical law and thus belong to the temporal order. When an apparently external miracle (whether spectacular or not) is performed by a human being, therefore, it may be argued that the miraculous element, that is to say, the transmission of power from the eternal to the temporal order, takes place entirely within the being of the agent, whose latent power to project psychical energy to the person or object affected is stimulated and activated. If this

process properly describes the mechanism whereby the miracle is performed then the miraculous element is perithaumatic, since it takes place wholly within the being of the person performing the miracle; but if the miracle is performed, not by enabling the agent to project psychical power, but by his projecting spiritual power, i.e., power residing in , or (as is more probable) specifically conferred by God on, the will as the soul's active agent, then the miracle is truly apothaumatic.
190. It is obvious that a final decision on this issue cannot be reached until we know a great deal more about the relation between matter and mind and the laws governing their interaction, and also on the manner in which the eternal order acts on the temporal order. Knowledge on these mysteries (the former a pseudo-mystery, since the knowledge required to enable us to solve it lies within the scope of the intellectual powers and processes already available to and exploited by us, i.e., the powers used in scientific investigation, but the latter is a true mystery, in that entirely new and at present inconceivable methods of attack and analysis will have to be brought to bear if progress towards a solution is to be made) is not at present available to us, and accordingly, unless we call upon the knowledge disclosed to us by faith, the questions whether human beings have the power to perform external miracles, and if so whether these are apothaumatic or perithaumatic, must for the time being remain open.
191. It may be thought that these questions are too academic to engage our attention, but this would be a false view. It is admittedly true that in present circumstances we would be unable, if the answers were suddenly to be revealed to us, to put them to any immediate use, but present utility is not the issue. For, bearing in mind that the powers exercisable by human beings have been and are still being acquired by evolutionary development, which is largely under the control of the human will, it is possible that, even if apothaumatic powers are not at present available to them, this will not always be the case; and we ought therefore to consider, first, how such powers might be used, and secondly, how the effect of apothaumatic action on the outside world (including the human beings in it) might differ from the effect of the perithaumatic actions

in which human beings already engage.

192. The answers to these question can in fact be readily given, and in both cases, and particularly when combined, are such as to give rise to apprehension, and to cause us to hope that, if apothaumatic powers are or should later become available, God will subject their use to very severe controls, ensuring that they are weak, confined within narrow limits, restricted to only a few exceptional individuals, and even by those rarely exercised. For it is certain, indeed it is axiomatic, that men and women will use all the powers available to them to further the achievement of the objectives selected by their souls for their development and, as we have seen in Chapters III and IV, these are stained by original sin and are bound to be largely in conflict with the will of God as laid down in his plan for the salvation of mankind[16]. In other words men will strive to use all their powers for evil as well as for good purposes.

193. To the second question the answer is that, whereas the power of perithaumatic miracles to affect the world is indirect and slow-acting, that of apothaumatic miracles, even when these are not spectacular (in fact *particularly* if they are not spectacular) may well be catastrophic. The distinction can best be shown by an example. On at least two occasions[17] Jesus exhorted his disciples to have faith, saying to them 'If ye have faith even as a grain of mustard seed, and shall say to this mountain, Remove hence to yonder place, it shall remove'. I suppose that most people, on reading this text, feel inclined to regard it as a picturesque exaggeration, but in fact Jesus meant exactly what he said. For we *have* had faith as a grain of mustard seed, and as a consequence are fully capable of removing this mountain to yonder place, not, admittedly, by simply saying a few words, but by placing a sufficient number of hydrogen bombs at appropriate points inside it and detonating them. And we are able to do this because, by perithaumatic activity over several centuries we have acquired the necessary scientific knowledge of the structure of matter and of the vast resources of energy locked up in the atom (of which we have so far unleashed only a small fraction). We have set ourselves the goal of mastering the secrets of nature and of using them, partly admittedly in the service of God, but also partly for the

aggrandizement of mankind and for achieving the object, suggested by Satan[18], of supplanting God and of denying our dependence on him, and we have used our perithaumatic powers to achieve this goal. The consequences have brought enough misery to mankind, but they have not yet proved to be catastrophic, for, as it has taken us centuries to arrive at this advanced state of knowledge we have had the opportunity of observing the development as it has taken place, and have therefore recognized the need of imposing some restraint (though obviously this has so far fallen short of what is required if the future of mankind is to be assured) on the use of the powers which it has placed in our hands, in so far as such use indirectly affects the external world. We are of course unable to assess the effects on man himself but must believe that, inasmuch as they derive from an attitude of mind in which the supremacy of God is rejected, they must contain a substantial admixture of evil.

194. It is characteristic of perithaumatic powers that although we are constantly using them we are normally entirely unaware that we are doing so[19]. This is a consequence of our faulty evolutionary development, whereby a barrier has been raised between the soul and the mind which, although it allows the will freely to create desires, is so nearly impenetrable by the intellect that we now have little knowledge of the existence of our own souls, not to mention those of other people, and consequently locate the will in some part of the mind and attribute to the psychical element of our personalities functions which properly belong to the soul. This barrier prevents our being aware of the continuous perithaumatic activity of our wills; and part of the process of regeneration and reorientation which it is our duty, with God's help, to aim at bringing to fruition, consists in breaking it down, so that we may regain awareness, not only of the fact that our wills are continuously exercising their miraculous power to mould the desires and to guide the evolution of the human race, but also of the objectives they have selected for these activities.

195. The use of apothaumatic powers, if available, would not normally be thus hidden from our intellects. For, in contrast to the mode of operation of a perithauma, the act constituting the

miracle and the effect on the object affected are simultaneous, or are separated only by the time taken for the transmission of spiritual energy; thus the effect and its cause would be seen to be linked. Moreover it is, I think, certain that in most cases the initiative would be mental rather than spiritual. The idea of the miracle would originate in the agent's mind, and would be seized on by the soul and put into action by the will. We cannot go so far as to replace, in the definition given in paragraph 183, the word 'purposeful' by the words 'consciously purposeful', for in some instances they would not be applicable, but normally the agent would be fully aware of what he was doing, although he might not realize that it was apothaumatic, but might attribute the effect of his action on the outside world to the transmission of mental force rather than to the direct action of his will.

196. It is of course unlikely that anyone, knowing himself to possess apothaumatic power, would use that power to dislodge a mountain, even if he were moved to do so, for he would be bound to reflect on the consequences of his action. He might, however, be moved to inflict irreparable damage on someone whom he disliked or whom for any reason he wished to incapacitate, e.g., by causing certain cells in his body to become cancerous, or by inflicting some other damage on his body, his mind or his property, damage which is at first infinitesimal and therefore not suspected but which, having taken root, may be irreversible otherwise than by a countervailing miracle.

197. It is obvious therefore that the possession of uncontrolled apothaumatic power would be extremely dangerous, and that as the whole of mankind is in a state of original sin and men are consequently unable to distinguish which of the courses of action open to them is most likely to lead them out of the wilderness of almost total confusion in which they now find themselves, are in brief unable to distinguish good from evil[20], that power would undoubtedly be used, deliberately or inadvertently, for purposes which would be in conflict with the will of God, and which, if not overridden by God's intervention, might lead to the frustration of his plan for mankind and the destruction of the whole human race. There is some danger

that even the exercise of perithaumatic power may be thus cataclysmically disastrous; how much greater then is the risk attaching to the use of apothaumatic power.

198. Nevertheless there is evidence that, although the power may at present be in abeyance, it is not, by *a priori* necessity, as an inescapable feature of the created universe, outside the range of human capacity. In other words, the power to perform apothaumata is not essentially inconsistent with the quality of eternal being possessed by human beings and its relation to the inhabitants of the temporal order, although God may have (temporarily) exercised his overriding power to prevent its use. As I have already said[21], this evidence rests on faith, and is therefore to be found in the pages of the New Testament[22].

III. The Miracles of Jesus

199. The Gospels record nearly forty occasions on which Jesus performed miracles, and most, possibly all, of these miracles were apothaumata. Of course, like every other man or woman, he also performed perithaumata, but as these were internal and therefore not spectacular they were unobserved and could not have been recorded. Indeed it is obvious that only those acts that were clearly seen or believed to be miraculous would be written down and it is therefore possible that in addition to the miracles recorded in the gospels Jesus performed other apothaumata of which we have no knowledge. Of the recorded miracles two thirds are cures of the sick, and these are particularly important in relation to the question of human apothaumatic power. They do not, however, require individual treatment, and may therefore be dealt with under a single head; but before setting out what appear to be the chief lessons to be learned from the healing miracles, it will be useful to consider briefly some of the other miracles which have distinctive characteristics.

200. *The miracle at Cana.* This, the first of Jesus's miracles[23], was clearly an apothauma. It has been pointed out[24] that temporal being is maintained only by the continuous activity of God; if this is withdrawn from anything whose being is temporal being

it ceases to exist. It is evident therefore that what Jesus did at the wedding feast at Cana was to withdraw the activity whereby the water in the jars was maintained in being, and simultaneously, by an act of creation, to replace it with wine. The water ceased, the wine commenced, to be. No doubt it will be objected that no one else has ever claimed to transform matter in this way, and that the description fails to render credible what is clearly incredible. But any such objection would be not only pointless but foolish. For even if human beings may (and, as I hope to show, do) possess apothaumatic power, this most certainly does not extend to enabling them to usurp the creative power of God (although, as I have already shown[25], they exercise creative powers within their own personalities). It is to be expected, therefore, that the miracle at Cana should be unique, for it was certainly unnecessary for Jesus to repeat it in order to establish who he was.

201. A more sophisticated, but equally false, objection would be that the power of creation, and of maintaining the temporal world in being, is for God the Father alone, but this objection can also be shown to be unsound. For what is claimed of Jesus is that he is the second Person of the Trinity in human form, and we are told that responsibility for creation, and presumably also for the preservation of what has been created, rests with God the Son or, as St John describes him, The Word[26]. It would therefore be entirely within the powers of Jesus, and also within the ambit of the responsibilities entrusted to him, that a miracle such as that performed at the wedding feast at Cana should be performed. It is also appropriate that it should have been the first of his miracles, as it served to establish his identity and his authority at the outset.

202. *The feeding of the multitude.* Matthew and Mark record two occasions[27] on which Jesus, although apparently supplied with only a small amount of food, was able miraculously to provide a satisfying meal for some thousands of people. Only the first of these two miracles finds a place in the gospels of Luke and John, and it has been suggested that in fact only one miracle took place, but that two accounts, substantially the same but differing in detail, were handed down orally and later incorporated in Mark's gospel. The question whether Jesus per-

formed miracles of this kind on more than one occasion is, however, unimportant; what is important is that a miracle in which a few loaves of bread and a few fishes were multiplied so as to provide a meal for a large number of people is recorded by John, who otherwise shows little interest in miracles[28]. And the reason surely is that John's chief object in writing his gospel is to display Jesus as the Word, the Son of God[29], endowed with creative power, for the multiplication of the loaves and fishes was clearly a creative act. The point may also be made that the inclusion by John in his gospel of an account of this miracle provides strong evidence of the authenticity of at least one of the records appearing in the gospels of Matthew and Mark[30].

203. *The resurrection miracles.* It is recorded that on three occasions Jesus raised people from the dead; the three people whose lives were thus preserved were the son of the widow of Nain[31], the daughter of Jairus, the ruler of a synagogue[32], and, probably the best known, Lazarus, the brother of Martha and Mary[33]. It is obviously more difficult to give a rational account (i.e., an account conforming to eternal as well as temporal reason) of these than of most of the other miracles, as such an account requires that we should first define what is meant by death. The task, however, ought not to be shirked, as the resurrection miracles are obviously of particular significance in the life and work of Jesus, but in view of the difficulties the conclusions reached must be regarded as carrying no more than tentative validity.

204. In the preceding chapter it was stated[34] that the distinction between living and non-living matter lay in the fact that in the former God has implanted a principle of development, an urge to survival by experimentation towards greater complexity[35]. Activation by this principle, which I have called the telos, suffices to distinguish life from death in the case of all plants and all animals other than man. When a dog dies, the telos is withdrawn, physical corruption sets in, the elements of which its body is composed are absorbed into their natural surroundings (even bony structures, although in certain conditions they may be preserved for thousands of years, cannot be regarded as preserving the individual which originally built them), the link between the dog's physical and mental ele-

ments is severed and the latter are absorbed into the general psychical continuum. The dog ceases to be, and although God might, by a creative act, reassemble the elements, physical and mental, of which it had been composed, it is by no means clear that we would be justified in saying that the resulting animal would be the same individual as the original dog.

205. The case of human beings, although in many respects similar to that of other animals, differs from it fundamentally and essentially in that every human being, during his earthly life is activated not only by the telos but also by the soul, which co-ordinates the physical and mental elements, together with the telos, and unites them into a unique personality, and which, through its agent the will, co-operates with the telos where possible but when necessary overrides it, in order to achieve the purposes which it has selected as the goal of its development.

206. Thus the death of a human being involves two separate events, the withdrawal of the telos and the severance of the soul, with its accumulated mental furniture, both created and resurrected[36], from the body and the mind. Probably these two events are normally roughly simultaneous, but there is no reason to suppose that this is necessarily the case, although it would seem to be unlikely that they would be separated by any long interval of time. Probably also bodily decomposition sets in with the withdrawal of the telos. Of course, even if this had occurred it would be within the power of God to restore the body to its original form, but it is unlikely that in the case of the resurrection miracles he would have so ordained events as to add this further dramatic display of power to an already sufficiently dramatic miracle. It is noteworthy that Jesus, in his miracles, never indulges in unnecessary display; he does what is necessary to make his point or to give expression to his compassion for those who are innocently afflicted, but does not mar the effect by histrionic displays.

207. We may suppose, therefore, that in all the resurrection miracles the close association between the eternal and temporal elements in the person restored to life had been partially but not wholly severed, so that he (or she) appeared to be dead, but that the telos was still active. What Jesus did was to restore the

link binding the soul to the body to its full effectiveness, thereby enabling the telos to discharge its proper function of manifesting its host as a living person.

208. *Walking on the water*[37]. If this incident was truly a direct miracle, and there can be no doubt that the three evangelists who recorded it regarded it as such, then it was clearly apothaumatic. But it may be questioned whether the apparent disturbance of the laws of nature was truly miraculous. It appeared that the law of gravity was defied. But this has been done by a few human beings[38], and although their actions were a cause of wonderment to those who observed them, and possibly also to themselves, it is not certain that they were regarded as miraculous. In fact it is probable that, although few people can, at will, exercise the power of levitation, it is a natural power. Once we recognize that the mind is part of the natural universe and that, in addition to the laws peculiar to the physical world and the mental world, there are also interactive laws, it is not difficult to believe that psychical energy can be used to affect, not only objects existing in space-time, but also the structure of space-time itself. Since gravity is the visible manifestation of the effect on physical bodies of the curvature of space-time, it is certainly possible that some minds, equipped with the necessary specialized faculty, may be able to modify the curvature of space-time in their immediate vicinity in such a way as temporarily to negate the force of gravity in that area. It is indeed possible that this power is present in all people, but latent, or in a state of atrophy resulting from disuse and disbelief in its existence; but available to be brought out and developed by the perithaumatic activity of the will.

IV. Healing Miracles

209. It is surely significant that although Jesus did nothing to relieve poverty or homelessness, or any of the other evils that weigh so heavily on our modern consciences, he expended a great deal of energy on healing the sick. It is true that fewer than thirty specific cures are actually recorded in the Gospels,

but the evangelists also mention several occasions on which he healed 'many that were sick of divers diseases' or 'all those who were lame, blind, dumb or maimed'[39]; and no doubt there were many similar occasions that have not been recorded. His attitude to the evils that may befall mankind appears to have been that in a fallen world they are for the most part inevitable – indeed he declared roundly that 'ye have the poor always with you'[40] – but that the task of coping with these evils ought not to be made more difficult by physical or mental disease or disablement.

210. This is an important point. The problem of pain is of course an enormously difficult one, and many of those who have tried to solve it have been forced, almost in despair, to suggest that sickness, disease and disablement are part of the means employed by God to strengthen, purify and ennoble the souls of men. It is of course true that God can bring good out of evil, and it is also true that many of those who are condemned to a lifetime of physical pain or disability display courage of such high order that they arouse in those of us who are not called upon to bear such a burden feelings of deep humility and thankfulness. The lives of such people provide to the more fortunate of us not only examples of shining fortitude, but also strong evidence that divine aid will be given to those who seek it.

211. Nevertheless these cases cannot be adduced as evidence that pain and disease were preordained by God as necessary disciplines for the souls of men. It is true that suffering is a necessary element in any world created into the temporal order, and it is probably also true that in such a world the incidence of physical and mental disease and disablement is inescapable[41], but it does not follow that it was God's intention that any of these should be a life-long burden. The fact that Jesus devoted so much of his time to healing the sick is conclusive evidence to the contrary. This fact makes it clear that he did (and does) not regard disease as a necessary discipline. (It is worth noting also that it is not a punishment for sin[42]). His attitude to physical and mental disease was, in fact, as David Cairns has pointed out[43], precisely the same as that of any good modern physician, although his method of

treatment was of course entirely different. 'He always assumes that disease is part of the kingdom of evil, and never once does he give the slightest sign to the contrary. Not only does he try to heal all those who are brought to him, but he sends his disciples forth with a general commission to heal indiscriminately. His unvarying assumption, when there are failures, is that there has not been enough faith either on the part of the healers or of the sick or their friends and neighbours. His underlying idea can only be that God is always on the side of health rather than of disease, and that where the latter triumphs, something is as it ought not to be'[44].

212. It is possible that some of the cures performed by Jesus were examples of what today would be called psycho-therapeutic treatment or faith healing, but certainly the majority of those recorded in the Gospels were true miracles and therefore apothaumata. We may indeed suppose that Jesus had perithaumatically acquired the power to project psychical energy, and that on occasion he used this power to transmit to those who sought his help a conviction that they would recover from their illnesses or lose their disabilities, a conviction so strong that nature's work of restoration was accelerated and supplemented. But such cures would not usually have been spectacular, and must therefore have remained unrecorded.

213. In the recorded cases therefore we must conclude that the cure, which in most instances appears to have been dramatic and instantaneous, must have been effected by the transmission of spiritual rather than psychical energy, and it would seem also to be beyond question that this apothaumatic activity involved a far greater expenditure of energy than is involved in any perithaumatic miracle. This may be deduced from the fact that when the woman with the issue of blood touched the hem of his garment, Jesus immediately knew that power had gone out from him[45].

214. It is in fact reasonable to suppose that, although all human miracles are acts of will, an essential factor distinguishing perithaumata from apothaumata is that for the former the necessary power is drawn from the reserves held within the will itself, but that for the latter these reserves are wholly insufficient, and it is necessary for the will to draw on supplies

obtainable only direct from God. There need therefore be no surprise that Jesus was able to perform apothaumata, for in him the divine and human wills were perfectly attuned, and the necessary concentration of spiritual energy was therefore readily available for transference to the person or object affected by the miracle.

V. Human Apothaumatic Power – the Need for Recovery

215. Although it appears probable that the power to perform apothaumata has been largely lost or has been suspended, and has always been at best available to only a very few people, we can be certain that, as a form of therapeutic treatment, it does not lie outside the range of possibilities of the human will. For this the evidence of the New Testament and other early Christian writers is overwhelming. Thus Matthew and Luke tell us that Jesus conferred the power of healing on the twelve disciples[46], and from Luke we learn that when he sent seventy apostles to prepare the way for him he commanded them to heal the sick in whatever city they might enter[47]. Further, after the apostles had received the Holy Spirit, they were able to perform miraculous healings and other miracles (including in one case the restoration to life of a woman who had died)[48], and Origen, in his book *Contra Celsum*[49], tells us that healing by the power of the Holy Spirit was customary until his own time (c. 185 – c. 254) although the practice was becoming less usual. Finally, many saints have displayed the power to heal the sick and to perform other miracles.

216. Why then is this power now so rare? To this question two answers can be given, both of which are no doubt valid. The first is that, as a result of the vast increase in the range of scientific knowledge and the assurance attaching to it, men have ceased to believe that miracles of any kind are possible. And this sceptical attitude of mind has produced and continues to produce a reaction whereby the ability to perform apothaumata is reduced or even destroyed. For the will, which is the agent involved in the performance of all miracles, takes note of,

and adjusts its objectives and the exercise of its powers to, the ideas present in the mind. These are, of course, in some measure its own creation, but in regard to the interpretation of the laws governing the universe are to a much greater extent absorbed by the individual mind from the prevailing opinions of society at the relevant time. Thus when the prevailing opinion is that all phenomena are explicable in terms of cause and effect and the application of laws which, though not yet all known, are in principle discoverable, the wills of individuals do not put forth their strength to disturb this opinion. This may be thought to be regrettable, but may in fact be a wise decision, for if, at a time when temporal rationality is held to be the only valid form of rationality, too blatant an interference by a faculty having access to eternal rationality might lead men to distrust the rationality of their minds altogether or even of the whole governance of the universe, with potentially disastrous results[50].

217. Thus disability engenders disbelief and disbelief engenders disability, and unless this circle can be broken the advance of mankind must be impeded. For the position now is that when apothaumata occur we are tempted to explain them away, but by allowing ourselves to be thus misled we have inevitably come to hold a false view of the potentialities of human beings, and this has distorted our vision of the future. We equate our potentiality to perform miracles, i.e., the power which God intended that we should be fitted to exercise, with our present abilities, which we assume to be non-existent; and we fail to grasp the important truths that the potentiality has not been annihilated but is merely latent, and that it must be rebuilt by a long and possibly painful evolutionary process if the kingdom of God on earth is to be realized[51]. This process involves a new alignment of our wills, but so long as we remain in a state of unbelief these, on seeking an intellectual basis for reorientation, can find none, and are therefore discouraged from making the necessary effort.

218. The second answer to the question why human apothaumata are now so rare is readily derivable from what has already been said. For whereas the energy required for perithaumatic activity is available at all times (indeed if in any

individual that activity were to cease it would mark the end of his humanity[52]), that required for apothaumatic activity has to be supplied by God[53]. And we have also seen that if the energy to perform apothaumata were made generally available it would, as a result of the Fall, certainly be misused[54]. We must suppose therefore that one of the reasons why apothaumata are now so rare is that God has deliberately withdrawn the power to perform them, or rather has withheld the necessary supply of spiritual energy, except from a very few people. Of course the power was never widely conferred, but it would seem that in the early years of the Christian era many of those who were firm believers were allowed to draw on it for curative purposes. The same may be true today, but the wider diffusion of belief during the Middle Ages led to its being infected by errors which have not been eradicated, but have rather been fostered and enhanced by the rise, during the past four centuries, of what is erroneously called 'rationalism'. The result has been a reduction in the number, relative to world population, of those who claim to be Christians, and a marked dilution, even among those who make this claim, of the strength and fervour of their belief, with the inevitable consequence that the number of people to whom God is now prepared to make apothaumatic power available must be very small.

219. And this is a situation which, as will become increasingly obvious, it is the duty of man to remedy. For although it is unlikely that God will ever make apothaumatic power generally available, it is clear from the fact that Jesus commissioned the apostles to perform miraculous cures that he is very willing to supply the power to selected people to heal the sick and disabled. And it is also clear that this power is becoming more and more necessary to close the widening gap between the need for remedial treatment of one kind or another and its availability. For the increasing complexity of the types of illness with which we are afflicted and the increasing sophistication of the physical and psychological methods of treating disease are likely soon to bring about a situation in which the supply of curative methods will be unable to meet the demand.

220. To see that this is the case we must note that there are two possible lines of development for the future. The first is that

man will continue in his attempt to subdue nature to his desires[55]. The conflict inherent in this situation – a conflict between the wills of men and the laws of nature, fought out within the being of man himself – must inevitably lead to an increase in the incidence of various existing forms of physical malfunctioning (and probably also in the appearance of many new forms), and although in some cases the immediate observable cause will be readily found (e.g., in the use, or the circumstances of the use, of some new technological device), in others no obvious cause will be discoverable. Moreover, in most cases, whether the immediate cause can or can not be pinpointed, the basic cause will be the lesion in the whole being of man brought about by the effort to conquer nature which, as we have seen, is one of the manifestations of original sin. Thus the removal of the immediate cause, if this is discoverable, will not effect a cure – all that will happen will be that one set of symptoms will be replaced by a different set, occurring perhaps in a different group of people. (For it must be borne in mind that we are dealing here not only with individual cases of sickness but with instances of disease or malaise affecting whole groups of people – possibly a nation or possibly even the whole of mankind.) Even more intractable will be the increase in psychological disorders. Already the number of people suffering from one or another form of mental illness provides grounds for serious concern, but if we continue to pursue the goal of subduing nature and harnessing it to a hubristic purpose there can be no doubt that the number will grow and will become a matter, not merely of concern, but of alarm.

221. It may be argued that advances in medical science will keep pace with the new forms and greater incidence of physical and psychical disorder. The devotion of the medical profession to the relief of suffering and the imagination and skill which have been displayed by medical research workers are, of course, not here in question, and it is certainly true that the development of technology, while creating new evils, often also provides the means of combatting them, or at any rate of mitigating their more obvious manifestations. But the cost of the remedies mounts so rapidly that it will be impossible to provide them to more than a fraction of those who will need

them.

222. Moreover, the physical and mental consequences of the conflict with nature described above, being essentially a conflict between human wills and the will of God, cannot be avoided or cured by any remedial techniques that do not themselves involve the intervention of the eternal order. This is because eternal beings cannot be affected by changes in the temporal order unless those beings themselves take the initiative, from which it follows that, unless the wills of men are realigned in the direction of collaborating with, rather than subduing, nature, the progress of medical science and of therapeutic techniques (other than that of miraculous healing) can never keep pace with the increasing problems with which they will have to contend.

223. Consideration of the incidence of disablement and of the means of dealing with it lead to the same conclusion. Whereas in the pre-industrial era it was nearly always possible for a disabled person to find some useful and satisfying work to do, the accelerating complexity of modern life renders such work more and more elusive. There can be nothing but admiration for the efforts that are made to enable disabled people to fit themselves into society, but we live in a world in which economic factors play a predominant part, and the types of equipment required to enable those who suffer from some disability to overcome it, or at least to avoid its worst consequences, become more elaborate with every advance in technology. Here again it is likely that demand will outrun supply.

224. These forecasts are based on the supposition that the present trend towards increased complexity of life and its dependence on ever more advanced technology for its maintenance will be continued. But there is also the alternative possibility that this trend will be halted or even reversed. This might ultimately lead to a lessening of the incidence of physical and mental disorders of conflict, but it would also create enormous economic disturbances, and would probably halt the advance in the discovery of remedial techniques. In this case also, therefore, the ability of medical science to meet the demands made on it would be bound to decrease.

225. Whatever the future holds in store, therefore, the tradi-

tional methods of healing must fail to secure the maintenance of physical and mental health which, if the will of God were paramount (that is to say, if God had not willingly surrendered part of his omnipotence to preserve man's freedom), would be the birthright of every human being. Of course the ideal state of affairs can never be realized while man remains in the wilderness in which he is now wandering with little sense of direction as a result of the accumulated evolutionary deviations which constitute original sin, but part of his search for the best path through this wilderness must take the form of a devout effort to solve the problem of health. This requires that we should recover the power of miraculous healing, and we must therefore devote some of our efforts to learning how to bring this about.

226. We learn from the Gospels that a prerequisite of miraculous healing is faith[56]. As David Cairns has pointed out in the passage quoted above[57], Jesus assumes that failure is invariably due to lack of faith. Now, although in Mark xi, 23 faith seems to be identified with freedom from doubt, and although this is certainly necessary, it is also certain that the requisite degree of faith involves much more than intellectual assent to a proposition, or even than a conviction that what one asks for will come to pass. What is required for the performance of apothaumata is a supreme act of will, leaping over all obstacles to effect a union with the will of God, to enable the will to draw on the energy which God is ready to make available. Faith, in the sense of belief, is of course necessary, in that such a leap cannot be made except from a firm ground of assured conviction that the power of God is available, but this alone provides merely the foundation; faith in its full sense is a positive act, and it is obvious that it must be an act of will operating in the eternal order.

227. Moreover, it must be a communal act. No progress towards the desired goal will be made if the effort is confined to a few people. For although it is within the power of the human will to direct the course of evolution, major developments can only be brought about if there is a general consensus of will, and the first step towards such a consensus is the universal acceptance–first among the Christian community but spread-

ing from them, by the power of their unshakable conviction, to the whole community – of the fact that what is desired is achievable. It is not to be expected, of course, that even when the general consensus of will has been reached, more than a few men and women at any one time will be endowed with the power of miraculous healing, and this fact suffices to ensure that it will not be abused, for those who possess it will be in such close communion with God that the desire to abuse it will not arise in their minds. The onset of such a desire would, in fact, immediately destroy the healing power, since the two could not co-exist in one mind.

228. One final point remains to be made. The miracles of Jesus and the apostles and saints were at one time, and by many people are still, very rightly regarded as the glories of the Faith. Later, with the spread of rationalism, the miracles of Jesus came to be looked on as proofs of his divinity – in fact the truth of the Christian faith was held to be attested by the fact that Jesus, its founder, was able to perform miracles. It ought, however, now to be clear that although the creative miracles do establish his status as the Word of God incarnate, his healing miracles point to his humanity as surely as to his divinity. Jesus, in his life on earth, behaved as a sinless man would necessarily behave, and thus established a norm to which it is possible for man to approximate. Like all men, he was born into a world of accumulated original sin, but this did not act as a barrier between his will and the will of his Father. Nor need it be so with man. If the obstacles created by original sin can be overcome by faith in the case of miracles, we may be certain that faith can also enable us to overcome them in other cases. In other words we need have no doubt that it is within the power of man to enlist the aid of God in redirecting his steps towards the true evolutionary path. This is not a counsel of easy optimism. Man has been wandering from the true path for perhaps a million years or more, and the consequences of this errancy cannot be simply wiped out. They display themselves in an innumerable variety of forms in the conditions of our everyday life – in the apparent inevitability of all the evils against which, both in public and in private life, we are continually struggling, often seemingly with little effect. By

them our desires are conditioned and the vision of our wills is obscured.

229. In spite of this, however, we need have no doubt that from time to time men and women with exceptional spiritual insight will appear, whose faith will be sufficiently strong to capture the imagination of mankind and to guide his steps along a path of escape from further entanglement. And the conclusion to which this points is that, if all Christians start by casting aside the pseudo-intellectual arguments against belief by which they are constantly assailed, and reaffirm their own certitude that the age of miracles is not past, they will set the stage for the wills of all men to seek a new direction for the path of evolution, and for the rise of prophets to help them in this task. Though the time for the recovery of belief may be running short, progress towards the building of the kingdom of God through the exercise of man's miraculous powers can, must and will be made, for God will not allow his great experiment in freedom to fail.

CHAPTER SIX

NOTES AND REFERENCES

(The numbers in brackets indicate the paragraphs in which the references occur)

1. (180) In paragraph 76.
2. (181) See paragraph 64.
3. (181) It is assumed here that the mode of being of the temporal order is temporal being, and this is reasonable as otherwise it would be necessary to postulate a different order or mode of being to accommodate the temporal order. In contrast to this the mode of being of the eternal order (or eternity) is not eternal being but supra-eternal being, since eternity is not created but *proceeds* from God (see paragraph 22).
4. (182) The notion that a distinction can be drawn between the temporal being of a person and that of other inhabitants of the temporal order, including the temporal being of other persons, will probably be readily accepted; but in fact it is very difficult to define. No full analysis will be attempted here, but the nature of the difficulties should be pointed out. For it is possible (though highly improbable) that the whole physical universe is, basically, continuous, the sub-atomic particles of which it appears to be composed being no more than singularities – points at which energy is concentrated – in a continuum. It is possible also (though again highly improbable) that the whole of the mental universe is a continuum, in which concentrations of psychic energy appear in those beings which are possessed of minds. Certainly there is constant interchange between the elements constituting the physical part of the temporal being of a person and those constituting the rest of the physical world, and the same may be true of the mental elements. Nevertheless we are intuitively certain that, for every

person, his temporal (physical and psychical) being is peculiar to himself, even though the elements of which these are composed are interchangeable with those of the outside world. This intuitive conviction of individuality is not a function solely of the fact that eternal being is welded to temporal being in every person, for the concept of individuality (though not of course that of personality) is applicable to other species besides man.

Thus it will generally be admitted that this dog or this cat is distinct from that dog or that cat; that each of these is a distinct individual; and it would probably also be admitted that the same applies to two amoebae, although there might be some difference of opinion as to the precise moment at which one individual becomes two individuals when an amoeba is in the process of propagating its kind by fission. Equally, individuality would generally be accorded to each of two oak trees, or of two rose bushes, or two roses on the same bush, or even to each of two blades of grass. There might be some difficulty in deciding how the concept of individuality should be applied to the spores of plants bearing no flowers, and no doubt other similar troublesome cases could be cited, but it is probable that all such difficulties could be overcome. On the other hand, no-one would accord individuality to a stone or a lump of earth, or even to a crystal such as a diamond. Two diamonds are certainly distinct, but neither can properly be called an individual. In fact it is clear that the concept of individuality can only be applied to living creatures, and must therefore be a function of the telos, but it is probably no easier to define precisely what that function is than it is to define life. We know, however, that the telos is continuously active in creating organization consciousness (see paragraphs 142 *et seq.*) and the simplest supposition is that it is in this organization consciousness, which is associated with the basic consciousness of every particle or element, physical or mental, forming part of a person or other living being, that the basis of individuality is to be found.

5. (184) See paragraph 51.

6. (184) It is of course possible for God or an eternal being to *observe* the development of events in the temporal order without

in any way disturbing the operation of its laws, but observation is not an 'act affecting that order'. The essential characteristic of the temporal order is that it is deterministic (see paragraph 15); that is to say it consists of events in time whose sequence is governed by law, and any active interference from outside must be displayed as a disturbance of this ordered sequence, that is to say, as a suspension or modification of the laws of the order.

7. (184) One of the two most important apothaumata in the history of the world – the conception of Jesus by the Holy Spirit – was wholly unspectacular; the fact that a miracle had occurred was at first known only to Mary and Joseph. The spectacular events recorded by Luke (if they occurred) were related to the *birth* of Jesus, which was not miraculous, rather than to his conception, which was. (See paragraphs 239 and 240).

8. (185) This statement amplifies the statement in paragraph 22 that the three orders of reality are ontologically distinct. But the fact that God is absolutely distinct from what he has created is not to be interpreted as meaning that he is not involved in the eternal and temporal worlds or that he regards them without interest; in fact, as we have seen in paragraph 23, it is only by God's continued activity – an *apothaumatic* activity – that the temporal order is maintained in being, and of course beings inhabiting the eternal order, which are free, have only to open the door to God to be the recipients of the Holy Spirit. But God's existence is independent of his creation, and the distinction between God and his creation, i.e., the temporal order and the beings which inhabit it, and the beings which inhabit the eternal order (but not that order itself – see Note 3 above) must be constantly borne in mind if we are to avoid the error of pantheism, which *identifies* God with the created world, and which underlies much of the false thinking about God and man current today.

9. (185) Paragraphs 52-55.
10. (185) cf. Chapter II, Note 21.
11. (186) See Chapter II, Note 10.
12. (187) See paragraphs 136 and 146.
13. (187) Paragraph 167.

14. (187) I have called this a suggestion, and the reader may regard it as carrying no more weight than an idea for consideration, but I have no doubt whatever that it is true. See paragraphs 171-174, also paragraph 116.
15. (189) In paragraph 45.
16. (192) See paragraphs 65-68.
17. (193) Matthew xvii, 20; Matthew xxi, 21 (= Mark xi, 23).
18. (193) Genesis iii, 5.
19. (194) cf. paragraphs 91, 154.
20. (197) It is ironic that the very act, which Satan promised would give man the power to know good and evil, has had the diametrically opposite effect.
21. (198) In paragraph 190.
22. (198) We must distinguish between the unusual events recorded in the Old Testament and the miracles described in the New Testament. The historical books of the Old Testament, and also those prophetic books which are in part historical (e.g., Daniel) were written long after the events they record, and almost certainly contain a good deal of fictional material which had been handed down by word of mouth, and had in the process become more and more divorced from reality. Moreover God, as described in those books, is sometimes represented as a tribal god, ready to manifest his superiority to other tribal gods by intervening, and overriding the laws of nature, on behalf of his chosen people. Thus we need not accept as true all the marvellous events recorded in the Old Testament, such as the destruction of the walls of Jericho (Joshua vi), the barrel of meal and the cruse of oil which were replenished daily (1 Kings xvii, 14-16), Daniel in the lion's den (Daniel vi, 4-23), or Shadrach, Meshach and Abednego in the furnace (Daniel iii, 19-26); but if we reject them we may not legitimately do so on the ground that, being apparently miraculous, we find them incredible, but because the concept of God to which they give rise is primitive, that of a tribal deity. Even on this ground, however, we should be chary of dismissing them as without foundation, for our own twentieth century vision of God is too distorted to enable us to form a true or even a rational judgement.

There is the further important point that in all or almost all the Old Testament miracles, the agent is God and not man. It was not Aaron who miraculously turned his staff into a serpent (Exodus vii, 8-10), but God using Aaron to break down Pharaoh's obduracy; Joshua's priests may have sounded the trumpets, but it was God who caused the walls of Jericho to fall; Elijah's prayer may have been instrumental in restoring the widow's son to life, but it was God who actually performed the miracle (1 Kings xvii, 17-24). It is indeed true that in all human apothaumata the power of God has to be invoked (see paragraph 214); but in the case of most of the Old Testament miracles it seems clear that the part played by the human beings concerned was not that of an agent on whom power has been conferred but that of a petitioner to God to use his own power. These miracles are therefore less relevant to a discussion of man's apothaumatic powers than those recorded in the New Testament.

23. (200) John ii, 1-11.
24. (200) In paragraph 23.
25. (200) In paragraph 144.
26. (201) John i, 1-3.
27. (202) Matthew xiv, 13-21 (= Mark vi, 30-44 = Luke ix, 10-17 = John vi, 1-13; Matthew xv, 32-39 (= Mark viii, 1-9).
28. (202) The only miracles recorded by John (apart from the Resurrection) are the turning of water into wine (ii, 1-11), the healing of a nobleman's son (iv, 46-54), the healing of a paralytic man at the pool of Bethesda (v, 1-16), the feeding of the five thousand (vi, 1-13), Jesus walking on the water (vi, 15-21), the healing of a blind man (ix, 1-38), and the raising of Lazarus (xi, 1-46). In all but one of these cases the miracle has special significance, either providing the basis of a discourse or showing Jesus as the Lord of creation (i.e. as having creative power), or as having power over life and death (John specifically records Jesus as claiming that the power of resurrection belonging to God is vested in the Son – v, 21), or of healing at a distance. The exception is the occasion when Jesus walked on the water, and this, as I suggest later (paragraph 208) may not have been a miracle at all. It is indeed interesting to note that John treats this apparent miracle summarily, whereas both Matthew and Mark develop it into a story, to show the

connection between faith and miraculous power, and evidently attaching to it greater weight than John does.

29. (202) See, e.g., John i, 34; iii, 16-18; v, 17-27; ix, 35-38; xi, 4. The other gospels also make the same claim (e.g., Matthew viii, 29 = Luke viii, 28; Matthew xiv, 33; Matthew xvi, 13-17 = Mark viii, 27-29 = Luke ix, 18-20; Matthew xxvi, 63, 64 = Mark xiv, 61, 62 = Luke xxii, 69, 70; Matthew xxvii, 43; Matthew xxvii, 54 = Mark xv, 39; Mark i, 1); but the affirmation is particularly insisted on in John. Moreover, it is chiefly from John that we learn of the triune nature of God; see John i, 32, 33; xiv, 26; xv, 26, in which it is stated that the Spirit *proceeds* from the Father; xx, 21, 22; and more particularly 1 John v, 7, where it is explicitly stated that the Father, the Word (i.e., the Son) and the Holy Ghost are one. But this fundamental fact is also implied in Matthew xxviii, 19, where the risen Jesus exhorts the eleven disciples to baptize all nations in the name of the Father, the Son and the Holy Ghost.

30. (202) It is necessary to make this point, because foolish attempts have been made to deny that the feeding of the crowd involved anything beyond the power of Jesus, by virtue of his personality, to persuade the people to share the food that they had themselves brought. This attempt to 'explain' the miracle is so obviously contrary to what the evangelists record that it is not worthy of serious consideration.

31. (203) Luke vii, 11-15.

32. (203) Matthew ix, 18, 19, 23-25 = Mark v, 22-24, 35-42 = Luke viii, 41, 42, 49-56.

33. (203) John xi, 1-44.

34. (204) In paragraph 142.

35. (204) Attempts have been, are being, and no doubt will continue to be made to show that living matter can arise from non-living matter by natural forces alone, but all such attempts are bound to fail. It is possible that in certain physical and chemical conditions molecules may combine to form organic compounds and may grow and split into two or more similar groups of molecules, thus apparently displaying the properties of survival, growth and reproduction. But all such examples of pseudo-life can have no permanence; the process must come to an end as soon as the conditions change, for the groupings have

no *urge* to bring about internal change so as to adapt themselves to the environment or to produce mutations, or to seek a new environment in which they can continue to 'survive' without change. Life began on earth when in these molecular groupings, which possessed (in the prevailing environment) the physical and chemical structures required as a basis for life, God implanted the telos, i.e., the urge towards survival. It may be noted that this urge is not necessarily an urge for the survival of the individual living creature or even of the species to which that individual belongs, although it usually manifests itself in these forms; it is primarily an urge towards the survival of the telos itself. At first this urge cannot have had any mental component, but ultimately, with the uniting of mind and matter in the higher species, it manifested itself as desire.

36. (206) See paragraph 146.
37. (208) Matthew xiv, 22-33 = Mark, vi, 45-51; John vi, 15-21.
38. (208) The most famous case is probably that of St Theresa of Avila, who records that the experience of levitation caused her great distress but that she was unable to resist the force lifting her up. (See *The Life of St Theresa*, translated by J.M. Cohen; Penguin Classics, 1957; chapter 20). Another well-known instance is that of Daniel Douglas Home (1833-1886), of whom Sir William Crookes, FRS wrote in the *Quarterly Journal of Science* (January, 1874): 'On three separate occasions have I seen him raised completely from the floor of the room . . . There are at least a hundred recorded instances of Home's rising from the ground, in the presence of as many separate persons . . . the accumulated testimony establishing Mr Home's levitations is overwhelming.'
39. (209) Matthew viii, 16, 17 = Mark i, 32-34 = Luke iv, 40, 41; Matthew xii, 15 = Mark iii, 10, 11 = Luke vi, 17-19; Matthew xiv, 14; Matthew xiv, 35, 36 = Mark vi, 54-56.
40. (209) Matthew xxvi, 11 = Mark xiv, 7 = John xii, 8.
41. (211) See paragraph 113. Jesus was, of course, aware that the intensity with which men and women are capable of experiencing pain is far greater than is necessary for the survival of the human species or for the fulfilment of God's plan for mankind, and that this enhanced capacity, which he

himself shared to the full, since he was a man like other men (cf. Hebrews iv, 14, 15), was due to faulty evolutionary development, i.e., to the accumulated effect of original sin.
42. (211) John ix, 1-3. As John has recorded only three healing miracles particular weight must be attached to the points he was anxious to make. In the other two cases (iv, 46-54 and v, 1-16) this was the need for faith on the part of the beneficiary as well as power in the hands of the healer, and the importance of subordinating rules, however well founded, to the principles underlying them, or, in other words, of observing the spirit rather than the letter of the law.
43. (211) *The Faith that Rebels*; SCM Press, 1954; p. 16.
44. (211) *op. cit.*, pp. 16, 17.
45. (213) Mark v, 24-34 = Luke viii, 43-48. The incident is also recorded by Matthew (ix, 20-22) who, however, omits the vital point that Jesus knew that healing power had been forcibly drained from him.
46. (215) Matthew x, 1; Luke ix, 1, 2.
47. (215) Luke x, 1, 8, 9.
48. (215) The woman raised from the dead was Tabitha (or Dorcas), and the miracle was performed by Peter (Acts ix, 36-42). For healing miracles see Acts iii, 2-10; ix, 33, 34; xiv, 8-10; xvi, 16-18; xix, 11, 12; xx, 9-12. For other miracles see Acts ii, 4-11; xii, 5-10; xvi, 25, 26; xix, 6.
49. (215) Celsus was a pagan philosopher who lived about the end of the second century AD. In his book *The True Discourse* he criticized Christian doctrine, particularly the Virgin Birth and the resurrection of the body (since, like the Manicheans he regarded matter as evil – cf. paragraph 79) and he dismissed the miracles of Jesus and the apostles as mere inventions. The fact that Origen thought it necessary to write a book refuting his ideas indicates that his teaching probably had great influence on contemporary thought.
50. (216) It may be noted that, even without the intervention of the wills of men to impose the logic (or rationality) of eternity on that of time, distrust of rationality, manifesting itself as superstition, is widespread. This situation is potentially even more disastrous than that envisaged in the text, for instead of subordinating one form of rationality to a higher

form, men are left without any rational foundation for the control of their thoughts and for the ordering of their lives and their future.

51. (217) It is essential to understand that it is only by such a process, and not by any political means, that this can be brought about. There is no short cut. This is not to say that political action may not – in fact it obviously will – be necessary as part of the process, but all such action must be secondary and consequential, subordinate to the universal, or nearly universal, realignment of the wills of men. One of the greatest and most dangerous errors of the second half of the twentieth century is to suppose that regeneration and salvation can be brought about by political means. (cf. paragraphs 58 and 99).

52. (218) See paragraphs 56 and 62.
53. (218) See paragraph 214.
54. (218) See paragraph 197.
55. (220) See paragraph 111.
56. (226) Both Matthew and Mark record that when Jesus was at Nazareth he was unable to do many mighty works because of the people's unbelief. His reception in his home town led to his remarking that 'a prophet is not without honour save in his own country and in his own house' (Matthew xiii, 57 = Mark vi, 4 = Luke iv, 24 = John iv, 44). Nevertheless, he did not entirely relinquish his power to heal, for we are told that 'he laid his hands upon a few sick folk, and healed them' (Mark vi, 5).
57. (226) In paragraph 211.

7

THE TWO GREAT MIRACLES

I. The Virgin Birth

230. The fact that Mary, the mother of Jesus, was a virgin and that Jesus was 'conceived by the Holy Ghost' is recorded by Matthew and Luke[1] and is included as an article of faith in early creeds, including the so-called Apostles' Creed and the Nicene Creed, which was put into its present form at the Council of Constantinople in AD 381. It is still a central tenet of Christianity and belief in its truth is asserted regularly by millions of people in churches throughout the world. But there are also thousands, perhaps millions, of others, professing Christians, who accept without question many of the doctrines of Christianity, including the doctrine that Jesus Christ was both divine and human, but who nevertheless regard the birth stories in the Gospels as picturesque fictions, and who either include the virginity of Mary among those fictions or keep an open mind on the matter[2]. There are of course also millions of non-Christians to whom the idea of a virgin birth is so obviously absurd that they regard those who assert their belief in it as being either liars or at best woefully deluded, and in support of their point of view point out that other religions besides Christianity have held a virgin birth to be an important item in their theology, but that these are dismissed by Christians as mere fabrications.

231. If the story of the virgin birth is true then it is clear that the event itself must have been a miracle. For if it was not a miracle it must have taken place in accordance with the laws of nature, and it must have been either unique or not unique. If it

was not unique there is nothing for the sceptics to criticize in the belief of Christians that it occurred; rather it is for the Christians to ask their critics to produce evidence of other occasions when human virgins have given birth. If on the other hand it was unique, then the fact that it occurred and that its occurrence was in accordance with natural law needs explanation. And this will certainly prove to be a much more intractable problem than the problem of giving a rational explanation of it as a miracle.

232. It is therefore important to analyse what is involved in the confession of belief 'in one Lord Jesus Christ, the only begotten Son of God, begotten of his Father before all worlds, . . . who for us men and for our salvation came down from heaven, and was incarnate by the Holy Ghost of the Virgin Mary, and was made man'.

233. In this statement of belief there are four separate elements. The first is that God the Father is also God the Son and God the Holy Ghost. The second is that at a particular moment in time God took on manhood and appeared as a man on earth. The third is that the circumstances of his appearance on earth were 'conception' by a virgin mother, the paternal agent in the conception being the Holy Ghost, that is to say, God himself in his form as a revelation to men on earth, followed by a normal pregnancy and birth. And the fourth is that these events were ordained by God for the salvation of mankind.

234. As regards the first, I have already shown[3] that if we accept as authentic and meaningful the instruction to address God as Father, then God must consist of at least two Persons. Moreover, we know that he is active and that his activity is a logical consequence of his freedom[4], and we have seen that these facts lead to the conclusion that he expresses himself in the form of a third Person, which is consubstantial with him and proceeds from the first two Persons, the three Persons constituting one supra-eternal Being.

235. The second element in the statement is a fact which has to be accepted as any other historical fact must be accepted, but it differs from all other historical facts in that although neither the event itself nor the time and place of its occurrence could have been predicted by reasoning from first principles or from

other facts established by observation, with hindsight both the event and the circumstances of its occurrence are seen to be entirely in accordance with a rational view of reality. For although it is never possible to predict by the use of reason how God's activity will express itself, to the eye of faith all his actions are seen to be reasonable. Thus we can now see that it is entirely reasonable to expect that God, having set man on his path to salvation, and having seen that man, in the exercise of his free will, has wandered far from the path into the wilderness, would decide to help him by making himself more fully known, and would select for this revelation a time when man was sufficiently developed, intellectually and spiritually, to grasp the message, but not so far developed that his powers of spiritual understanding had become (as they have now become) subordinate to his intellect. It is also reasonable to expect that he would decide that the most effective revelation would be to clothe himself in flesh and appear as a man among men, and moreover, that he would choose, for the race to be thus honoured, not the most intellectual but the most spiritual race, not perhaps the most moral race but the race most aware of God, not the race with the most highly developed political and administrative system but the race whose instinct prompted them to determine every issue by reference to their religious teaching, the race who, although they believed that God was especially *their* God, nevertheless recognized that there is only one God, that this God is the God of all men and that he is a personal and not merely a metaphysical God, the race who would have found it incredible that anyone should seriously propound the utilitarian principle rather than the commandments of God as the criterion of right and wrong and therefore as the basis of government; in short, the race of the Jews. And so it was, and we can now see that it could not rationally have been otherwise.
236. This brings us to the third element, the assertion of the Virgin Birth, to which many people, even among those who accept as genuine other miraculous stories recorded in the Gospels, feel they must take exception. Granted that God is Father, Son and Holy Spirit, and that at the time and place deemed by him to be appropriate he decided to take on the

nature of humanity, to appear as a man among men, we have to consider the historical assertion that he did so, not by appearing suddenly on the scene as a full grown man, but as an infant, born in a stable of a virgin mother. It is not for us to question why he decided to manifest himself in this way although we must continually seek to learn what lessons can be drawn from the fact that this was his decision, but we are not only entitled, we are also bound, to consider whether the accounts given by the Evangelists are in all respects true or whether, bearing in mind that all human achievements must be imperfect, those accounts may not be false in some particulars. In other words we have to consider whether there is anything in those accounts which appears to be inconsistent with what God has otherwise revealed of himself to us, or which is so incomprehensible as to appear to be incredible. Even if some such difficulty does present itself we must, of course, further consider whether this may not be due to our limited understanding and not to any error in the record.

237. We may, if we wish, dismiss the accounts of the appearance of the angel Gabriel to Mary[5], of an angel to Joseph[6], and of 'a multitude of the heavenly host' to the shepherds[7] as stories, even as childish stories, included for edification, rather than as true records of actual events, but in fact we have no *rational* grounds for denying their authenticity. For, as I have shown in Chapter I[8], the existence of angels is a logical consequence of the existence of God and of his independence of the created universe; and although it is no doubt true that angels do not often appear to men or women there is no logical or scientific reason why they should not do so. For being eternal beings they are able to communicate with the souls of human beings and to act, either directly or indirectly (through the mediation of their souls) on their minds; and it is certainly possible that the effect of such action may be to produce 'visions'. It would be pointless to attempt to inquire into the 'mechanism' of this communication, but it is important to note that the visions, though extraordinary psychological experiences, are not in any way hallucinations. For a hallucination is an experience which takes place entirely within the temporal order, an experience in which some part of the mind or of the

body acts on the mind in such a way as to produce the experience of a sense impression, whereas in a vision, such as that of the shepherds, there is a transmission of energy from the eternal order into the temporal order. And this, of course, is a miracle.

238. We are left, then, with the claim that the conception of Jesus was miraculous, in that no human father took part in it. Now parthenogenesis is not a logical or an ontological impossibility. It may or may not involve an overriding of the laws of nature, but this is very different from saying that it is impossible. Some things are absolutely impossible, in the strictest sense of that word; thus it is impossible, even for God, to undo the past (although he can, of course, nullify the effects of past actions) or to foretell the future *specifically* (although he can foretell it in general terms, since he can always intervene to ensure that what he wills is not frustrated), or for any inconsistency to reside in God, or for any man, who is not also God, to be perfect. It is also impossible for any two things to be identical, since they must differ either in time or place or both and, more fundamentally, they must differ in the 'being' (*esse*) they possess, since God can withdraw his creative activity from one, thereby annihilating it, while allowing the other to remain in being. All these are absolute impossibilities; a statement asserting that any of them had occurred or could occur would be a contradiction in terms or would involve a breach of the logic of eternity. Moreover, they all relate to the nature of God or of his creation; they do not inhere in or arise from the laws by which the created universe develops in time, for although those laws, when not subject to interference, determine the behaviour of the whole universe, and therefore the range of what is contingently possible or impossible, they can always be overridden by a being possessing eternal being.

239. It is clear, therefore, that although parthenogenesis may be very rare, although among human beings it may have occurred only once in the history of the world, it is certainly not an absolute impossibility as the examples quoted above are impossible. If it occurs it is, as we have already seen[9], a miracle, but it is only an elaboration, at the physical level, of the miracle that occurs in the conception and birth of every human

being. For in the creation of new human life the essential miracle (apart from the quickening of matter by the telos, which may or may not be miraculous[10]), is the uniting of the newly created soul, having eternal being, with the temporal being of the physical and psychical elements of which the child's body and mind are and will be composed. Compared with this, the miracle of parthenogenesis does not appear to be so very remarkable. It is, I imagine, questionable whether any biologist could say precisely what takes place *at the molecular level* when a sperm fertilizes an ovum or, even if he could describe the sequence of events in all their ultimate detail, whether he could show conclusively that every stage takes place in accordance with the known laws of physics and chemistry. If, then, one particular stage in this sequence of events is, in one particular case, effected by a specific act of God, can anyone claim to be so well informed that he can positively deny that such divine intervention has taken place? Viewed in this light, it becomes obvious that those who deny, or cast doubt on, the Virgin Birth are not directed to do so by the exercise of reason, but are moved by an irrational, and probably emotional, dislike of the whole notion of parthenogenesis.

240. Moreover, their scepticism is vain, even from their own point of view. For, unless they are prepared to deny the divinity of Christ altogether, in which case their opinions on the matter can carry no weight with Christians, their denial of the Virgin Birth in no way relieves them of the necessity of conceding that in the conception of Jesus a miracle was involved, over and above the miracle that takes place in the creation of all new human life. For the essential miracle was that, whereas in every human conception eternal being is, miraculously, united with temporal being by a specific act of God[11], in the unique case of Jesus supra-eternal being was also added, so that throughout his earthly life, as well as being activated by the telos, he combined all three modes of existence. This was a unique miracle, transcending the quickening of life in Mary's womb, transcending even the implantation of a soul, and as such should command our attention so fully that arguments about the Virgin Birth would be seen to be

relatively foolish.

241. These considerations lead directly to the fourth element in the credal statement, which is that this miracle was performed to bring about the salvation of mankind. A book on the power of miracle is not the place for an analysis of the full meaning of salvation, but clearly one element in this supreme expression of God's grace is that mankind as a whole should ultimately fulfil the destiny laid down for him in God's plan, and that every individual human being should play the part assigned to him in this overall task. When therefore we say that God, in the Person of Jesus Christ, 'for us men and for our salvation came down from heaven, and was incarnate by the Holy Ghost of the Virgin Mary, and was made man; and was crucified also for us under Pontius Pilate', we are declaring our conviction that although God will not force the fulfilment of his plan on mankind, leaving it to every human being to play his rightful part in it by the exercise of his free will, he will go to the utmost limits, short of compulsion, to teach everyone who genuinely seeks guidance what his role is, and to give help and strength in the performance of that role.

242. We are also acknowledging that an inescapable condition of receiving help and guidance from God is that our wills should be in a state of humility, recognizing that without God's aid they are unable either to learn what they are required to do or, having learned it, to perform it. Further, we are acknowledging that this basic and eternal truth has been revealed to us, not only intellectually but also in practical form, by God himself who, in order to implant it firmly and ineradicably in our souls and minds has put on the garb of humility, constricting his infinitude within the limits of one of his own creatures, while retaining both his divine will and his human will unsullied by their imperfections. It is as if a man should be willing to lay aside his humanity and become as one of his own machines in order to ensure that the purpose for which that machine was constructed should not be frustrated. And finally, we are asserting that, if their wills are thus rightly aligned, men and women may, as St John puts it, be born again[12], that societies, nations, and even the whole world, may be miraculously transformed, and the kingdom of God (which of course

does not resemble any utopia imagined by man[13]) realized on earth.

II. The Resurrection

243. This, the greatest miracle of all time, is also its greatest mystery. It is perhaps hardly necessary to say that, although all the events in the life of Christ on earth are significant, the Resurrection is the most fundamentally so, because it is from the fact that Jesus rose from the dead that the Christian religion sprang, and it is on this fact, much more than on the moral teachings of Jesus, which can be largely parallelled in the scriptures of other religions, that the whole of Christianity rests. We may recall the words of Ronald Knox, who pointed out that the message which electrified the world of the first century was not 'Love your enemies', but 'He is risen'[14]; and in this he was surely right. Furthermore it is by the fact of the resurrection of Jesus that the survival of Christianity throughout all time, its ultimate victory in the natural world and its governance of eternity, are assured.

244. It is therefore our duty to discover, as far as is possible, what actually occurred. Before attempting this task, however, let us dispose of a suggestion put forward by those who are anxious to confine reality within narrow limits by denying the existence of the supernatural. They concentrate on the fact that on the morning after the sabbath the tomb in which the body of Jesus had been laid was found to be empty. This fact they explain by assuming that Jesus did not die on the Cross, but was taken down while unconscious and laid in the sepulchre, and that later Joseph of Arimathea or one or more of the disciples came and, finding that Jesus was still alive, removed him and nursed him back to health[15]. If we ask them why we hear so little about the subsequent life of Jesus and nothing at all about his true death, their answer is that after having endured one crucifixion Jesus was not willing to run the risk of a second condemnation by the authorities and therefore retired into private life, or joined a monastic sect such as the Essenes. Of course if this construction of the events of the first Easter

were correct the subsequent appearances of Jesus to the disciples (and others) would present little difficulty, but it is impossible to reconcile it with the accounts given by the Evangelists and by St Paul (even allowing for the fact that these accounts do not all agree), or with the behaviour of the disciples as recorded in the Acts of the Apostles, and there is no need to treat it seriously.

245. These appearances alone, even if not supplemented by the fact of the empty tomb, would provide sufficient evidence that something very unusual and significant occurred between the Friday of the Crucifixion and the following Sunday morning. Many articles have indeed been written and many sermons preached to draw out the lessons to be learned from them. Thus it has been pointed out that each appearance was designed to drive home some particular truth about the power of God, through his Son, to guide, influence and control the lives of men and women even after he had ceased, as a man (in the fullest sense), to meet and talk with them – his power to overcome disillusionment, sorrow and despair (the meeting on the road from Jerusalem to Emmaus[16]), to overcome doubt (the showing of his wounds to Thomas[17]), to help mankind to achieve and maintain economic sufficiency, provided that the methods dictated by human (and for the most part selfish) aspirations are discarded in favour of those dictated by God ('let down your nets on the *other* side'[18]), to teach those appointed to be leaders of thought and action that their task is not 'to express their personalities' or 'to reflect reality as they see it'[19], but to convey to those whom their words and actions can reach the truths which God has revealed or is willing to reveal to them ('Feed my sheep'[20]), and finally to effect a complete transformation of outlook and an infusion of supreme courage into the lives of all men, even of those who have tried to resist the revelation of God in Christ, provided that they repent of their former ways (the vision of Saul on the road to Damascus[21]).

246. These are important lessons, and no doubt other moral and spiritual guidance can be derived from the manner in which Jesus revealed himself after his resurrection, but for our present purpose, which is to describe in simple terms, as far as it

is possible to do so, the nature of the Resurrection as a miracle, and the meaning of that miracle today, the important points to note are that the accounts given by the Evangelists of the post-resurrection appearances of Jesus present no coherent pattern, and that this fact is evidence of their reliability. If the accounts were fictions created by the early church to support its claims, it might be expected that the narratives would have displayed more consistency, and that the risen Lord would have been shown convincingly as being constantly with his disciples, teaching them in some detail the meaning of his resurrection, warning them to prepare for his ascension, and instructing them how to carry on his work thereafter and how to found his church. But according to the records he does none of these things. He appears on only a few occasions, usually without warning, gives a few generalized instructions (e.g., 'Feed my sheep'; 'Go and teach all nations'[22]), and either disappears or is not further reported. We may therefore justifiably claim that the incompleteness and inconsistency of the narratives and the elusiveness of the teaching are guarantees of the authenticity of the records.

247. It must of course be understood that neither the task of describing the precise nature of the miracle that occurred on the first Easter Sunday nor that of interpreting that miracle can ever be fully discharged; our efforts in regard to the first must necessarily be speculative, and in regard to the second must always be incomplete, since the Resurrection is relevant to all times and all circumstances and must therefore reveal new meanings as the evolution of mankind leads him to acquire new knowledge and to adopt new objectives. The brief discussion that follows will therefore be confined to generalities.

248. The manner in which Jesus appeared to his disciples after his Resurrection makes it abundantly clear that he did not rise from the dead with the physical body that had been laid in the sepulchre. He appeared and vanished without warning[23]; he was not always recognized even by those who had known him intimately[24]; and finally he was 'parted from' his disciples and was 'carried up into heaven'[25], and 'a cloud received him out of their sight'[26]. Thus the resurrection of Jesus was totally unlike the raising of Lazarus[27]. Those who were miraculously

restored to life by Jesus or the apostles were restored in their natural bodies and minds; they continued to live as they had lived before their first deaths and they ultimately died again. We are not dealing, in the case of Jesus, with a suspension of the action of the telos and of its subsequent restoration, or with the re-uniting of his temporal being with his eternal (and supra-eternal) being. Jesus died fully on the Cross – the telos which had activated his body and his mind was totally withdrawn and the link between his temporal being and his other two modes of being was finally severed. The body which was laid in the tomb was an ordinary physical body, subject to corruption and ultimate absorption into the substance of the earth around it, and in the ordinary course of events would have ended as a small collection of bones.

249. Nevertheless, when Mary Magdelene (and possibly other women) came to the tomb on Sunday morning, the body had disappeared, although the tomb had been sealed and was closely guarded[28]. Moreover the linen clothes in which the body had been wrapped were lying in the tomb[29], (John even mentions that the napkin that had been wrapped around the head of Jesus was lying separately[30]). The facts alone suffice to refute the suggestion that the body was removed by Joseph of Arimathea or the disciples, for it is most unlikely that they would have taken it away unclothed or that they would have thought it necessary to bring other clothing with them. They also reinforce the conclusion already recorded that the risen body was not a physical body, and it would seem that only one explanation covers all the facts. This is that the elements of which the body had been composed, and the atoms and sub-atomic particles of which those elements were constituted, were annihilated by the withdrawal by God of the activity whereby their maintenance in being had been sustained. These elements and particles therefore ceased to exist.

250. There is thus a close parallel between the first miracle performed by Jesus, the replacement of water by wine[31], and the last, in that in both the power of God over the existence of matter was manifested. It seems probable that John who, as we have seen[32], records few miracles, was inspired to include in his testimony an account of the miracle of Cana precisely because

it prefigures the final miracle. We need not suppose that this was deliberate, in fact it probably was not; for if John had consciously intended to draw the parallel between the first and last miracles he might be expected to have done so explicitly. We may therefore believe that in recording the miracle at Cana, as in other parts of his gospel, he was writing under the guidance of the Holy Spirit, and that it has been left to us to recognize in both miracles not only the power of God over the world he has created, but its absolute and unceasing dependence on him for its continued existence.

251. We must not, however, pursue the likeness between the first and last miracles too far. For whereas at Cana the replacement of the annihilated water by wine involved an act of creation, no specific act, beyond that which took place in the Incarnation, was involved in the survival of Jesus after his physical death or in his continued existence today. The Incarnation and the Resurrection are in fact two elements in the single act of the salvation of mankind. In the Incarnation God the Son, or in John's phrase the Word, whose being is supra-eternal being, added to that mode of being both temporal being and eternal being[33], the mode of being which he had created to be the being of the angels and for infusion into mankind, as the vehicle of his great experiment in freedom. When the physical body of Jesus was annihilated in the sepulchre in which Joseph of Arimathea had laid it, his temporal being ceased to exist, but both his supra-eternal being, which is independent of any creation, and his eternal being which, although created, is indestructible except by a positive act of God[34], continued and continues to this day, as it will continue until the end of time and beyond, outside time and independent of it.

252. How then can we explain the seemingly physical appearances of Jesus after his resurrection? We have however only to ask this question to realize its impropriety. For it is in the nature of things that no answer can be given in any words that would constitute such an explanation as we might seek if we were investigating a natural phenomenon. For the appearances were miraculous, in the strict sense of that word as already defined[35]. The supra-eternal being of Jesus, or his

eternal being, or both, acted on the elements of the temporal order in his vicinity in such a manner as to cause electromagnetic radiations to enter the eyes, and sound waves to enter the ears, of those who were present, leading them to see and hear a man whom, with some hesitancy, they recognized as Jesus, exactly as though a physical body were actually present and speaking to them. Alternatively, though I think less probably, an actual physical body, together with appropriate clothing, was created spontaneously at each of the appearances and annihilated when the message for which the appearance was the occasion had been given.

253. Either of these hypotheses would account for the recorded facts, and neither need give rise to scepticism, for we know, from the facts that miracles occur and that human beings are continually performing them, that eternal being can act on temporal being, causing effects in the temporal order which would not or perhaps even could not occur otherwise than by action from outside that order. We also know that supra-eternal being certainly, and eternal being probably, can act apothaumatically on the physical world outside the personality of the agent. We cannot however explain the mechanism of such actions, for if we could they would cease to be miraculous and we would, in effect, be reducing the supra-eternal and eternal modes of being to the level of temporal being, to being in fact no more than specialized aspects of temporal being; and no greater error than this is possible or even conceivable. The inevitable outcome of this error is either atheism or the disastrous heresy (unfortunately all too prevalent today) of creating God in our own image, and of reducing ourselves, and God with us, to the level of mere animals, specialized perhaps, but in no essential way different from the rest of the natural world.

254. As the resurrection of Jesus is the central fact of Christianity we must believe that its significance is inexhaustible, and as the goal towards which Christianity points is the building of the kingdom of God we must also believe that if we were as firmly convinced of the truth of the Resurrection, existentially as well as intellectually, as each of us is of his own existence, the world would be transformed. But although mankind has

certainly advanced since the time of his creation it is clear that the world has not been transformed; we are indeed only too well aware that evil persists on a vast scale, and is seemingly even more widespread and more potent during the present century than at any previous time in the history of man. It is evident therefore that belief in the Resurrection is spread too thinly, and even among those who accept it as a fact of history is held with too little conviction and with too little understanding of its full implications, to be a really active force in the development of mankind.

255. The use of the word 'existential' to describe the quality of belief required for the building of the kingdom of God is not to be taken as implying that belief in the truths of Christianity must be linked with adherence to any of the philosophies included under the generic title of 'existentialism'. The implication is rather that belief must form part of and possess the will as well as the mind; only thus can it affect the individual and the community at the eternal level, only thus therefore can it play its rightful role in promoting the advent of the kingdom. The nature of belief required might therefore be more accurately described as 'thelematic'[36].

256. The fact that, to be truly effective, belief must be thelematic should not be held to carry the implication that psychical belief, that is to say, conviction of a truth at the level of the intellect, is valueless. On the contrary, it is extremely important; it is indeed not only important, it is essential. It is important because any firmly held intellectual belief is bound to affect behaviour. This is true even of relatively trivial beliefs, e.g., a belief that the weather next week will be fine; it is true with even greater force in the case of more important, though still temporal, matters, e.g., a belief that the economic condition of the country is likely to improve or to decline. *A fortiori*, the influence of intellectual belief on behaviour must be greatest where eternal as well as temporal matters are in issue. Thus the behaviour of a man who believes that his being is annihilated when his body dies must necessarily change if he later comes to believe that his essential self continues in being after his physical death, even though at first this belief is no more than assent to a proposition (intellectual belief) and does

not enter into the being of his soul and his will. Judged by worldly standards his behaviour may not be thought to improve, but it must certainly change.

257. And intellectual belief is essential because a thelematic belief (especially if it not only resides but originates in the soul) will certainly be unable to discharge effectively its function of directing the will to adopt the objectives to which that belief points and which are compatible with it, or to endow the will with sufficient force to pursue those objectives in the face of opposing temptations, unless the belief is supported by intellectual conviction. We may indeed say that thelematic belief which lacks (or loses) the support of the intellect must wither away, with inevitable consequences on the objectives pursued by the will. For although the will is free whereas the mind is not, so that causal action must flow from the former to the latter, the extent to which the will freely draws on the mind is considerable[37]. This is true even of the goals which the will assigns for itself, some of which are in the first instance formulated in the mind and, when examined by the soul, are found to be attractive to it or to be conducive to the attainment of some larger goal already adopted for the exercise of the soul's activities. And it is true to a very much greater extent in the case of beliefs. For, although some beliefs, particularly those relating to the existence, nature and content of the supraeternal order (i.e., beliefs as to whether God exists, and if so whether he is a personal God or a demiurge, and in the former case what are his characteristics), originate in the soul[38] and express themselves through the activity of the will, most beliefs, being the result either of direct observation or of rational argument based on such observation, originate in and reside in the mind. Thus in the interrelationship between the mind and the soul, beliefs are normally the province of the former and aspirations of the latter, and although the will has the power to, and does, take over and transform such beliefs as conform with its aspirations, it does not thereby displace the mind as the guardian of temporal rationality.

258. From this it follows that intellectual belief, soundly based on truth, is essential to a healthy attitude of the will, and thus to the creation of the individual character and the evolution of

the human race along the right lines. We can express this vitally important conclusion in other words by saying that doctrine, so far from being a useless excrescence on the religious life or even, as many people assert today, an impediment to it, is both basic and absolutely essential. The importance of doctrine is immense, it can indeed hardly be exaggerated, for the soul is bound to take note of what the intellect holds to be true, and may be led to modify its objectives accordingly; from this it follows that the duty of seeking, arriving at and holding to true doctrine is paramount[39], for if this is not done it is impossible for mankind to carry out his prime duty of building the kingdom of God. And among the basic doctrines, to which intellectual as well as thelematic assent must be given, we must accord pride of place to the belief that the historical Jesus, the incarnate Son of God, having died on the Cross for the salvation of mankind, rose again on the third day and lives throughout all time and all eternity.

259. Three elements in the complex of beliefs deriving from or supported by the Resurrection of Jesus deserve mention. The first is that it provides evidence that we ourselves will survive physical death, with the corollary that our sojourn on earth is only part of an infinitely greater whole. If we are truly convinced of this fact the certainty we feel must inevitably affect our outlook on life and its meaning. A man who is convinced that an illness from which he is suffering is fatal and that he has only a few weeks to live will have an entirely different outlook on the remainder of his life from one who is convinced that his disease is curable. And if the contrast between the prospect of a few weeks and that of many years of earthly life can vitally affect his outlook, how much greater will be the effect of the contrast between the prospect of a few years of earthly life and that of life in a new dimension, unbounded and infinitely richer than his present life!

260. One particular aspect of the outlook characterizing a belief in eternal life concerns the reaction to bereavement. Of course the sorrow, the sense of personal loss, the possible loneliness, that must accompany the death of a dearly loved husband or wife, parent, child or friend, cannot be lessened, nor can the difficulties of adjusting to a new way of life be

eliminated, much less overcome, by any particular belief. But although the pain of bereavement cannot be avoided, it may be partially offset by the certainty that life on earth is only an incident in a life of infinitely greater fulness, and that in this greater reality, in which the limitations imposed by a linear time, and the distress of waiting for renewed contact, have no place, those who have already cast off their temporal being have not lost sight of or forgotten us, and will in due course recognize and resume conscious communication with us when the time comes for us to join them in eternity[40].

261. The second point is that what survives death not only has being, it also has life. The distinction is important, for although the possession of eternal being implies freedom, which is normally accompanied by purpose and activity, that is to say by life, a free being can renounce life, even though by so doing it destroys itself. It is eternal life, not merely eternal being, that is promised to the believer[41], and from this we deduce that we continue to evolve and develop after death[42], and that our evolution will be purposeful and active. We shall indeed be active in a manner and degree that must immeasurably transcend earthly activity, for although all thelematic activity is carried on in the eternal order, the determinations of our wills are, during earthly life, translated into action through the medium of our minds and bodies in the temporal order. In eternal life development takes place not by change but by metallassis, and the limitations imposed by attachment to the temporal order (other than the freely accepted links by which communication is maintained with those on earth whom we wish to help and guide) will no longer apply. Since, however, our minds have become so conditioned by our bodies that they find difficulty in transcending experience, and do so only by revelation from the eternal order, it follows that the nature of our activity and development after death can only be partially imagined, and that even partial understanding is given only to those who seek it with the eye of faith.

262. In particular we can, while on earth, have only a vague idea of the processes by which we shall continue our individual development after death, and an even less clear idea of those by which the human race continues its evolution towards 'perfec-

tion'[43], that is, towards fulfilling the role laid down for it by God in the beginning. As regards the first, we have already seen[44] that the will can both create spiritual consciousness and transform temporal (organization) consciousness into spiritual consciousness, and that the total consciousness thus produced has eternal being. It is entirely reasonable, therefore, to suppose that the will, in furtherance of its objectives, which in eternal life will be formulated in the light of the fuller knowledge of God then available, will continue to create spiritual consciousness, so that the building of character can continue without limit. In fact, so far as the eternally essential features of individual life and character are concerned, the processes of development in heaven, apart from the fundamental fact that they take place by metallassis and not by change, and are therefore not necessarily linear, are probably not markedly different from those of development on earth.

263. The same cannot, however, be said of evolutionary development. For whereas on earth evolution among the higher species takes place by means of death and birth, in the resurrection there is neither death nor birth, neither marriage nor giving in marriage[45]. The processes of earthly evolution, whereby the offspring in every generation differ slightly from their parents, the differences being physically expressed in genetic mutations, some of which, in the case of human beings, are initiated by their wills, are necessitated by the fact that the space available for accommodating the bodies of living creatures is finite, so that the old must continually die to be replaced by the young. These processes are not necessary in heaven, even if, as may well be the case, the creation of new souls by God is continued indefinitely after the end of time, for in eternity neither space nor time can impose any restriction. It is probable therefore that the evolution of the human race in eternity is carried forward by, and is identical with, the development of the individual souls, both resurrected and newly created, that inhabit it.

264. Although the considerations of the two preceding paragraphs are necessarily speculative, the fact from which they derive, namely that development and evolution, both individual and communal, continue in the life after death, is certain;

and from this fact we make the important deduction that the opportunity to arrive at the belief spoken of by Jesus as the condition of eternal life is not closed at death. This must obviously be true in the case of those who during their earthly lives have had no means of knowing the Christian revelation, but it is also true of those to whom this revelation has not been denied, but has been rejected or ignored. It may indeed be expected that those who deliberately reject the eschatological teaching of Jesus while still on earth will be limited immediately after death by having certain restrictions placed upon their freedom and therefore on the quality and fulness of their eternal life. Such restrictions will doubtless be necessary, lest those who are disposed to deny their need for salvation and to reject the means of achieving it offered to them should succumb to the temptation to join the ranks of Satan and the evil spirits led by him who, though the scope for their activity is probably less than on earth, are certainly not inactive in heaven. On the other hand we may also be certain that the limitations thus imposed need not be permanent; those who are at first reluctant to acknowledge their insufficiency will have the opportunity, even while under condemnation, of renouncing their disbelief in the truths of God's revelation, and as they begin to accept those truths they will also be released from the restrictions imposed on their freedom, thus enabling them to develop their latent capacity for eternal life in its fulness. Only those who finally and irrevocably refuse, even in eternity, to accept those truths, and we may be sure that the opportunity to accept them will not be withdrawn until their refusals number seventy times seven and more, will be condemned to losing the life that ought to be associated with their eternal being, reducing them ultimately to a state which, being static and therefore the negation of all that characterizes the eternal nature of humanity, must lead to the annihilation of being, a process that can only be described as hell[46].

265. The two elements in the complex of beliefs associated with the resurrection of Jesus which have been discussed in the foregoing paragraphs, namely that existence is not terminated by natural death and that in eternity we possess life as well as being, are in some measure common to many religions. The

third element to which attention must be drawn is, however, peculiar to Christianity; it ought therefore to be particularly stressed by Christians and its implications particularly displayed in their lives. It is the belief that the Incarnation, Crucifixion and Resurrection of Jesus marked a critical point in the history of the world. The condition of the world and particularly the circumstances in which men and women conduct their lives have been radically altered by the advent of the Christian era. Before the Incarnation God stood aside from his creation and was separate from it. Of course he had laid down its physical and psychical laws; at the appropriate time he introduced the telos and thereby created life, at a later date he united mind and matter in the higher species of animals, and finally he introduced eternal being into the world by the creation of man. Moreover, he intervened from time to time to ensure that his plan for mankind should not be frustrated. But all these activities were carried on from outside his creation; God and the created world were in no way identified.

266. Since the conception and birth of Jesus, however, this relationship has been entirely changed. In those events God the Son, the second Person in the supra-eternal Being, having created both temporal and eternal being, having implanted into some of his creatures the principle of temporal life, and having united temporal and eternal being in the race of men and women, took on and subsumed into himself all these aspects of his own creation. When Jesus died on the Cross he renounced the telos, and when he rose from the dead he annihilated his temporal being. But he retained his eternal being, with the result that since the Resurrection eternal being and supra-eternal being are united in the second Person of the Trinity. Thus whereas the relation of man to the Old Testament God was that of creature to Creator, of servant to master, these relations are now supplemented by a relation of partial identity of being, since all human beings, including those who lived and died before the Incarnation, now share their possession of eternal being with God the Son. It is of course possible to renounce the implications and consequences of this identity of being, but the fact itself is inescapable. And those who accept both the fact and its implications, including the duties which it

imposes, are given a new status, for they are entitled to call themselves the friends of God[47] and, as I have already pointed out, the opportunity to accept the offer of friendship will remain open throughout all time and all eternity. This is vouched for by the final words of Jesus, as recorded by St Matthew: 'Lo, I am with you always, even unto the end of the world'[48]. It is on these words that the aspirations of Christians throughout the world, and the conviction that these aspirations will be fulfilled, are centred, and it is the message of hope and certainty they contain that it is their duty to proclaim to all the world[49].

CHAPTER SEVEN

NOTES AND REFERENCES

(The numbers in brackets indicate the paragraphs in which the references occur)

1. (230) Matthew i, 18; Luke i, 26-31. It is true that some people have argued that these gospels do not necessarily support the doctrine of the Virgin Birth, on the ground that the word '*parthenos*' may be translated 'a young girl' rather than 'a virgin', but such arguments ignore the other circumstances recorded by the evangelists. In fact Matthew does not use the word '*parthenos*' in verse 18 (though he uses it later, in verse 23, when he refers to the prophecy of Isaiah vii, 14), but says that Mary was found to be with child before she and Joseph came together. And in verse 20 he says that it was revealed to Joseph, who was considering whether to break off his betrothal to Mary, that 'that which is conceived in her is of the Holy Ghost'. Luke is equally specific – he records that the angel Gabriel said to Mary, 'The Holy Ghost shall come upon thee, and the power of the Highest shall overshadow thee: therefore that holy thing which shall be born of thee shall be called the Son of God' (Luke i, 35). (As regards these angelic appearances, see paragraph 237).
2. (230) see J.A.T. Robinson, D.D.: *But That I Can't Believe* (Fontana Books, 1967); p. 25.
3. (234) In paragraphs 35-41.
4. (234) see paragraphs 62 and 65.
5. (237) Luke i, 26-38.
6. (237) Matthew i, 19-21.
7. (237) Luke ii, 8-14.
8. (237) Paragraph 10.
9. (239) In paragraph 231.

10. (239) I have said (in Chapter V, Note 18) that the telos is a temporal entity, implying that its being is temporal being. This is probably true, but we can only speculate on its ontological status and its manner of operation. Two questions in particular suggest themselves:

> (i) Is the telos simply an additional natural principle which, having been implanted in matter, thereby giving rise to the emergence of life on earth, has thereafter formed part of the laws of nature applying to living beings, and to living beings only, or does it, in its operation, override those laws?
> (ii) Is the telos transmitted through the agency of living matter in procreation (of whatever type), or is a quantum of the telos newly implanted by God as a distinct entity in every new living being at the moment when that being becomes a separate individual (see Chapter VI, Note 4)?

Two important features of the telos which may be relevant in seeking answers to these questions are:

> (i) Where the telos is acting the second law of thermodynamics (see paragraph 142) is locally and temporarily reversed, although the law is not thereby invalidated, for the increase of organization displayed in the living organism must be accompanied by a greater degree of disorganization elsewhere than if the organism had not existed;
> (ii) Whereas the whole of nature points to the existence of a First Cause (God) and to the operation of efficient causes, the evolution of living beings is clearly seen to be directed; thus where the telos is in action we find evidence of a Final Cause. In this the action of the telos resembles a miracle, for it follows from the discussion on freedom, activity and purpose in Chapter II that the distinction between what is governed by law and what is governed by miracle is that the latter is directed by a vision of the future.

11. (240) It is the possibility that this act, which is clearly an act of immeasurable significance, may take place at the moment of conception that renders the problem of deciding in what circumstances abortion is not a sin, and should therefore be permitted by the law, so difficult.
12. (242) John iii, 3.
13. (242) See paragraph 110.
14. (243) Ronald A Knox: *Caliban in Grub Street*, Sheed & Ward, 1931; p. 113.
15. (244) Matthew records that the chief priests and elders, fearing the consequences of the resurrection of Jesus, bribed the soldiers who had been set to guard the tomb to say that the disciples had removed the body while they slept (Matthew xxviii, 11-15). cf. also paragraph 249.
16. (245) Luke xxiv, 13-35.
17. (245) John xx, 24-29.
18. (245) John xxi, 6.
19. (245) cf. paragraphs 120, 173, 174, 187 and 188.
20. (245) John xxi, 15-17.
21. (245) Acts ix, 1-9.
22. (246) Matthew xxviii, 19, 20.
23. (248) Luke xxiv, 31, 36; John xx, 19.
24. (248) Luke xxiv, 16; John xxi, 4.
25. (248) Luke xxiv, 50, 51.
26. (248) Acts i, 9.
27. (248) John xi, 1-46; see paragraphs 203-207.
28. (249) Matthew xxvii, 60, 62-66.
29. (249) Matthew xxvii, 59; Luke xxiv, 12.
30. (249) John xx, 5-7.
31. (250) John ii, 1-11; see paragraph 200.
32. (250) Paragraph 202.
33. (251) cf. paragraph 35 of the Athanasian Creed, where it is clearly stated that in the Incarnation manhood was added to the Godhead, not *vice versa*.
34. (251) See paragraph 23.
35. (252) In paragraphs 48 and 51.
36. (255) From the Greek *thelema*, meaning the will.
37. (257) cf. paragraphs 34, 89.
38. (257) It is of course difficult, if not impossible, to trace the

origin of a belief, other than a belief resting on direct observation, but it is clear enough that knowledge of the existence of God or the divinity of Christ or the power of the Holy Spirit is not available to those creatures which do not possess souls. All such knowledge must therefore originate in the soul. Many attempts have admittedly been made to reverse the order of the apprehension of supra-eternal truths or to provide intellectual support to the spiritual apprehension of those truths, by devising rational arguments, based either on logical or ontological premises or on observation, to prove the existence of God. Of these 'proofs' the best known are the ontological proof of St Anselm, the five proofs of St Thomas Aquinas, and the arguments advanced by René Descartes and William Paley. It is, however, generally agreed that the existence of God cannot be rigorously proved by any argument, although it can be shown to be so probable that it is foolish to reject it. (See Chapter II, Note 11).

39. (258) It was at one time generally acknowledged that 'Theology is the Queen of the Sciences', but it is indicative of our present distorted outlook that few people would accord so honourable a place to that science today.

40. (260) See paragraphs 149-174.

41. (261) John iii, 15, 36; vi, 47, 54.

42. (261) cf. paragraph 165; also paragraph 64, where it is shown that development in eternity will not be free from conflict.

43. (262) cf. Matthew v, 48.

44. (262) In paragraphs 144-146.

45. (263) Matthew xxii, 30 = Mark xii, 25 = Luke xx, 35. It should be noted, however, that we must not deduce from these texts that there are no sexual differences in heaven. On the contrary, it is certain that these differences exist and are recognized (see Genesis i, 27). For it is not only the bodies and minds of women that differ from those of men; their souls also have their distinctive characteristics, of which one of the most important is that while the souls of men are more concerned with being than with life, in the case of women the order of priority is reversed. (The statement by St Paul in Galatians iii, 28 that in Christ there is neither male nor female must be

understood as referring to equality of worth, not to identity of being).

46. (264) Although in this paragraph words having temporal connotation (e.g., 'permanent', 'static', 'process') have been used, (inevitably, for we have no others), the references to the fate of those who finally reject God are references to events (or occasions) in eternity, which cannot be brought within the limitations of temporal description. The annihilation of being, therefore, (if any are condemned to such a fate) may well be experienced by those who suffer it as boundless.

47. (266) John xv, 15.

48. (266) Matthew xxviii, 20. The translation is that of the Authorized Version, but it is important to understand that 'the end of the world' is not to be interpreted as meaning 'the end of life on earth', or 'the end of the earth's existence as a planet', or 'the end of the universe', or even 'the end of time'. Other translations are 'the close of the age' (Revised Standard Version), 'the end of the age' (C.K. Williams), 'the end of time' (Revised English Bible), 'the consummation of the world' (Ronald Knox). The most misleading of these is that of the Revised English Bible, but none is entirely satisfactory. Probably the translation that comes nearest to expressing the assurance that Jesus (whose thought was never bounded by temporal concepts) intended to convey, not only to his disciples, but to all men and women at all times and in all places, would be 'Lo, I am with you always, even unto the consummation of eternity'.

49. (266) Matthew xxviii, 19.

INDEXES

Note: References in the form 126 indicate paragraph numbers; references in the form **VI 34** indicate notes.

SUBJECT INDEX

abortion, **IV 28**, **VII 11**
abstract concepts, 12
accident, and substance, 41, 176-177, 179
action, human, 78, 83, 89-92, 95, **III 5**, 96
    reflex, 78, 85, **III 1, 5**
action at a distance, 189
activity, implied by freedom, 62, 65, **II 21**
    implies purpose, 64, 65
    thelematic, 261
aesthetic sense, 30
    perversion of, 120, 173
aggrandizement, of mankind, 94, 193
    see also self-aggrandizement
allegiance, 94, 108, 111
analogy, for God's plan, 118
    for modes of being, 12
    for time and eternity, 18, 21
analytic thought, 30
angels, 10, 22, 41, **II 21**, 93
    as active, 18, 167
    appearances, 237, **VII 1**
    communication from, 167, 173-174
    fallen, 173-174
    and imperfection, 68, 187
    and salvation, 66, **II 30**, 129
    will of, 22
animals, death of, 204
    have no freedom, 60
    individuality of, **V 36**, **VI 4**
Anselm, St, **II 11**, **VII 38**
anthropology, given status of theology, 112, **IV 27, 32**
Apostles' Creed, **V 3**, 230
apothaumata, definition, 76, 180-184, 253
    and human miracles, 182, 189-193, 195-198, 215-229
    and miracles of Jesus, 199-214
    range of, 185-198
appearances, post-resurrection, 244-246, 248, 252-253
Aquinas, St Thomas, **II 11**, **V 55**, **VII 38**
Aristotle, **V 55**
art, works of, 40, 116
artifacts, 52, 71, 98
artist, duty of, 116, 120
astrology, **I 6**
Athanasian Creed, **VII 33**
atomicity of temporal order, 139-140, 176
awareness, 150-154, **V 11**

Babel, Tower of, 118
Barth, Karl, **IV 27**
beauty, search for, 114, 116, 120
begetting, 37-38, 40
being (*esse*), annihilation of, 23, 264, 266
    and essence, **I 17**
    eternal, see eternal being
    hierarchy of, 56, 101, 127
    modes of, 10-23, 137, **VI 3**
    supra-eternal, 8, 10, 14, 17, 22, 41, 52, 185, 234
    of Jesus, 251-252
    see also God;
    order, supra-eternal
    temporal, see temporal being
    transformation of, **III 12**, 136, 143-147, 178-179, **V 35**, 262
beings (*entia*), eternal, activity of, 51, 187-188, 222, 237
    and apothaumata, 187-188
belief, existential, 254

origin of, 257
psychical/intellectual, 256-258
thelematic, 255-257
bereavement, 260
Bettenson, Henry, **V 3**
biochemistry, 119
birth, as miracle, **I 29**, 239-240
birth of Jesus, *see* conception, of Jesus;
 Virgin Birth
body, 24-25, 27, 33, 79, 123
 post-resurrection, 248-251
 resurrection of, 137-138, 143, 145-146,
  148, 153
 see also temporal being
Boethius, Annius Manlius Severinus, **II 3**
Bultmann, Rudolf, **IV 27**
But That I Can't Believe (Robinson), **VII 2**

Cairns, David, 211, 226
Caliban in Grub Street (Knox), **VI 14**
Cana, miracle at, 200-201, 250-251
Cause, First/Final, **VII 10**
Celsus, **VI 49**
chance, *see* randomness
change, and eternity, 19-21, **I 37**, **II 22**
 see also metallassis
 and time, 19, **IV 40**, 141
character, creation of, 78, 85-92, 103,
 108-110, 128, 132, 134, 262
charity, 99, 105, 114, 117, 121-127
Christian Faith, The (Moss), **II 35**
Christianity, constriction of, **IV 32**
 full means of salvation, 127
Christianity and Evolution (Teilhard de
 Chardin), **V 27**
*Christian Philosophy of St Thomas Aquinas,
 The* (Gilson), **V 55**
Christs, false, **II 16**
chronon, **V 10**
City of the Gods, The (Dunne), **IV 13**
cognition, and soul, 153-154
Cohen, J.M. (translator), **VI 38**
communication, between living and dead,
 168-173, 187
 spiritual, 164, 167, 168, 187, 237, 260
Complexity and Consciousness, Law of,
 139-142, 144-145, 175

conception, of Jesus, **VI 7**, 233, 238-240
conflict, and eternal beings, 64, 67-69,
 93-94
 in human personality, 80, 92, 94, 108,
  118
consciousness, **IV 40**, 139-146
 organization, 140, 145, 146-147, 175,
  177-179, **VI 4**, 262
 spiritual, 143, 144-145, 262
 and substance, 175-178
Contra Celsus (Origen), 215
Copleston, Frederick S.J., **V 9**
creation, and God the Son, 201-202,
 VI 28, 266
 God's action in, 9-10, 22, 40, 52-54,
  VI 8
 of man, 5, 47, 107-108
 as self-expression, 65, 66
creeds, **V 3**, 230
crime, **II 20**
 disposition to, 61
critical points, 143
Crookes, Sir William, **VI 38**
Crucifixion, 129, 265

death, and awareness, 150-152
 definition, 204-206
 as process, **II 23**, 147-148
De Consolatione Philosophiae (Boethius), **II 3**
deism, **I 12**
Descartes, René, **II 11**, **VII 38**
desire, 78-80, 82-85, 89-91, 96, 113
 action, 89, 95, 96
 and genetic change, 103-104
 intellectual, 114
 origin of, 82, 86-88, 102, 108, 128,
  194, **VI 35**
 and pain, 113
 parent, 85-90, 95, 96, 101, 102-103,
  113-114, 156
 sexual, 83, **III 10**, **IV 28**
 as temporal, **IV 29**
 see also will, and desire
determinism, 2-4, 46, **V 10**
development, in eternity, 18-19, 21-23,
 63, 165, 261-264
 see also metallassis

difference, sexual, after death, **VII 45**
directedness, 138-139, 141
disarmament, **IV 33**
disease, 123-124, 210-211, 219-224
doctrine, as essential, 93, 258
Documents of the Christian Church
    (Bettenson), **V 3**
dualism, **III 3**
Dunne, John S, **IV 3**
duty, of artists, writers, 116, 120
    concept of, 103, 108, 187
    of forgiveness, 91
    to align will with God's will, 99
    to build God's kingdom, 109, 118, 258
    to extend bounds of knowledge, 37
    to guide others, 187
    to monitor the will's objectives, 106
    to overcome evil desires, 78
    to promote discovery of God's will,
      IV 6
    to promote freedom, 58
    to recover apothaumatic power, 219
    to recover awareness of soul, 194
    to resist perversion of talent, 173
    to reveal God's essence, 116, 120
    to seek salvation, 109
    to use thaumaturgic power, 56

Eden, garden of, 107
End of Time, The (Pieper), **II 27**
energy, psychical, 189, 208, 212-213
    spiritual, 14, 213, 214, 218
    and transformation of being, 90, 144, 195
entertainment, influence of, 120
environment, **II 20**, 86-87, **III 2**, 96, 130, 134, 162-163
Essay on Man (Pope), **I 2**
Essenes, 244
eternal being, 8, 10, 21-23, 41, 47, 93, 265
    as active, 18, 20, 21, 62, 74, 167
    and awareness, 150
    and change, 18-20
    and consciousness, 143-146, 178-179, 262
    and duty, 187
    of human will, 82, 96, 104, 107, 134, 136-137
    of Jesus, 251-252, 266
    of soul, 26, 33-34, **II 9**, 55, 57, 81, 96, **IV 40**, 134-136, 155-156
    and time, 18, 21, 156, **VI 41**
    and will, 22
    withdrawal of, 23
    see also eternal order, freedom
eternal order, 13, 34, **I 32, 35**, 50, **II 10**
    action on temporal order, 51, 74, 81, 136, 189-190, 198, 253, 266
    and change, 18-23, *see also* metallassis
    God as active in, **II 10, 15**, 186
    laws of, 51
    link with supra-eternal order, **IV 27**
    and miracle, **II 10**, 188
    as necessary, 22
    procession of, 22
    as rational, **VI 50**
    as uniform, 168
    see also eternal being
eternal rationality, 166
eternal truth, revelation of, 171, 172
eternal verities, 114, 174, 188
eternity, 18-21, **I 37**, 82, 129, **V 2**
    consummation of, **VII 48**
    development of, 18, **I 37**
    logic of, Preface, 51, **VI 50**, 238
    and miracle, **II 10**
    procession of, 22
ethics, and Christianity, **III 4**, **IV 32**
    distortion of, 174
evil, **II 35**
    conquered by good, **V 30**
    and evolution, **V 30**
    origin of, 109
    problem of, 94
    and Satan, 94
evolution, 2, 4-5, **II 19**, 97-111
    after death, 64, 165, 261-264
    as continuous, 5, **I 19**
    as directed, 138-139, 141-144
    as discontinuous, 5
    genetic, 103-105, 134, 154, 263
    man's responsibility for, 91, 97-98, 194
    and salvation, 127, 131-132

social, 97, 103, 134
  and will, 102-103, 107-111, 114-118,
    128, 131-132, 154, 191, 194, 229, 263
existentialism, **IV 13**, 255
experience, of God, **II 11**
  mental, 27, 29-32
  personal, religion as, **IV 32**
  psychical, 169-170
experiment in freedom, 119, 229

faith, communal, 227
  and healing, 211, 226, 228-229, **VI 42**
Faith That Rebels, The (Cairns), **VI 43**
Fall, of man, 107, 122, 128-129, 218
  see also original sin
feeding miracles, 202
forgiveness, by man, 91
  divine, 19, 21
freedom, as active, 62-65, 67
  definition, 57, 69
  and eternal being, 21-23, 38, 60,
    67-69, **II 10, 21, 22**, 261
  of God, 54, **II 21**, 234
  implies purpose, 54
  is positive, 62, 71
  limitations on, 58, 61, 71
  of man, 54, 56, 57-74, 80, 109
  and natural law, 59-61, 70, 74
  and purpose, 54, 67-74
  of soul, 26, 34, 62, 69-72, **II 21**, 80,
    96, 135, 137, **V 19**
  of will, 4, 46, 68-70, 74, 89, 257
friendship, in eternity, 166
  with God, 266
Future of Man, The (Teilhard de Chardin),
  V 9

genes, changed by will, 103-105, 134, 154,
  263
genetic engineering, 119
Gilson, Etienne, **V 55**
God, as active, 14, 17, 20, 73, **II 21**, 93,
    234-235
  as active in begetting, 38
  as active in creation, 9-10, 40, 52-54,
    65, **VI 8**
  as active in eternal beings, 185-186

  as active in eternity, 10, 22, 63, **II 10**
  as active in temporal being, 96, 200
  cannot forget man, 40, **III 21**, **IV 18**
  characteristics/attributes, 8, 17, 39,
    I 10, 257
  distorted vision of, **VI 22**
  enjoyment of his activity, 10
  essence of, 116, 120
  as expressed in man, 38, 65, 66
  as Father, 6, 8, 36-38, 50, **II 11**
  as First Cause, **VII 10**
  freedom from constraint by, 69
  friendship with, 266
  his actions reasonable, 235
  his experiment in freedom, 119, 229
  his freedom absolute, **II 21**
  his kingdom, *see* kingdom of God
  his plan, *see* God's plan, *below*
  his purpose, *see* purpose of God
  his will, alignment with, 99, 174
    conformity with, 89
    conflict with, 108, 109, 192
    frustration of, **I 36**, 54, 69
  as immanent, 7
  independence of (objective), 94, 112,
    193
  independence of (subjective), 38
  as infinite, 14
  is love, **I 10**
  no conflict in, 65
  as omnipotent, 225
  rebellion against, **II 24**, 93
  rejection by, 130
  rejection of, 10, 22, 23, 94, **IV 2**, 174,
    264, **VII 46**
  response to, 10
  search for, 120
  sees all possible futures, **V 41**
  as Son, 38, 39
  submission to, 94, 99, 109, 111, 174
  supremacy of, 95, 193
  as transcendent, **IV 32**, **V 16**
  triune nature of, 35-41, **VI 29**, 234
  as unchangeable, 8, 14, 17, 20, 51, 53
  understanding of, through art, 187,
    188

235

vision of, 169
see also being, supra-eternal, creation, Trinity
God's plan, allows for imperfection, 68
   creation as part of, 65
   divergence from, 109
   of evolution, 37
   frustration of, 186, 197, 265
   man a participant in, 66
   for mankind, 94, 95, 97, 98, 103, 108, 116, **VI 41**
   man's failure to understand, 67, 68
   not imposed, 97, 241
   for salvation, 186, 192, 197
   for the whole creation, 72
good, *see* right, and good
good and evil, absolute standard of, 95
   knowledge of, **IV 13**, **VI 20**
gullibility, Preface, 7

hallucinations, 257
healing, and medical science, 219-225
   miracles, 199, 209-214, 219-220, 225-227
heaven, 6-8
   and conflict, 64, 67-69, 93-94
   kingdom of, 110
Hegel, G.W.F., **V 9**
Heisenberg, Werner, **II 3**
hell, 264
heredity, 37, **II 20**, 86-87, **III 2**, 96, 130, 134, 162-163
   laws of, 37
heresy, **II 35**, **III 3**, **IV 28**, 253
hermeons, **V 10**
history, essence of, **II 27**
History of Philosophy, A (Copleston), **V 9**
Holy Spirit, 40, 96, 110, **VI 29**
   and apothaumata, 215
   and conception of Jesus, 230, 233
   inspiration by, 250
   procession of, 40, **VI 29**, 234
Home, Daniel Douglas, **VI 38**
Honest to God (Robinson), **IV 27**
hubris, 173, 174, 220
humanism, ethical, **IV 32**
human nature, fundamental change of, 109
regeneration of, 58
humility, 121, 124, 127, 131, **IV 29**, 174, 242
hunger, 123-124
Hymn of Man (Swinburne), **IV 25**

identity, personal, 152, 156-157
illness, physical, 28, 123-124, 210-211, 219-224
   psychological, 28, 211, 220-221, 224
immortality, and resurrection, 137
   see also life, eternal
imperfection, of eternal being, 67-68, 93, 174, 187
   of man, 109
Incarnation, 10, 251, 265-266
   see also Virgin Birth
independence, of man, 112
individuality, **V 36**, **VI 4**
   see also personality
infant, **IV 1**, 151
inspiration, by eternal beings, 170-173, 187-188

James, H.R. (translator), **II 3**
Jericho, **VI 22**
Jesus, and apothaumata, 199-208
   eschatological teaching of, 264
   healing miracles, 199, 209-214
   and perithaumata, 199
   resurrection miracles, 203-207
Jews, 235
judgement, moral, 67
   of others, **II 28**, 91, 161-163

Kant, Immanuel, **II 11**
Kerygma and Myth (Bultmann), **IV 27**
kingdom of God, 99, 105, 109-110, 118, 123, 128, 217, 242, 255, 258
   building/realization of, and apothaumata, 217
   and belief, 255
   cannot be abandoned, 110
   as duty, 109, 118, 258
   as essence of charity, 99
   as final objective, 123

    not impossible, 128
    and regeneration, 242
    and salvation, 118
    as task for communal will, 105
knowledge, branches of, **IV 32**, 171
    duty to extend, 37
    interpretations of, 171
    pursuit of, 114, 115, 119
Knox, Ronald A, 243, **VII 48**

law, constraints imposed by, 57
    inadequacy of, 58
        see also political action
    interactive, 33, 61, **II 2**, 208
    moral, 38, 40, 108
    natural, 15, 16, 59-61, 108
    physical, 21, 33, 37, 52, 265
        and evolution of man, 100-102,
            109, 115-117
        and freedom, 59-61, 70, 74
        and miracle, 5, 42, 45-47, 142,
            183-184, 189, 208
        and temporal being, 15-16
        and virgin birth, 231, 238-239
        and will, 91, 96, 97, 145, 220, 222
    psychical, 33, 37, 55, 265
leaders, responsibility of, 174
Leibniz, Gottfried, **V 52**
levitation, 189, 208, **VI 38**
Lewis, C.S., Preface
life, eternal, 129, **IV 40**, 135, 146, 259-265
    modes of, 12
Life of St Teresa, The (Cohen, translator), **VI 38**
Lord's Prayer, 6-7, 35-36

man, as able to perform miracles, 1, 5-6, 25, 47, 56, 74, 75-76
    see also apothaumata, perithaumata
    as agent of God, 55
    cannot forget God, 40, **III 21**, **IV 18**
    creation of, 5, 47, 107
    as expression of God, 38, 65
    made in God's image, 87
    nature of, 1-6, 10, 21, 23-24, 56, 64, 138

    relationship with God, 8, **I 20**
    role in God's plan, 65-69, 72-74, 89, 94-95, 96-98, 108, 241
    as trustee for nature, 111
Manicheism, 79, **III 3, 4**, **VI 49**
Marxist theory, 47
matter, living/non-living, 2-3, 137, 142, 204
    and mind, *see* mind, and matter
media, secularisation of, 120
Medieval Manichee, The (Runciman), **III 3**
memory, 147, **V 10, 32, 41**
metallassis, 19-21, 51, 64, **II 10, 22, IV 1, 40**, 164-165, 261-262
Milton, John, **II 12**
mind, 24-26, **I 9**, 89, 261
    and aesthetic sense, 30-32, 116
    and awareness, 150, 153-154
    definition, 33-34
    and eternal beings, 188
    and evolution, 100-101
    and matter, 9, 27-30, 33, 47, 190, 265
    and natural law, 60
    and recognition, 157
    and will, 34, 89, 257
    see also temporal being
miracle, as active force, 47, 90
    definitions, 42-46, 48-51, **V 10**
    denied, 3, 45, 93
    divine, 47, 52-55, 179, 185
    and existence of God, **II 11**
    see also apothaumata, healing miracles, perithaumata, resurrection
Miracle, a preliminary study (Lewis), Preface
monads, 176, **V 52**
Mooney, Christopher F, **V 9**, **V 14**
moral code, 174
moral law, 38, 40, 108
moral sense, 30, 31
moral values, 67
    scale of, 82
morality, and desire and will, 78-79, 82, 95, 96, 108
Moss, C.B., **II 35**

music, as revelation of God, 187
Muslims, 137
mutation, and will, 103-105, 134, 154, 263

nature, attitudes towards, 111, 220, 222
needs, and desires, 83-85
Nicene Creed, 41, **V 3**, 230

obligation, to God, 30, 38, 72, 95, 96, 108
Occam, William of, 2
Occam's Razor, 2, **I 3, 4**, 177
Old Testament, and miracle, **VI 22**
Omega, **V 16**
    Alpha and, 133
order, eternal, *see* eternal order
    supra-eternal, 13-14, 17, 22, 36, 39-40, 50-52
        see also being, supra-eternal
    temporal (spatio-temporal), *see* temporal order
orders of reality, either three or one, **IV 27**
organization, God as end of, **IV 40**
orientation, 142, **V 10**
Origen, 215
Origin and Propagation of Sin, The (Tennant), **IV 30**
original sin, 68, 74, **II 35**, 106, 107, 109, **IV 32, 33**, 192, 197, 220, 225, 228, **VI 41**
    definition, 68, 106-109

pain, 113, 210-211, **VI 41**
Paley, William, **VII 38**
pantheism, **VI 8**
Panthéisme et Christianisme (Teilhard de Chardin), **V 14**
Paradise Lost (Milton), **II 12**, 93
Pelagianism, **II 35**, 112
perfection, after death, 262
perithaumata, and creation of character, 78, 90-95, 96, 103-108, 128, 132, 134
    definition, 76, 77, 182, 189
    of Jesus, 199, 212
    and man, 189, 193-195, 197, 214
    and transformation of being, 134-179

personality, 10, 41, **I 35**, **V 36**, **VI 4**
    and conflict, 80, 92, 94, 108, 118
    and eternal being, 37, 67
Personality of Trinity, 41
Phenomenon of Man, The (Teilhard de Chardin), 138, **V 7**
philosophic insights, 171
physicons, **V 10**
Pieper, Josef, **II 27**
Planck, Max, **II 3**
pleasure, pursuit of, 113
political action, inadequacy of, **VI 51**
Pope, Alexander, 1
population, increase, 123-125
possibility, absolute and contingent, 238
pre-life, 142
procession, of eternal order, 22, **I 35**, **VI 3**
    of Spirit from Father, 40, **VI 29**, 234
proofs, of existence of God, **II 11**, **VII 38**
prophets, 229
    false, **III 16**
pseudo-life, **VI 35**
psychical continuum, 204
psychokinesis, 45, 189
psychological disorder, 220, 221
psychons, **V 10**
Puritanism, 79, **III 4**, **IV 28**
purpose, and eternal beings, 64-65, 67-69, **IV 40**, 181
    of God, 54, 55, 65-69, 72-74, 96, 108
    of man, 68, 74, 89
purposes, good, contain latent evil, **IV 32**

quantum, 140, 144
Quarterly Journal of Science, Article in (Crookes), **VI 38**

randomness, 15, 21, 46, 64, **II 3**, 105
rationalism, 218, 228
rationality, distrust of, **VI 50**
    temporal and eternal, 216
reality, misunderstanding of, **IV 32**
    orders of, 5, 13-22, 129, **VI 8**
recognition, after death, 152-153, 155-162, 164-167, 175, 187
redemption, 106, 128-131
    available to all, 23, 94

of eternal beings, 187
see also salvation
reflex action, 78, 85
regeneration, 58, 109, 194, 242
rejection of God, 10, 22, 23, 94, **IV 2**, 174, 264, **VII 46**
religion, subjective aspects of, **IV 32**
religions, non-Christian, 127
repentance, 19, 68, 130-131, 163
   death-bed, 148
   group, 131, 133
responsibility, 116, 174
   see also duty
resurrection, of the body, 137-138, 143, 145-146, 148, 153, 177, 206, 259
   of Jesus, 129, 243-259, 265-266
   miracles of, 203-207, **VI 28**, 248
   as process, 147-148
revelation, of God, 17, 35, 40, 235
right, and good, 82, **IV 28, 32**
Robinson, J.A.T., **IV 27**, **VII 2**
Runciman, Steven, **III 3**

salvation, of angels, 66, **II 30**, 129
   and disaster, as essence of history, **II 27**
   as fulfilment of God's purpose, 66, 68-69, 73, 95, 118, 241
   of human race, 66, 68, 127, 131-132, 186, **VI 51**, 233, 241, 251
   of individual, insufficient, 97
   moral interpretation of, **II 35**
   and will, 109
   see also redemption, regeneration
Satan, 22, 23, **II 24**, 93-95, **III 17**, **IV 2**, 129, 187, 188, 264
   and will of man, 96, 108, 110-113, 119-120, **IV 32**, 174, 193
schizophrenia, **V 36**
Science and Christ (Teilhard de Chardin), **V 51, 52**
science and Christianity, **I 24**
scientists, inspiration of, 187, 188
secularisation, Preface, 120
selection, natural, 83, 97, 100, 105, 144
self-aggrandizement, 38, 93, 94, 111, **IV 31**, 193

self-centredness, 161
self-consciousness, 151
self-denial, 110
self-esteem, 162
self-expression, begetting seen as, 37, 38, 65
self-recognition, 150, 155-157
sexual distinction after death, **VII 45**
sin, consequences of, 19, 21
   of man, 109
   see also original sin
sinfulness, undue dwelling on, 162
soul (*psuche*), 24-26, **I 9**, 123
   as active, 62, 81
   and awareness, 150-151, 153-154
   and cognition, 153
   and creative activity of God, 9, 26
   and death, 148, 155, 205-207
   and desires, 87-89, 194
   of infant, **IV 1**
   knowledge of, 32, 154, 194
   and mind, 32-34
   and will, 80-82, 90-91, 96, 145, 205, 257
   see also eternal being; freedom, of the soul; temporal being
species, survival of, 115, 116, **VI 35**
Spirit, *see* Holy Spirit
spirit (*pneuma*), 8, 24, **I 9**
spiritual energy, 14, 199, 218
structure, 139, 177-178
submission, to God, 38, 94-95, 96, 99, 109, 111, **IV 29**, 117, 133
substance, and accident, 41, 177, 179
   and consciousness, 175-178
   of God, 41
suffering, *see* pain
superstition, **VI 50**
Swinburne, Algernon, **IV 25**
Systematic Theology (Tillich), **IV 13**

taste, debasement of, 120
Teilhard de Chardin, Pierre, 138-143, **V 30, 33**, 175-178
Teilhard de Chardin and the Mystery of Christ (Mooney), **V 9, 14**

telepathy, 45, 189
telos, **VI 35**, 239-240, 265-266, **VII 10**
  and death, 204-207, 248
  definition, 142
  and Final Cause, **VII 10**
  and organization consciousness, 144, 145, 147, **VI 4**
  survival of, **VI 35**
temporal being, 8, 10-11, 15-16, 47, 74
  and activity of God, 23, 200-201
  of body, 26-27, 33, 96, 135-137
  and immortality, **III 12**
  as individual, **VI 4**
  of Jesus, 251
  of mind, 27-29, 33, 39, 96, 135
  and natural law, 60-61
  and soul, 135-137, 146, 154-156
  and will, 137, 143-147
  see also temporal order
temporal order, 13, 16, 20-22, 33-34, 50-52, 181
  and change, 15-16
  as contingent, 22
  as deterministic system, 50, **V 10**
  God as active in, 54-55
  man's attitude towards, 111-112
  and miracle, 181-184
  see also temporal being
Tennant, F.R., **IV 30**
theology, as anthropology, 112, **IV 27, 32**
  as Queen of the Sciences, **VII 39**
Theresa of Avila, St, **VI 38**
thermodynamics, second law of, 142, 144, **V 17**, **VII 10**
thought, secularisation of, Preface, 120
Tillich, Paul, **IV 13**
time, 18-19, 21, 39
  and eternity, 18, 21, 156
  is linear, 18
transubstantiation, 179
tribal god, **VI 22**
Trinity, 35-41, 201, **VI 29**, 233-234
True Discourse, The (Celsus), **VI 49**
truth, 30, 32, **I 24**, **II 1**, 114
  definition, **II 1**
  distortion of, 174

  inversion of, 154
  revelation of, **IV 20**
  search for, 115, 119
  truth, beauty and goodness, 30, 32, 114, 174, 188
  truths, heavenly, 172

Uncertainty Principle, **II 3**, **V 10**
universe, mental, as continuum, **VI 4**
universe, other parts of, **I 1, 14, 35**
  static, 141
universe, physical, as continuum, **VI 4**
utilitarianism, 58, **III 4**, 235
utopia, **II 35**, 109, 110, 170, 174, 242

violence, 61
Virgin Birth, **VI 7**, 230-232, 236-242
visions, 237

wealth, 119, 125-126
well-being, 58, 67, 99, 121-127
wilderness, 118, 225, 235
will, active organ of the soul, 81, 88
  after death, 262
  and apothaumata, 182, 189, 195, 214, 216, 226
  communal, **III 10**, 99, 105, 113-118, 131-132, 154, **V 30**, 227
  consensus of, 227
  and desire, 78-82, 88-92, 95, 96, 102-104, 108, 113, 128, 134, 156, 194
  of God, **I 36**, 89, 109, 117, 124, 130
  as good, 107-108
  of man, 69, **II 35**, 96-103, 112-113, 128-132, 174
  and natural law, 61, 102-103
  and perithaumata, 194, 214, 215
  see also eternal being; soul, and will; temporal being
Williams, C.K., **VII 48**
wisdom, higher, 171, 172
writers, responsibility of, 116, 174, 187
Zoroastrianism, **III 3**

INDEX OF BIBLICAL REFERENCES

OLD TESTAMENT

Gen. i, 26, 27, **III 9**
    i, 27, **VII 45**
    i, 31, **III 4**, **IV 12**
    ii, 2, **I 13**
    iii, 1, **IV 34**
    iii, 4, 5, **III 19**
    iii, 5, **VI 18**
    xi, 1-9, **IV 31**

Ex. vii, 8-10, **VI 22**

Jos. vi, **VI 22**

1 Kings xvii, 14-16, **VI 22**
    xvii, 17-24, **VI 22**
    xix, 11-13, **II 16**

Ps. viii, 5, **IV 3**
    lxv, 12, 13, **I 16**
    xcvi, 11, 12, **I 16**
    cxiv, 4, 6, **I 16**
    cl, 6, **I 16**

Is. vii, 14, **VII 1**

Dan. iii, 19-26, **VI 22**
    vi, 4-23, **VI 22**

Mal. iii, 6, **I 7**

APOCRYPHA

Ecclus. xliv, 9, 135, **V 1**

NEW TESTAMENT

Matt. i, 18, **VII 1**
    i, 19-21, **VII 6**
    i, 20, **VII 1**

i, 23, **VII 1**
iv, 1-11, **III 17**
v, 48, **VII 43**
vi, 14, 15, **III 13**
vi, 33, 125, **IV 36**
vii, 1, **II 28**, **III 13**
vii, 13, 14, **IV 14**
viii, 16, 17, **VI 39**
viii, 24-27, **II 15**
viii, 29, **VI 29**
ix, 18, 19, 23-25, **VI 32**
ix, 20-22, **VI 45**
x, 1, **VI 46**
x, 26, **IV 20**
x, 29, **I 5**
x, 34-39, **IV 21**
xi, 29, 30, **IV 22**
xii, 15, **VI 39**
xii, 26, **III 17**
xii, 30, **IV 40**
xiii, 57, **VI 56**
xiv, 13-21, **VI 27**
xiv, 14, **VI 39**
xiv, 22-33, **VI 37**
xiv, 33, **VI 29**
xiv, 35, 36, **VI 39**
xv, 32-39, **VI 27**
xvi, 13-17, **VI 29**
xvi, 21, **V 4**
xvi, 23, **III 17**
xvi, 24-26, **IV 21**
xvii, 20, Preface, **VI 17**
xviii, 6, **IV 38**, **V 48**
xx, 19, **V 4**
xxi, 21, **VI 17**
xxii, 29-32, **V 4**
xxii, 30, **VII 45**
xxiv, 8-11, **II 16**
xxiv, 24, **II 16**

241

xxv, 31-46, Preface
xxvi, 11, **VI 40**
xxvi, 63, 64, **VI 29**
xxvii, 43, **VI 29**
xxvii, 54, **VI 29**
xxvii, 59, **VII 29**
xxvii, 60, 62-66, **VII 28**
xxviii, 11-15, **VII 15**
xxviii, 19, **VI 29, VII 49**
xxviii, 19, 20, **VII 22**
xxviii, 20, 266, **VII 48**

Mark i, 1, **VI 29**
i, 32-34, **VI 39**
iii, 10, 11, **VI 39**
iii, 25, **III 20**
iv, 37-41, **II 15**
v, 22-24, 35-42, **VI 32**
v, 24-34, **VI 45**
vi, 4, **VI 56**
vi, 5, **VI 56**
vi, 30-44, **VI 27**
vi, 45-51, **VI 37**
vi, 54-56, **VI 39**
viii, 1-9, **VI 27**
viii, 27-29, **VI 29**
ix, 42, **IV 38, V 48**
x, 21, **IV 21**
xi, 23, **VI 17**, 193
xii, 24-27, **V 4**
xii, 25, **VII 45**
xii, 30, **I 9**
xiii, 22, **II 16**
xiv, 7, **VI 40**
xiv, 61, 62, **VI 29**
xv, 39, **VI 29**

Luke i, 26-31, **VII 1**
i, 26-38, **VII 5**
i, 35, **VII 1**
ii, 8-14, **VII 7**
iv, 24, **VI 56**
iv, 40, 41, **VI 39**
vi, 17-19, **VI 39**
vii, 11-15, **VI 31**
viii, 23-25, **II 15**
viii, 28, **VI 29**

viii, 41, 42, 49-56, **VI 32**
viii, 43-48, **VI 45**
ix, 1-2, **VI 46**
ix, 10-17, **VI 27**
ix, 18-20, **VI 29**
x, 1, 8, 9, **VI 47**
x, 18, **III 17**
xiii, 16, **III 17**
xiii, 24, **IV 14**
xiv, 14, **V 4**
xvii, 1, 2, **IV 38**
xvii, 2, **V 48**
xvii, 33, **IV 32**
xviii, 9-14, **V 42**
xx, 34-38, **V 4**
xx, 35, **VII 45**
xxi, 8-11, 25-28, **II 16**
xxii, 31, **III 17**
xxii, 69, 70, **VI 29**
xxiv, 12, **VII 29**
xxiv, 13-35, **VII 16**
xxiv, 16, **VII 24**
xxiv, 31, 36, **VII 23**
xxiv, 50, 51, **VII 25**

John i, 1-3, **VI 26**
i, 32, 33, **VI 29**
i, 34, **VI 29**
ii, 1-11, **II 15, VI 23, 28, VII 31**
ii, 19, 22, **V 4**
iii, 1-13, **II 18, IV 17**
iii, 3, **VII 12**
iii, 15,, 36, **VII 41**
iii, 16-18, **VI 29**
iv, 24, **I 8**
iv, 44, **VI 56**
iv, 46-54, **VI 28, 42**
iv, 48, **II 16**
v, 1-16, **VI 28, 42**
v, 17-27, **VI 29**
v, 21, **VI 28**
v, 28, **V 4**
vi, 1-13, **VI 27, 28**
vi, 15-21, **VI 28, 37**
vi, 37, **IV 41**
vi, 47, 54, **VII 41**
ix, 1-3, **VI 42**

ix, 1-38, **VI 28**
ix, 35-38, **VI 29**
x, 10, **IV 40**
xi, 1-44, **VI 33**
xi, 4, **VI 29**
xi, 1-46, **VI 28**, **VII 27**
xi, 24, 25, **V 4**
xii, 8, **VI 40**
xii, 31, **III 17**
xiv, 6, **IV 37**
xiv, 26, **VI 29**
xiv, 30, **III 17**
xv, 15, **VII 47**
xv, 26, **I 35**, **VI 29**
xvi, 11, **III 17**
xvi, 13, **IV 20**
xx, 5-7, **VII 30**
xx, 19, **VII 23**
xx, 21, 22, **VI 29**
xx, 24-29, **VII 17**
xxi, 4, **VII 24**
xxi, 6, **VII 18**
xxi, 15-17, **VII 20**

Acts i, 9, **VII 26**
ii, 4-11, **VI 48**
iii, 2-10, **VI 48**
ix, 1-9, **VII 21**
ix, 33, 34, **VI 48**
ix, 36-42, **VI 48**

xii, 5-10, **VI 48**
xiv, 8-10, **VI 48**
xvi, 16-18, **VI 48**
xvi, 25, 26, **VI 48**
xvii, 28, **I 20**
xix, 6, **VI 48**
xix, 11, 12, **VI 48**
xx, 9-12, **VI 48**

1 Cor. ii, 7-10, **II 25**
ii, 9, 10, **IV 19**
xiii, **IV 4**
xiii, 12, **IV 20, 23**
xv, 42-44, **V 5**
xv, 53, **V 6**

2 Cor. iv, 16, **V 31**

Gal. iii, 28, **VII 45**

Heb. ii, 7, **IV 3**
iv, 14, 15, **VI 41**

1 John, iv, 8, **I 10**
v, 7, **VI 29**

Rev. i, 8, 133
iii, 19-22, 133
xii, **II 24**
xxi, 6, **IV 41**